THE RISE OF MARGINAL VOICES

Gender Balance in the Workplace

Anne Statham

University Press of America, Inc.
Lanham • New York • London

Copyright © 1996 by
University Press of America,® Inc.
4720 Boston Way
Lanham, Maryland 20706

3 Henrietta Street
London, WC2E 8LU England

Library of Congress Cataloging-in-Publication Data

Statham, Anne.
The rise of marginal voices : gender balance in the workplace / Anne
Statham.
p.   cm.
Includes bibliographical references and index.
1. Women--United States--Social conditions. 2. Women--
Employment--United States. 3. Marginality, Social--United States. 4.
Sex discrimination in employment--United States. 5. Sex differences
(Psychology)--United States. 6. Feminist theory--United States. I.
Title.
HQ1421.S73   1996   305.42'0973 --dc20   96-9244   CIP

ISBN 0-7618-0444-7 (cloth: alk. ppr.)
ISBN 0-7618-0445-5 (pbk: alk. ppr.)

∞™ The paper used in this publication meets the minimum
requirements of American National Standard for information
Sciences—Permanence of Paper for Printed Library Materials,
ANSI Z39.48—1984

To Bettye and Lowell

who in so many direct and indirect ways

taught me to look for a better world

Contents

PREFACE

Writing this book has been like a journey for me. I want to invite you, the reader, to come along. Through the more than ten years I have been gathering material for this project, the world has witnessed dramatic change. The Soviet Union no longer exists. The Berlin Wall has fallen. The concept of "spaceship earth" has been firmly implanted in our psyche. We use e-mail to easily converse with people all around the globe. We have also seen a great explosion of groups, formerly under the yoke of some other group's oppression, seeking the right to autonomy and self-determination. These groups range from those in Eastern Europe to domestic subgroups within our own society.

One intent of this book is to try to make sense of all of this change, to chart at least part of the direction we humans may be heading. Of course, our direction is not entirely out of our control. According to the Symbolic Interactionists that I have spent a great deal of time reading, our thoughts and beliefs act to shape what exists in social life. True, these collective subjective realities become encoded as social structure, which in turn acts back upon us. But we do have a role in deciding what our direction will be.

We can be much more purposeful in our shaping if we have a clear sense of what it is we wish to see happen and where it is we seem to be heading. My purpose here is to help give that sense of clarity. I am asking you to suspend your normal predispositions and imagine the world as you would most like it to be. Most of us wish for a kinder world, one where all individuals are treated with dignity and respect -- especially people like ourselves! I have searched for evidence that we are moving in that direction, over the very long run, and for outlines of the process through which we are achieving that end.

One problem I have identified in this search for a better world is a tendency we have to resist emerging realities. Thomas Kuhn talked about this in his work on paradigm shifts among scientists, but I believe it is a tendency that we all have. We resist change; we try to recast the "new" into terms of the "old." This makes things more comfortable for us. Symbolic Interactionists talk about the need we have for predictability. Even positive changes, things we really want, cause stress in our lives. Thus, we often fail to see the direction we may be heading, or to make the most of our opportunities to shape things in the most positive way.

In this book, I offer a model for how our social world may be changing over the long run. I borrow from Karl Marx the notion that current social structures have internal inconsistencies that will ultimately lead to their destruction, a transformation to a new social arrangement. I incorporate Thomas Kuhn's notion of the importance of ideas in driving this transformation process, and the tendency we have to resist new perspectives. From Gregory Bateson, I use the idea of social structures as involving self-correcting mechanisms he called feedback loops, which allow the structures to incorporate more information and integrate it more fully through time.

Using this model, I have searched previous writings and my own data and experience to discern our social direction. I ask, what is the future of our social life? I believe the long term tendency is for us to evolve social systems that are increasingly egalitarian, that extend the dignity, respect, and autonomy all of us yearn for to ever wider circles in our population. As we have passed through numerous feedback loops through time, this notion has grown in complexity and depth. It is a world view that I find among many of our "left out" citizens. Those currently in control may find it especially difficult to accept a new direction, to give up the old system that does not quite meet these goals, given their level of investment in the way things are. Many more marginalized voices, articulating a new direction, are found in the pages of this book.

I have followed recent feminist imperatives that we look beyond white, middle-class America for accurate portrayals of our social realities. Here, I trace my own intellectual development in this regard, showing my first studies of gender differences, in which I found evidence that women, as a group, might have a different perspective on how management should be done. These findings have been greeted with charges of essentialism by those both within and without the feminist community. I found these reactions interesting in themselves, and used them as an opportunity to explore the process through which we accept new realities. I also moved on to looking at diverse groups -- American Indians and African-Americans, in particular -- finding this new or alternative perspective even more clearly articulated among these groups.

I hope you, either student or general reader, will find your own reality reflected in the voices heard here, and that you will be called to examine your own beliefs and role in this process. This message is meant for all groups in our society -- women, men, people of color, those of European descent. We have all played some role in maintaining our current social structure, and we can all play some role in implementing change. I hope that seeing the convergence in perspectives will increase our clarity and make it possible for us to shape our future in very purposive ways.

Anne Statham
Salem, Wisconsin
April, 1996

Acknowledgements

This work has been going on for so long, it is difficult to remember all who helped in some way. The freedom I have felt at the University of Wisconsin-Parkside to follow my heart has been most important. This support was provided by my colleagues (both students and faculty) all across campus, but most especially in Sociology/Anthropology and Women's Studies. Moral and intellectual support is the critical factor, but I also received financial support from various units on the campus for certain aspects of this work: the Department of Sociology and Anthropology, the Women's Studies Program, the Committee for Research and Creative Activity. Arthur J. Steinback also provided critical financial suport at just the right time. Marian Swoboda was also helpful in this regard.

Many individuals read parts of this manuscript and gave useful feedback. They include Spencer Cahill, Donna Carr, Roseann Mason, Eleanor Miller, Ron Pavalko, Judith Pryor, Pat Rhoton, Laurel Richardson, Helen Rosenberg, Mary Kay Schleiter, Kath Schoemaker, Jack Sparacino, Sheldon Styrker, Kathleen Tierney. Others have read the entire manuscript and have been enormously helpful with editorial and substantive suggestions. They include Julie King, Nina Smith, Mary Ritchie, Michael Zupan, Nancy Backes, and students in a Women's Studies Seminar class.

The preparation of this manuscript would have been impossible without the dedication and skill of Clare Weber. She took raw bits of chapters and turned them into a professional document, offering substantive help along the way. Luella Vines, Marge Rowley, Pat Jones, Kelly Corrigal, and Terri Eisenbart, Gloria Sikes, and Judy Gaal provided clerical support, as well. Mary Ritchie and Sheila Denise Neinhaus provided crucial research assistance and Dave Datta provided technical support. Despite all of this assistance, any errors that remain are mine. I finally want to thank my husband, Michael Zupan, who provided encouragement in good and bad times and a challenging intellectual atmosphere for these ideas to grow.

Chapter 1

Moving Back to the Future

...For me, the impact of feminism is connected to the insistence upon agency, subjectivity, self-determination and self-transformation.
Hester Eisenstein, 1991.

This book deals with the terrain of gender differences, what they are (and are not), how we come to understand them, and how we can use our growing knowledge about these differences and their total context to our benefit. Ultimately, it is about our ability to live in community despite our differences, our willingness to bring all perspectives to the table in an effort to create a more integrated and resilient society. Our way is often shrouded by a lack of awareness. This book represents an effort to lift that veil a bit so we can see more clearly.

Re-Cycling Ideas

We tend to think of the social patterns comfortable for us as having been around for a very long time. Ideas which seem new spring up and are adopted, sometimes accompanied by conflict, pain and struggle. We fail to realize they have been around before, maybe not in this culture, but in others, maybe not in this generation but in previous ones. Carl Jung believed such cultural imprints, archetypes that appeared in many places, were passed on, vestiges of experiences our ancestors had stored. But, we ask. where? In their genes, in an ephemeral subconscious?

In this book, I want to propose a theory of change that involves the apparently cyclical process whereby seemingly new ideas or notions tend to periodically re-appear, often with greater force or more intensive focus than they had before. In general, I believe that we are moving as a species to increasing levels of social complexity and integration. This systemic aspect of our social life acts a great deal like the process found in our biosphere where evolutionary processes push toward higher levels of complexity. Our earth is certainly a highly integrated system, a result of apparently oscillating cycles of increased specialization *and* integration over the eons.

Signs that we are moving socially toward integration are everywhere. Information technology makes it possible to communicate world-wide. Multicultural perspectives are demanded in our schools and workplaces. Corporations, foundations, financial organizations, and the U.N. use increasingly global strategies. The women's movement demands inclusion of all women's voices into the social order. Other groups press for full participation -- the differently abled, homosexuals, the elderly, the poor.

Inclusion on Multiple Levels

This integration of perspectives is occurring on several levels. Various groups attain greater access to societal resources. They swell the ranks of the workforce in new positions; this benefits individuals in those groups. But perhaps most importantly, their perspectives are incorporated into our general thinking; at least, there is the chance they will be. And this is important. Groups that are excluded from the mainstream of social life -- or from valued resources -- often have developed a unique perspective that influences their strategies in life and their outlooks. They often have valuable insights into our process of living on this planet, insights that if incorporated can lead to a more fully self-correcting and reliable system. One point I make in this book is that often something practiced by one or more of these excluded groups may be a good solution for an existing social problem. Hence, the more fully we pay attention to and incorporate those perspectives, the better our system.

Many social observers point to problems that can be recast in these terms. My argument, developed in the chapters that follow, asserts that suppression and exclusions of these marginal groups continues to lead our culture or society to periodic crises. Humanity is currently at such a point. Both in this country and abroad, western civilization is assailed for its negative impact on the earth and its colonizing effect on those who happen not to be white males. Although some of these assertions are being loudly debated (I'm thinking in particular of the political correctness debates currently exploding on our campuses), many social commentators argue that our society is in decline. Daniel Yankevolich (1981), observing U.S. culture, has noted several problems:

> ...the inability of our schools to teach; slovenliness in standards...decay of railroads, bridges...aging of our industrial plants; litigiousness of our overlawyered society; the decline of our political parties; the bland arrogance of the news media; the living-in-the-past of our labor unions; the irrelevance of our colleges (p. 261).

Lately, we see much dissatisfaction with the "old order," movements ahead, attempts to turn backward, in all areas of life. Corporations search for new management techniques, governments and world organizations explore new types of power arrangements. Multinational corporations are changing the face of our economic life. Technological change, particularly the information explosion, threatens to outpace our ability to comprehend that change. Very major changes in the way we live are moving us to the brink of a new era. Possibilities for a new order appear.

Widening Rings of Inclusion

I will develop the argument in these pages that our problems stem largely from the self-defeating tendency of our system to exploit, oppress, and marginalize the majority of our citizens -- women and people of color. As we squander these precious human resources, we foist apathy, alienation, bitterness, and worse on many of our citizens, becoming increasingly inefficient as we develop institutions designed to force unmotivated participants to comply with system needs.

Many revolutions in both the workplace and the home are direct reactions to this tendency. The left-out individuals are very important in fashioning the solutions to our dilemma for several reasons. First, as formerly excluded groups, they have much energy to contribute to this new endeavor. Some recent research shows women, for example, to be the most enthusiastic of workers. Second, it is often their perspectives that are so badly needed. For example, since "feminine" concerns have been excluded from the "male" world of work, politics, etc., many reformers are calling for their infusion into our workplace. And women, having been socialized to exhibit traits of cooperation, person-investment, relationship fostering, already possess those very traits corporations are now paying men to learn in training seminars. Thus, for the good of all of our society, inclusion of formerly excluded groups may be an important feature in the solution to our present difficulties. Growing equality, dignity, respect, and inclusion is the thread running through the many revolutionary cycles we have seen. This is the content of the "new order" that may well be dawning.

The Nature of Change

To fully understand the social space in which we now live, we must understand how change occurs, for we are truly living in a time of great change. Even fairly conservative forces have captured this rhetoric to advance their causes. For example, Newt Gingrinch speaks of "change" incessantly.

I do not, however, see this process as singularly linear; the overall, longterm trend may be toward increasing complexity, toward incorporating more perspectives. However, the full process also involves a series of cycles, often repeating, sometimes at different levels. In thinking of trends, we can have a very long-term trend in a certain direction (such as falling birth rates overall, globally), combined with many short-term oscillations (i.e., rise and fall of birth rates in the short run, according to variations in business cycles). My project here is essentially to combine notions of linear and rational change (often associated with the European, northern perspective) with notions of circular and creative change (often associated with southern, indigenous perspectives).

As an example of the combination of linearity and circularity, consider the pressures for inclusion that include a seemingly opposite trend -- that of fragmentation. As it becomes more desirable for all voices to be incorporated into our social systems, individual groups sometimes become pre-occupied with developing their own voices. They seem to withdraw from the whole. Ultimately, however, inclusion rests upon the ability of all groups to fully develop their sense of self, to throw off their oppression and come into an autonomous position.

This gives new insight to the "Think Globally, Act Locally" motto coined by the environmental movement, and makes more concrete the possibility that a long term process may be facilitated by cyclical oscillations.

One reason change is not always straight-forward or simple is the resistance exhibited by those in power -- and even from those not in power. While this resistance is often direct and explicit, it is sometimes less obvious, as when power holders seem to have problems in just perceiving that new ways exist. As a result, change often occurs gradually or in stages. For example, in examining the integration of alternative viewpoints into university curricula, Peggy McIntosh (1989) shows that individual instructors, even entire institutions, seem to go through stages. The sequence begins with viewing omitted groups (women or people of color) as curiosities, oppressed, or troubled peoples. The process ends with a truly diverse and integrated curriculum that uses issues of the omitted groups, not just those of the dominant groups, to actually structure course or curriculum design. And, of course, in this academic setting, a great backlash has occurred, with the dominant group claiming they are being "silenced" by the "thought control police," hence the outcry against "political correctness." Thus, this particular trend -- diversifying academic curricula -- will go through yet more cycles in the process of change.

There are many existing ideas of how change occurs for us to draw on. One of the oldest is the Marxian/Hegelian notion of thesis, antithesis, synthesis, which asserts that all social forms contain the seeds of their own destruction, a process that will lead to a new order or "synthesis." I use elements of this idea in my own framework to account for what seems to be happening in later stage capitalism. Many of us wonder, as each new phase unfolds, if the system can bear much more strain, if the amount of inequality developing will not cause a social eruption or explosion. Yet, somehow, an antithesis has not burst onto the scene, nor the long awaited synthesis.

I believe the Marxian model is flawed in one fundamental aspect: it fails to give credence to the power of ideas to transform our social order. In fact, this model quite clearly gives precedence to economic relations as the primary mover of our social evolution, with ideas following in their wake, serving as rationales for the existing order. While there is some truth to the Marxian argument, its failure to see the enormous impact of ideas on our development leaves it unable to account fully for the patterns we are now seeing in our society.

Other thinkers have focused more fully on the impact of ideas, and incorporating these approaches may give some balance to the overall model. They are particularly helpful in accounting for the gradual way in which change seems to occur, with much apparent backsliding. One of these is the notion of "paradigm shift," a very useful tool, I believe, to understand current social trends.

A paradigm shift is a totally new way of proceeding, not simply a re-ordering or modification of our current view. Many voices are predicting such a paradigm shift is indeed imminent, that our present order and ways of viewing things are outmoded and will not allow us to solve our many problems. In fact, the idea that we need a re-visioning of society has actually come from many sources simultaneously, from various groups which point to problems in our present social order. Many of these groups will be discussed in this book, as we take a very broad and integrated look at the process of change. From these perspectives, we get different insights into the process.

Compelling evidence suggests that our systems's tendency toward exploitation is indeed a type of "fatal flaw" that will, ultimately, force a major transformation upon us. Recurring themes appear in many formulations of a new order: new societal norms espousing openness to change, flexibility, consideration of individual rights and needs, and participatory democracy. Denzin (1996) argues that work toward democracy in today's post-modern world converges on the values of freedom, social justice, dignity, respect, nonviolence, and honor, seen as even more widely dispersed than in previous revolutions. I believe the growing, widespread adoption of these values thrusts us into a new realm. As outmoded, authoritarian, bureaucratic approaches become increasingly dysfunctional, calls for alternative approaches become more common. Some view the amount of change required of us as a negative development, as Alvin Toffler (1970) suggests in his book *Future Shock*. It seems certain we experience change as unsettling and painful, no matter how much we recognize its necessity. It is well-documented that even happy and welcomed transitions in our lives cause us psychic pain and require adjustment. Widespread societal-level change will require even more of us.

It is, however, possible to anticipate the benefits of change and to use our foresight to direct the change in a positive direction. For one thing, understanding the content of pending change may help us to adjust more readily. The notion of paradigm shift, discussed most thoroughly by

Thomas Kuhn (1977; 1965), provides one possible template for how the process proceeds. A paradigm shift occurs when we are pushed to re-think and re-craft our basic, underlying assumptions, affecting our over-all approach to life. It is a broad-sweeping change in the way reality is perceived and interpreted. His argument rests upon assumptions about how we function cognitively in a general sense. Thus, much of what Kuhn has written about scientific revolutions would apply to broad-scale social change, as well. Changes that appear to be sudden, even disorienting, have usually been building more gradually. The way we absorb and embrace change makes it so. As Kuhn has observed, we are slow to admit that current belief systems are not working, though it may be obvious in hindsight. Rather, the "failures to fit" appear as asides or footnotes until their prevalence becomes undeniable. At that point, they come to occupy center stage, generating a great deal of controversy, until a new synthesized perspective seems to suddenly burst upon the scene. This may well account for the fact that break-through discoveries tend to be made simultaneously by several individuals.

The same has been true of the social changes considered in this book. In retrospect, there have been many warning signs about serious problems with our society, that it has become increasingly dysfunctional, particularly in such areas as the world economy, world politics, and national problems of crime and poverty. In the "paradigm shift" style of slowly, gradually embracing change, we did not immediately opt for new approaches. We have attempted to make the old work by using a bandaid approach. This tendency to cling with fierce tenacity to the old seems to be a fundamental aspect of our psychological functioning. Experiments conducted by Kurt Lewin (1951) and his followers earlier in this century demonstrated our strong tendency to *perceive* the familiar even when it does not exist. A simple example includes seeing familiar names in lieu of actually existing rare names, something I often experience with the spelling of my last name, as people commonly pronounce or spell it "Stratham" because they have seen *that* name somewhere.

Partly because of this tendency, even widespread need for change can be ignored for a long while. In our current case, the signs something was amiss have been treated like footnotes in a scientific article -- interesting asides, nothing more. The slowness with which we come to recognize the need for drastic change can be seen in the evolutions apparent in one aspect of our last several presidential campaigns. Several campaigns ago, in 1984, Walter Mondale challenged Ronald

Reagan with fairly "old line" Democratic labor and race issues, adding as they did the gender issue by including a woman Vice Presidential candidate. The outlines of the new perspective may be seen in embryonic form, almost bleeding through to the surface in that campaign, as problems with deficit spending were alluded to and attempts were made to include women in the standard Democratic coalition. The next race in 1988, which included no women but did include a person of color, Jessie Jackson, found the parties still clinging to the past, refusing to directly confront the new issues and realities that had arisen. However, the price of clinging to our established viewpoints was beginning to be apparent. One could argue this from a moral standpoint, looking at our country's stands on such issues as global ecological crises -- or from an economic standpoint, looking at our huge budget deficit and declining world position. The feeling that something was very wrong was making many voters uneasy, yet this could not be articulated by the Democrats to challenge the Republican status quo.

Glimpses of a new reality, however, began to emerge in that campaign. Jesse Jackson, for example, *did* make major errors, such as his off-handed statements about Jews, but also spoke eloquently of the need for individual dignity for *all* persons. While the major candidates in the past several elections seemed locked in the old, outmoded debate, he consistently introduced new elements, most of them part of the new paradigm I see emerging. Through time, the notion of equality has grown steadily more expansive to now include not only women and blacks (our idea of equality early in this century) but also Hispanics, gays and lesbians, the physically disabled, those in Third World nations. During the 1988 campaign, both major parties began to talk about "diversity." Our view of how we "ought" to relate to these individuals is beginning to shift, though it may seem to many that this new perspective burst upon the scene quite suddenly.

During the 1992 campaign, though no women or people of color participated as candidates, the contours of the debate seemed to have shifted dramatically. We had a president who had spoken of a "new world order" but seemed to be using approaches to world politics developed at the end of World War II. The Democrats who ran in the primary had all adopted ideas put forward by Jessie Jackson, speaking about a commitment to equality and equal protection. Their proposals included access to health care and work. The Republicans were also pushed to embrace some of these concepts, at least on a superficial level. The consequences of the huge deficit spending begun in earnest by Ronald Reagan, predicted by earlier politicians, were becoming reality and the "trickle down" argument was being rejected. Policies aimed at helping the few rich seemed likely to be soundly rejected by the electorate, especially if our economic problems continued unabated. And Bill Clinton seemed in the beginning, more than any past president, intent upon drawing related concerns together and acting upon them in a holistic fashion, particularly concerns related to equality, participation, and access to opportunity. His administration was also enthusiastically embracing some notions in the new integrated society, such as making the information "super highway" readily accessible.

The ideas revolving around equality have been articulated by numerous movements and organizations, many of them consciously adapting the new paradigm terminology of Thomas Kuhn. Fritjof Capra (1976; 1982), a physicist, is often credited as being one of the first writers to clearly do so. He has written several books that explore the implications of changing paradigms in physics for the rest of our thought patterns, drawing heavily upon the Green Politics of Germany. For him, the old paradigm is characterized by four major beliefs: 1) our natural environment is a mechanized system to be exploited by interested groups, 2) life is a competitive struggle, 3) unlimited natural progress is highly desirable, and 4) females dominated by males is the natural order. According to Capra, the new paradigm is characterized by belief in: 1) oneness in life, 2) interdependence among all things, 3) life as a series of cycles of change and transformation (Capra, 1987). He notes that much of the old order is based upon the mechanistic principles of Newtonian physics, which have led us to erroneously believe that we could manipulate the environment, nature, and other individuals with no negative consequences. It was simply a taken-for-granted reality. We are just beginning to shed these views in our social philosophy and ways of dealing with the world in favor of a more relativistic view which sees humankind as one among many creatures on this earth, not necessarily the most important or highest order. From this view, he argues, flows a deep respect for and spiritual awareness of the natural world.

Challenging these mechanistic assumptions leads to radically different approaches to the environment, relations to animals, relations with one another. Domination as an ordering principle is questioned, rejected. New ways of relating must be found. According to Capra, our secure knowledge that we are "at least better than inanimate objects" is shaken by the discovery in physics that all objects in the world share similar "probability patterns of energy," and that boundaries between objects are more apparent than real. These new discoveries challenge our taken-for-granted methods of observation. Clinging to our mechanistic assumptions makes it impossible for us to account for all that is happening around us.

Capra argues that we have not yet truly integrated the implications of Einstein's relativism, but continuing discourses will force us to do so. That *all* is energy and that energy takes many different, shifting forms, are principles that have been with us since Einstein. But we are only now absorbing on a widespread basis the implications of these discoveries and incorporating them into our overall world view. For example, Marjory Kelly (1992a) in *Business Ethics* draws connections for how our work world is structured directly from the discovery in quantum physics that vibrational energy patterns are essentially the basis for all that exists. Since we are intricately connected to everything on the earth, as is the "divinity," she argues, this eventually ought to drastically alter how we do our business, treat each other and the earth.

For most of us, however, it seems difficult to understand exactly what is happening. Our models of change are often not very helpful for understanding the full complexity of the process. Two of the most popular theories of change, the Marxian model and the idea of paradigm shift, suffer from purely linear thinking. They do not account very well for the apparently contradictory trends around us. As we have seen from recent political events in this country, new ideas are not smoothly adopted. Much resistance or "backlash" occurs. Often, two realities seem to exist at once -- the old and the new. Some individuals living through this time of change find it difficult to give up old conceptions. Many others are simply confused. In our adversarial systems, society becomes polarized. Extremists on both ends of the political spectrum shout slogans at one another, creating ambivalence among many in the middle. Gradually, however, new ideas begin to develop. For example, opinion surveys show the majority of our citizens support notions of enhanced equality among all, including respect, social and economic support for our less advantaged citizens, despite the current political rhetoric of the radical right which seeks to deny safety nets to the less privileged and destroy other methods for establishing equality, such as labor organizations.

It seems that dual realities are coexisting, each blurring the outlines of the other. I am reminded of the pentimento process, when an original painting "bleeds through" one painted over it. Another way of understanding what is happening is with Gregory Bateson's idea of self correcting systems. He argued that social systems mimic biological ones, that they are self-organizing. As new information and perspectives are processed through our social systems, they pass through feedback loops that integrate the new with the old.

This tendency could account for the apparent stops and starts, the erratic course we seem to be on. For example, we could analyze the change cycles we have seen since the 1960's as a series of spirals or feedback loops with ever tighter integration of new insights and awareness of our basic social principles. We seem to move off in a direction of greater equality and individual autonomy, then as this cycles through our social structures, certain groups say, "But this idea of family stability is important." So, we pause to address that problem in the "new" thinking. We elected Bill Clinton, which Fritzof Capra said explicitly in his last Elmwood Institute newsletter signaled the success of new paradigm thinking, yet many people said, "But wait a minute...! He's doing things I don't agree with or that make me uneasy." The Republicans capitalized on this, playing on people's fears of change and loss of privilege. I see the 1995 U.S. Congress as simply one side of a large feedback loop, where the new ideas are being re-processed for greater eventual integration. Of course, this does not happen automatically. We all have an impact on the direction this will go and must exercise our initiative wisely.

These ideas of systemic change, of self-correcting systems and of pentimento, the old reality continuing to bleed through onto the new, hence appearing to co-exist, are helpful additions to Kuhn's idea of paradigm shift and Marx's notion that systems contain the seeds of their own destruction. Kuhn's notion was meant to apply to a rather narrow situation of expanding understanding in the natural sciences, specifically. It is not quite adequate to account for the totality of social change. Elaborations explaining how paradigms change in the social world are needed. And Marx failed to appreciate the importance of ideas in moving us toward a transformation, especially as that might be processed through cycles over the longterm.

Seeing Causes in Isolation

A major problem in our ability to understand what is truly happening is our penchant for tunnel vision. Perhaps this is why feedback cycles are necessary. We tend to focus on one aspect at a time, usually that which most immediately affects us, using old categorizations. Some of us focus on the impact of gender, others on race, others on class, and others on different personal characteristics or on such issues as success in business. Still other groups emphasize the importance of combating environmental degradation, saying that if we are not still able to live here, none of these other issues will matter. Most of us have very convincing reasons why our particular problems are the most urgent. Change becomes most likely when these apparently desperate viewpoints converge in a singular analysis.

I have attended many meetings and conferences recently where the tendency for tunnel vision is discussed with considerable alarm. The need for coalition politics is emphasized, though not well practiced. I have heard several individuals say that the fact only 1 or 5 percent of the wealthy have benefitted so much economically in the last several decades means by definition that the majority of us are more than likely being hurt in some way. If that majority could stand together, perhaps we could move our society in a different direction.

The idea that these issues can all be analyzed within a united framework is gaining favor in academic circles. Feminism here and abroad has taken great steps in this direction. For example, many of these disparate views are pulled together under the umbrella of eco-feminism, where many types of oppression, including worker exploitation, racism, sexism, and environmental degradation are seen as springing from a common thrust toward exploitation in our current economic and social order. In the pages that follow, I will attempt to make apparent the interconnections among these various trends, using this base to help clarify difference as it can be used constructively to build a better world. This is, after all, part of the integrated perspective thought to be part of the new order.

Feminist theories of change (see, for example, Chafetz, 1990) often do consider the backlash episodes that seem to accompany our steps forward. But because they have no conceptual framework for talking about how the two trends work together (forward and backlash), they remain essentially pessimistic about the possibilities for real change. They often focus on the possibilities for marginalized groups acquiring a greater share of the resources from the existing system, rather than considering the extent to which system transformation may be occurring. They also misuse categorizations as rigid dividers. For example, in a wonderfully insightful book by Linda Gordon (1994) on the history of women and welfare, she laments the lack of a collective feminist voice in the social movements during the Great Depression and the lobbying for New Deal legislation (p. 212). Yet, pages later (p. 217) she casually mentions the great involvement of women in many of the radical labor and unemployed movements that prevented evictions and demanded greater government support for the unemployed and the poor. Was this not some sort of "feminist" influence? Has that been explored? I find it fascinating that even 50 years later, we still fail to see inter-connections between movements toward equality. As Eisenstein (1991) says about her experiences in Australia, "We have got somehow to get beyond the obsessive polarity and pendulum swing between sameness and difference, and get used to new ways of thinking about gender in its social, economic and political context" (p. 112).

Organization of Book

To explore these issues, I have organized the book into three main sections, an organization that models my own growing understanding of gender and difference and, hopefully gives a concrete example of how a change in perspective occurs, the various stages we might pass through. Part I deals with the notion of gender as an isolated issue, the perspective many of us took in the early 1980's. I first discuss gender imbalance on a general level (Chapter 2) and move on to consider that women have some unique approaches to offer (Chapter 3). I deal with the controversy that notion has spawned, even in feminist circles (Chapter 4) and end with the problematics that surround the notion of the "feminine" in our society (Chapter 5). This section deals with gender alone, not in the context of the other issues we now see to be intimately related.

Part II begins the process of analyzing gender in relation to other issues of concern, particularly those of class and race. It considers how class issues are involved in workplace problems and how gender issues intertwine with those of class (Chapters 6 and 7). Race is also considered as a factor that can transform our understandings about how gender operates in a specific setting (Chapter 8). This section illustrates the beginning stages of a change in conceptual awareness when old moorings are abandoned.

Part III deals with gender in total cultural context, something much in the background in our beginning work (Part I). For grounding, it begins with a consideration of leadership in Native American context specifically, making the point that the idea of "difference" is greatly enriched by looking at the total cultural context in which gender is played out (Chapter 9). It also gives greater power to the notion of an alternative way of proceeding among many marginalized groups, not just among women, resolving to some extent the issue of essentialism. This section then moves on to consider explicitly how the marginalized voices I explore might transform our workplace (Chapter 10), drawing implications for society (Chapter 12). I also take some time to elaborate about what we have learned about the process of change in relation to these issues (Chapter 11).

I take a consciously feminist approach throughout, both in theoretical orientation and in methodological practice (cf. Harding, 1987), using a variety of sources. I draw heavily from others' research and writing on related topics. I use many types of methodologies, including qualitative and quantitative, in the considerable research I have done with hundreds of men and women. I incorporate personal experiences as a source of data, drawing upon the feminist belief that public realities are often echoed in personal experiences. And always, I am looking for confirmations across my sources of information. (See Statham, Richardson, and Cook, 1991 for a discussion of the importance of this triangulation approach.)

I have been gathering these data for more than ten years. I began in the Spring of 1983, first choosing three worksites in southeastern Wisconsin -- a technical institute, a bank, and a multinational manufacturing company -- for a qualitative (structured interview) study with men and women managers and their secretaries. This original study provided a wealth of information but also pointed out further issues to explore. Since then, I have completed four survey and three interview studies. One was a survey administered to secretaries in the same geographical area where the interviews were done; another was a community survey in the same area, asking about general community reactions (male and female) to women managers; a third was a follow-up survey of women who had received advanced degrees (Ph.D.'s, M.D's, J.D's, D.V.M.'s, D.D.'s, etc.) from a major midwestern university between 1964 and 1974, asking about their experiences as managers; fifth was a study of women and men administrators in a different large midwestern university system; sixth was a follow-up of the forty managers I had interviewed originally, more than five years later, asking how they were doing then and what their thoughts were about the workplace; seventh is an interview study done of African-American managers in the same geographical area as the original study;

and eighth is a study of leadership in the context of various American Indian communities in the state of Wisconsin. Details of all of these studies can be found in the Appendix. In addition to these surveys and interviews, I have also done a content analysis of advertisements for seminars for women managers collected over the last eight years. This has given me a slightly different view of the situation, from the perspective of those monitoring the market of women managers.

All of this information, combined with my personal experiences as academic department chair, division head, and coordinator of a women's studies program (which I have also analyzed from a diary I kept), contributes to what I hope is a well-grounded analysis, both empirically and theoretically, one intended to be much more comprehensive than other treatments of this topic. This book attempts to look at this issue from the standpoints of several literatures or bodies of thought, integrating them into a new viewpoint. I hope more than moving us to consider the as yet inconceivable, different world with more equality and dignity for all, the story told here will spur us to *action* toward that end.

PART I:

A First Look At Difference

In this section of the book, earlier approaches to gender are illustrated in my original writing on the topic. At this stage, the field was struggling with the issue of whether progress meant women achieving the same position as men or if it meant revisiting the qualities seen as feminine, working to have them seen in a new positive light, "valorizing" them, as postmodernists have come to say (see Clough, 1994, for example). This debate raged through feminist circles for quite a while leading to the infamous controversy about essentialism, the question of whether men and women were innately or biologically different. Another related issue being debated at this time was that between "liberal" and "radical" feminists: whether the purpose of feminist activity ought to be assuring women an equal share of existing resources or working to totally transform current social structures.

These chapters, then, should be seen in this historical context, as not necessarily representing contemporary feminist thought, but as providing a backdrop. By modeling some of the controversy resulting from this early work, I hope to give a good illustration of how multiple realities co-exist when new ideas begin to emerge and of how feedback loops begin to generate more tightly integrated modes of perception (part of the change process discussed in Chapter 1). I believe such developments in awareness are integral to the process of social change and that they occur mostly in stages. These chapters begin to tell that story.

Chapter 2

The Missing Feminine

The notion that women have something vital to contribute to society has been popping through the veneer of our cultural understandings since the women's movement experienced a revival in the 1960's. The first version of this innovation consisted of pointing out that women could do what men had been doing -- doctoring, lawyering, managing, politicking -- that women had been unfairly excluded from these fields because of ignorance and bigotry. The notion that women *can* perform these functions has come to be widely accepted. In working out this idea, considerable progress was made along the way. However, in the process, another problem arose, brought on by a strong resistance to any attempt to assign women to the traditional realm of "female," be it biological or social.

Now, women were expected to act like men, to give up our primary commitment to home and family, to focus on our work with the same intensity that men did. If we did not, we would not be as successful. This troubled us, made us feel we had to choose between our personal and work lives, take one road or the other. It was difficult to feel satisfied either way we went. For one reason or another, we felt cheated. And many of us who chose work began to dream nostalgically about the "world of our mothers" we, even many of our mothers, ultimately had left behind.

At this stage, the less desirable realities of men's lives had become painfully clear to women, and this often weakened women's resolve to enter that world full-force. "Is this what we really want?" women around the country began to ask. In one of my own early studies, a woman attorney, who had left a lucrative career in private practice for one with more "reasonable hours," said to me:

> I used to wish I was a man, so I wouldn't have so many obstacles in my way. Now that I've seen the male world of success, I'm not interested. They can *have* their careers. The people I've liked have been more balanced than that. They had a heavy influence on my decision.

As many more of us had these experiences, clarifications in the feminist dream for a new kind of social order began to take shape. We advanced from marking the inequalities and unused talents in women's lives to critiquing the entire social order. We worried about the dualisms inherent in the predominant world view; the hierarchies; the choices between private and public, home, and work; the ranking of those choices; the personal implications for those choosing to live without intimacy and personal sustenance in their lives. As Segal has put it, "We did not want to be like men; we wanted something new, and better" (1987:5). We began to develop a holistic critique of society at its basis, not only of its exclusionary tendencies. The changes envisioned would benefit men as well as women, giving them both the latitude to develop closer family ties and personal relationships.

From this thinking, distinctions arose between "reform" and "radical" feminists, the former wanting only to open the current structure more fully to women. Suzanne Gordon (1991), in her book, *Prisoners of Men's Dreams*, terms these two perspectives equal opportunity and transformative feminism. Radical or transformative feminists asked that we alter the social structure (for example, see Balsamo, 1985). Even at this point, we began to move beyond a singular focus on gender in our critique. Is it not true, we asked, that *any* form of oppression works against us? Does not the sexist nature of our society lead in large part to many other types of oppression, this white, macho, male-controlled society of ours?

Putting a few women in some powerful and prestigious positions may not change things a great deal. Certainly, it can be argued that women's basic position in our society has not changed much, despite increasing representation in all job categories. The gender gap in earnings has remained stubbornly constant; women have remained largely concentrated in a few sex-typed occupations such as clerical jobs, teaching, and nursing, and have retained primary responsibility for home and children. The same is true of the position of people of color in our economic system; they remain segregated in certain occupations and receive lower pay overall. These facts point to the co-existence of two realities: new opportunities for women (and other groups), along with continuing inequality.

The more radical, transformative line of feminist thinking has evolved into a consideration of multiple sources of oppression. One example is eco-feminism, an awareness that the hierarchical, dominator type of social arrangements can also be seen in how we relate to the earth itself, that there is a common thread running through our society's tendency toward warlike, classist, racist, sexist, ecologically damaging behavior.

A first stage in gaining our new awareness was the realization that to solve these problems, we must create a new type of society. In asking what type this might be, we began to look at the "feminine" values that have been missing. In doing this, we gained a new appreciation for women's traditional characteristics. We were attempting to become whole persons, not predominantly nurturing/emotional *or* rational/instrumental. And this led to other questions. How would women do things differently? What special talents, insights, and practices could women bring to the old order, possibly (and hopefully) transforming it in the process? Writers such as Jean Baker-Miller, Mary Daly, Germaine Greer, Adrienne Rich, and Dorothy Dinnerstein took this perspective and used it to produce works delineating women's strengths and potential contributions to our world in many different areas.

In today's world, several potential causes are given for our many problems, including the breakdown of the family, loss of traditional values, and lack of moral fiber. The thought was crystallizing in feminist circles that a more fundamental cause exists: a lack of balance between male and female forces or qualities. We began to argue that the "feminine" has too long been absent from our culture, that "masculine" values and traits have governed its development. Feminists have bemoaned women's lack of influence, arguing that giving women input could only make things better.

While masculine principles of aggression, rationality, autonomous justice, and feminine principles of nurturance, intuition, connection to the earth are often ascribed to individual males and females in our culture, I mean them as more universal or archetypal forces as described by Jung (animus or anima) or Eastern philosophers (yin and yang). A correspondence between the global and individual levels exists, of course, but it is not perfect. Thus, individual women (Thatcher of Britain, Ghandi of India, Meir of Israel) -- and men -- may well exist who do not fulfill such predictions, in terms of their willingness to use violence or force or other aspects of their particular leadership style. Jung believed important components of the self arose from a balanced interaction between masculine and feminine tendencies (Campbell, 1971). Many ancient and current systems of philosophic thought emphasize the balance or harmony necessary between these qualities -- the aggressive and the nurturant, the light and the dark.

The need for balance is stated most explicitly in Eastern religions, but many other religions and mystical schools stress this need, as well. For example, *The I Ching* or *Book of Changes* emphasizes both The Creative and The Receptive. Much of its philosophy deals with needed balance between these forces, if not simultaneously, then in succession, as life moves through various cycles. According to Wilhelm (1967), The Receptive signifies:

> The dark, yielding, receptive primal power of yin...its image is the earth. It is the perfect complement of The Creative...not the opposite...The Receptive does not combat The Creative but completes it. It represents nature in contrast to spirit, earth in contrast to heaven, space as against time, the female-maternal as against the male-paternal. (p. 10)

Lao Tzu also emphasized the need for such a balance:

> The myriad creatures carry on their back the *yin* and embrace in their arms the *yang* and are the blending of the generative forces of the two. (Tzu, 103)

Various mystical societies in this country also emphasize the need for balance and attunement to our connections with all that is around us. Such a view is evident in this excerpt from a *Rosacrucian Digest*:

> The evils of the world are due to the ego's insistence that we are all separate from one another and separate from the Cosmic. The motto of the ego is "do unto others before they do unto you." And so we go

about our daily business trying to establish dominance over nature and other people. (Huff, 1993)

Somehow, in our society, the wisdom about balancing "male" and "female" has been lost. Such is the essential critique feminism makes of modern society, that it denigrates and suppresses half of the human personality, in the process, projecting those denigrated qualities onto half the human race -- women --and, so, suppresses them as well. It is in this sense that we all suffer. None of us is whole.

In our own country, Native American groups attempt to achieve balance between male and female. Paula Gunn Allen (1986) argues that Western colonists misunderstood the balance that existed at the time of contact, mistaking separate responsibilities for oppression of women. She further argues contact with Western societies disrupted that balance, a balance these groups are once again attempting to achieve. After showing the strength of women in these traditional communities, she says:

> Every part of the oral tradition expresses the idea that ritual is gender-based, but rather than acting as a purely divisive structure, the separation by gender emphasizes complementarily. The women's traditions are largely about continuity, and men's traditions are largely about transitoriness or change. Thus, women's rituals and lore center on birth, death, food, householding, and medicine...all that goes into the maintenance of life over the long term. Man's rituals are concerned with risk, death, and transformation...all that helps regulate and control change.

She stresses both factors are extremely important for a healthy society that serves its members well.

In our society, the lack of balance causes problems. Our system emphasizes and rewards certain human characteristics over others, among them rationality, logic, strength, persistence, independence, thinking in linear progressions, and abstract reasoning. These qualities are heralded as the highest by important institutions, such as business and education. This is not all that we are as human beings; we are also emotional, nurturant, creative, spontaneous, tied to the universe and all of creation, and in need of social and intimate connections. These qualities are defined in our culture as "weakness." They are shunted aside into the "private sphere," defined as inappropriate for the public realm. Only a few extraneous "characters" are allowed the license to exhibit these qualities publicly, without sanction, and these persons are usually not in "real jobs" but more often artists, writers, actors, professional sports players, etc. This is not to say such individuals cannot and do not have a tremendous influence upon our society, but they are not usually permitted to run powerful organizations.

The idea that "feminine" qualities ought to be restored to prominence is bleeding though our cultural landscape in many different forums. Elizabeth Dodson Gray, an eco-feminist writer, argues the survival of the species depends upon our moving toward balance and away from a monolithic culture that is a "scientific, industrial, militaristic [worldview] created out of the male consciousness." (1982:129). Gene Marshall, an independent writer and ecologist who lives in an alternative community, sees a need to rid ourselves of "[T]he inherited intellectual climate...characterized by qualities like: analytical fragmentation; mechanistic imagery; efficient technological activism; and abstract, feelingless libraries of fact devoid of any value orientation." (1988:22) Kristine Culp, writing about women's religious involvement, urges that we embrace a "feminist ecclesiology...a two-sided movement...[which moves us] to denounce the life-denying forces [of the old order]...and announce the life-giving possibilities in the present [new] order." For her, the hierarchical, authoritarian, dualistic aspects of the old order are the most troubling.

Others also show evidence of this thinking about women and the feminine. The Women's Studies literature has critiqued the male biased perspective in much of our extant knowledge. Many influential writers speak of the "female experience" (Thorne and Luria, 1986) and decry the fact that our institutions "...deprive of authority to speak, the voices of those [women] who know the society differently" (Smith, 1974:12). As Elizabeth Dodson Gray has said, "The human species has been driving down the highway of life with one eye (the female) held firmly closed...[T]he unique experience of women has been ignored or disregarded" (1982:129). And Leah Fritz (1975), a peace activist, in her collection of earlier essays, says that women have the responsibility to save the world. She writes:

> I think the method we [women] have evolved will ultimately serve the best interests of all human beings...[W]omen [are] struggling everywhere, each in her own way...to write, in Jane Austen's phrase, sense and sensibility...to make the world whole. (p. 148-9)

Earlier, she said our way of ending the "millennia of men's misrule," would be to "bring the government down in a strange way...lightly spanking men, sending them out to play." She seems to believe we need simply to assert our power. In all these sources, we see the evidence of revolutionary consciousness -- the insight that there is "another way of knowing," of seeing the world, looking through the eyes of those formerly denied participation in our construction of reality.

Ways Women are Denied Input

A brief sojourn into earlier ways of thinking gives some notion of the process through which women were denied this influence. As early as 1911, sociologist George Simmel argued that women have not had input into the creation of "objective culture," according to him because of women's "essential nature" (making her incapable of contributing to any form of objective culture, lest it destroy her nature.) Newman (1985) shows how women's sphere was made highly restrictive, then trivialized and denigrated during the time when Simmel was writing. Later, Beauvoir, in her classic work *The Second Sex*, interpreted women's lack of input as the direct result of the patriarchal order existing at the time.

> As long as woman remains a parasite, she cannot take part in effectively making a better world. (1953:606)

It seems that Beauvoir bought into the prevailing notion that woman's position in society actually made it impossible for her to contribute to its development. Rather, woman stands as the inessential, The Other, the reactant to man's designs. According to Beauvoir, it is man who has shaped the world. In some ways, Beauvoir's writing simply illustrates less developed or insightful thinking; later feminists would argue women *were* contributing in many unrecognized ways. However, it is also true that her words, written more that 30 years ago, are still very relevant today. While much has changed, much remains the same. With women moving away from the home exclusively into the labor force in record numbers, they are finding a chance for an independent expression of an authentic life, as Beauvoir would say.

This trend, however, obscures certain key realities. The essential responsibilities for home and work remain gender-divided; in a marriage, a woman's work or occupation is often seen as secondary to her husband's. Also, working women tend to remain segregated in a relatively small number of occupations and are less often in managerial positions. Though women are in the labor force, with the possibility of an independent life, men are still basically in control of it. And many women doubt their ability, with good reason, to adequately support themselves without the combined income of a man in their lives. However, despite these traces of the previous order, Beauvoir believed that the forces for change were sufficiently in motion that, ultimately, women would attain an equal footing with men.

I argue that the structure of patriarchy as we know it is, ultimately, seriously undermined by the fact that women no longer find themselves being confined mainly to the home, but are now much more likely to be in the labor force. And men are slightly more often attending to matters of the home. The power dominance of male over female inherent in patriarchy is also shifting. Despite continuing problems, women are gaining more independence and power in families and other relationships. They are also moving into supervisory positions in the work force in record numbers. In this book, I will examine the ways in which women's input in the work world might improve it substantially.

Change in Perceptions

Later feminists have reinforced and expanded de Beauvoir's view, more explicitly showing the routes through which women will and have entered more fully into the public world. Here, we see the paradigm shift process operating as discussed in Chapter 1. This new view of the feminine, in our own time, began with Betty Friedan (1963) in her book *The Feminine Mystique*. However, women's discontent was treated as interesting footnotes to the "real purpose" of society, and resources were spent helping women to "adjust." Over time, more attention was paid to their problems until many individuals suddenly burst upon the scene with proposals for alternative social arrangements, proposals that have become increasingly specific through time, proposals which have much in common with one another.

Friedan's work was followed by several other very influential books that made conscious our taken-for-granted reality about gender inequality. Germaine Greer's *The Female Eunuch* and Shulamith Firestone's *The Dialectic of Sex* were among them, followed by *many* other books, the creation and publication of *MS Magazine*, and countless other periodicals. Today, the alternative thought pattern is well-developed. Nearly every publishing house makes it a point to publish feminist works and many exclusively feminist presses exist, a National Women's Studies Association has again begun to flourish, and popular magazines such as *Ladies' Home Journal* and *McCall's* have drastically altered their coverage to include many articles about working women and related issues. In all of these cases, we see a move toward balancing the power distribution between men and women; discrimination is recognized, as is women's role outside of the home. The subordinate position of women is no longer a taken-for-granted, "natural" reality. Granted, backlash and controversy abound, but progress has been made.

Many works focus on incorporating women's perspectives. By doing so, what do we stand to gain? How would this change things? Many areas have been touched upon in the feminist literature. Take, for example, the area of spiritually. Some writers argue that women have developed a deeper concern with the "inner life." Recent research shows that between 1977 and 1991, young women were consistently much less concerned than young men with materialistic success and much more concerned with finding meaning and purpose in life (Beutel and Marini, 1995). Anais Nin (1976) has given us one of the most telling accounts of a woman's concern with developing the inner life. She casts this struggle against that which comes so naturally for men, saying "the purely feminine experience...is part of...the added struggle we have, which men don't have in becoming an independent person" (p. 81) largely because we live in a patriarchal culture that trivializes concerns such as this. Women's ability to turn inward is a very different journey than that of many men. As we search to the depths of our beings, we find the whole, powerful selves that will grow and enrich the lives of those around us. This is Nin's philosophy. It is also the philosophy of many feminist spirituality women who are currently uncovering evidence that such self-reflection was ritualistically encouraged in past societies that honored women (cf. Eisler, 1987; Hall, 1980; Spretnak, 1982). Evidence exists that in ancient times, feminine qualities were revered and women actually formulated many early religious beliefs and practices (Drinker, 1948).

Psychologist Anne Wilson Schaef (1981) asserts that even in the present, for many women, learning about "god" is a process of getting in touch with the internal, since women more often view god as an internal rather than external reality. This characteristic of women was put quite succinctly by Yoko Ono in her last interview with husband John Lennon:

> Maybe it's just that I have strength, a feminine strength. Because women develop it -- in a relationship I think women really have the inner wisdom and they're carrying that while men have sort of wisdom to cope with society, since they created it. Men never develop the inner wisdom; they didn't have to. So most men do rely on women's inner wisdom, whether they express that or not (1981:93).

As Ono implies, women's concern with spiritual development is related to their concern about inner life *and* interpersonal relationships.

A recent study of women's spirituality, *The Feminine Face of God*, (Anderson and Hopkins, 1991), shows that many women are on this inner journey. These researchers find a very diverse group of women using this process to make conscious, risky, active choices. A process of "woman-centered spiritual questioning" that they chronicle leads, often, to powerfully felt connections to the life force.

Others in the area of women's spirituality (Daly, 1984;1978; Spretnak, 1982) and peace philosophy (McAllister, 1982) make similar arguments concerning "woman's perspective." In the past, it was commonly argued that women have been the keepers of our spirituality, our cultural conscience. Indeed, women have spear-headed many moral movements: temperance, peace (Mothers Against War, Women Strike for Peace), and nuclear disarmament. Many studies show women to be more religious than men in their beliefs and church participation (Bendix and Lipset, 1958), though it is not clear whether those researchers considered this to be a positive or negative trait. This concern with spiritual development often includes altruism, a concern for the other instead of the self. Hence, women are also seen as the nurturers, the care-takers of humankind; this image has persisted since ancient times (Hall, 1980; Spretnak, 1982).

Another important, related issue is that of the environment. Charlene Spretnak (1986), speaking from a cultural and eco-feminist perspective at a conference organized by Frijof Capra for the Elmwood Institute he established, talks of the need to see more clearly our connection with nature. If we continue to believe we control nature, rather than coming to see ourselves as *part* of nature, we will ultimately destroy ourselves. Capra himself asserts that the belief that males dominating females is the natural order of things is one of the more troubling aspects of our current system. New Society Publishers have produced many books dealing with this issue, including their most integrated contribution on this topic, *Healing the Wounds: The Promise of Ecofeminism* by Judith Plant (1989).

Countless authors have detailed the devastating impact of the mechanistic, controlling belief and action system upon women themselves, effects ranging from physical abuse to labor market discrimination. Others have begun to note the consequences to society in general, effects that include, among others, loss of talented women's input into many levels of society and the dependence of unwed mothers on our welfare system. And also, on the more global level, are the implications of suppressing "feminine concerns" like nurturing and connection in most of our institutions.

As I will suggest in later chapters, women and other marginalized groups are, perhaps unconsciously, actively participating in the creation of a new order, both conceptually and pragmatically. Some of these activities consist of recovering awareness and critiquing/rejecting the old order. Elizabeth Dodson Gray (1982) says:

> Male culture must accept responsibility for the fact that we have conceptualized ourselves as separated, and that all this is a product of the male psyche. It has indeed been "a man's world" (p. 122).

In fact, she says:

> We are not separated from one another. Nor are we apart from the air and water and energy which flow through and are vital to our bodies and our well being (p. 124)...What is emerging now is that women have a very interesting and different religious consciousness which includes a strong sense of connectedness to the natural world...Under patriarchy

we humans have been attempting to become as gods and transcend our morality. We have mythed ourselves as "apart from" and "above."

Put simply, she says, "The unique perspective and potential of women has been ignored or disregarded" (p. 128). LaVerne Francis Collins (1990), national president of Business and Professional Women, when addressing a gathering of women in Racine, Wisconsin, similarly said: "What we need is full participation in decision making so that all societal concerns are considered." Women are working in many professions to incorporate this philosophy. For example, Sarah Conn (1991) proposes a totally new way of doing psychotherapy, one which encourages development of connections to the "outside world," rather than *dis*couraging this, as she argues traditional psychotherapy does.

In Gray's view, "One cannot think systemically or holistically and still think in hierarchies (p. 130)...You can't rank diversity in a system because each element has its part to play." She believes that we are headed for a more holistic order (p. 133). Martha Long Ice (1987) reports similar trends. She found clergywomen to be articulating this new order in their emphasis on egalitarian social relationships:

> Their worldviews clearly lean to the holistic. They show strong awareness of the complex dynamism of modern social change...With just a few uneasy exceptions...they are nonabsolutist and process oriented in their conceptual approaches to truth and morality. The full participation of persons in their social arrangements is a high priority consideration for the women. All of them place responsible caring at the heart of their moral commitments. As they talk about intentions for shaping institutional structure, all profess attention to how it serves individual members' needs...(p. 184).

Mary Hembrow Snyder (1988) notes Rosemary Radford Reuther's discovery that "women have continually emerged from periods of repressive social and ecclesiastical history with a vision of equality" (p. 13). Charlene Spretnak (1986) also believes that women's contributions have to do with rejecting patriarchy and hierarchy, the source of which is experiential:

> ...women are telling the truth about our experience to ourselves and also to the culture at large. We tend to see things in certain ways (unless patriarchal culture has taught us to suppress it) because of our

three core areas of experience: unbroken relational experience with the mother, the body parables inherent in women's sexuality, and the deep caring for others inherent in childrearing (p. 39).

Another potential contribution of women concerns re-fashioning our perceived relationship with the environment. Relevant concerns range from the pragmatic, such as demands that women's issues be recognized as important health and environmental issues (Williams, 1993) to showing the substantial contributions women can and have made to solving our environmental problems. A woman working to preserve the Kenai River in Alaska, Devony Lehner (1993), believes women's interpersonal strengths "have much to offer natural resources work -- they can build bridges between factions on opposite sides..." (p. 13) And the proceedings from a conference showcasing women's solutions to environmental problems in countries around the world makes this point:

> Women's knowledge, expertise, and contribution to natural resources and environmental management are essential if the world is to achieve sustainable consumption, sustainable lifestyles, and sustainable livelihoods by all...Despite years of debate and discussion, both gender and environment are still marginal issues yet to be fully incorporated into development programs. (Ofosu-Amaah and Philleo, 1992)

Marion Woodman (1988), a psychotherapist specializing in addictive relationships, believes the feminine principle is "the healing way" because it accepts paradox as the way of things, the way of life.

> Microcosm and macrocosm mirror each other...Just as we rape our own bodies, we rape the Earth...The feminine soul that would move with the majestic rhythms of nature into creative, whole living is considered slow, stupid, and irrational...The feminine is rumbling with rage and grief. The frenzied addict eventually has to look her in the eye. And so does our frenzied world (p.).

Women are also rethinking our approaches to business structures and technology. Rothschild and Whitt (1986) find that women are playing important rolls in developing cooperative structures which permit the desired integration between work and play spheres of life. Oerton (1994) examines women's sensitivity to the need for autonomy, control, and dignity which influence preferences for cooperative structure. Riane Eisler (1987), creator of new partnership models, hopes that technology may actually work in our favor. She notes that we now have technological capabilities that cannot only provide instant destruction but also massive communions. With them, we can "exponentially accelerate the major transformation" in consciousness that it will take for us to move from a dominator to a partnership mentality. New Zealand politician Marilyn Waring (1988) shows how we could, by incorporating women's concerns, create a totally new system of world economics.

In sum, we see here many sources for thinking differently about women's contributions to society. This new view seems to entail the belief that we lose much by excluding women and other groups in fashioning our social institutions. Many of our serious problems may well be solved by incorporating those perspectives. From a feminist perspective, we would all stand to gain by doing so. In a more egalitarian situation, power would be shared responsibly along with the short-comings of being in charge: stress, physical and mental pressure, responsibility for failure. All of these things keep the traditional male from living the female side in their lives. If these things were valued, our lives might all be more rewarding.

But more telling, from this growing awareness, are the implications of suppressing the feminine principle in modern society. As a cultural feature, we look not only to *individuals* to re-assess their sense of self. We also seek to incorporate elements considered "feminine" into our broad social fabric. The need to do so becomes clearer as the analysis is expanded to incorporate other factors, such as race and class. In the meantime, the next several chapters will continue looking at the impact of gender in isolation from the other factors, exploring specific contributions women might or have made to the world of work.

Chapter 3

Are Women Different?

If our society as a whole suffers from lack of balance between what are traditionally thought of as "masculine" and "feminine" forces or characteristics, surely the same would hold for particular institutions. Here, I focus specifically on implications for the work world, looking especially at how women as managers or leaders at work might transform the workplace. I am also interested in the process through which we come to accept these new approaches.

My understanding about the different levels of insight currently existing about a "new way" first crystallized more than ten years ago with a particular incident. I was at a university in a different part of the country to present one of my first papers on the differences between men and women managers. The conference brought together academics and business people in order to ponder the future of women in the workplace. I really enjoy presenting my data and ideas to this type of audience, as it gives me an opportunity to see that my work has some significance for the "real world," something academics may not always realize. Further, it was a women's conference, and audiences at these conferences always seem to identify with what I am saying.

In the spirit of this conference, I had invited my cousin, a high level manager for a large international company, to attend my session and comment on my paper. I had been sending him papers and asking for comments and thought this would be one way to hear what he had to

say.   In my presentation, I explained my findings, that two very
different management models seemed to exist, that men seemed
engrossed with their image, position, and power in the company, while
women were occupied with doing their jobs and accomplishing the
related tasks.   These were the first topics mentioned by members of
each sex in the focused interviews I had done with them.   Also, men
managed others with a strictly hands-off approach, not making contact
until work was completed, while women maintained contact along the
way.   Neither appreciated the other's approach, and each group felt its
method superior.   The men went so far as to assert women *had* no
approach but rather needed to be taught how to manage (presumably,
their way!).   I finished my paper to enthusiastic nods and questions
from the audience.   My cousin later remarked, "They *really* seemed to
identify with what you were saying."

At the time, however, he got up to say we were cousins and then
continued with the statement, "What Anne says is true; women often
don't have the larger picture..." He followed with some comments about
women managers he had observed.   He did as many in business also do:
analyze women managers using the traditional management model
derived from men's experience.   I was astounded.   He had missed the
point.   He had not heard that women were using a different model.   This
tendency exerts pressure against change, working to keep the old
viewpoint intact.

I was struck by the ease with which he had translated my words back
into his own framework.   This is exactly what was emerging from my
interviews: men and women talking to one another, working together,
but totally misunderstanding one another.   Later that day, several
women approached me to remark how interesting it was to see the male
and female perspective side-by-side.   No one said this at the session.
Instead, the women surrounded my cousin in order to get information
about the company for which he worked.

Though I was struck by what had happened, I did not immediately
grasp the full implications.   The impression left on me has deepened
through the years, coming back to me again and again as I have probed
further into this difference between the genders, problems in the
workplace, and implications for the world in which we live.   The
incident points to both the difficulty and the promise that are some of
the main premises of this book: that women's (and other excluded
groups') potential contributions to our world are enormous, that they
have been virtually ignored, but men and women have great difficulty

communicating about this because they tend to see and interpret the world very differently. I call this "the battle of the sexes framework." What I hope to do in the following pages is present a compelling argument that both views must be incorporated into our worldview, that women's potential absolutely *must* be used and that it is there, intact, ready for implementation.

By outlining the process through which the new reality competes with and gradually (seemingly suddenly) overtakes the old reality, I hope to enhance the process through which the new reality is seen clearly, as a basis for action. Needed reforms are suggested by this new reality, yet those in power may resist them or fail to see what is even being said. The issues are much broader, involving more encompassing workplace revolutions, as well as changes in our government, economy, and the marketplace. We are in an awkward phase, with the "new" bleeding through the "old," both realities existing simultaneously.

Three components of the new reality emerge: first, women as a group tend to approach various challenges in ways different than men as a group would (or have) proceed(ed); second, these new or different approaches offer vital, useful solutions to current social problems; and third, all of society would ultimately benefit from the transformations resulting from the inclusion of such perspectives. Considering the female experience, listening to the "voice of those who know society differently," involves looking at the oppression of women and considering the impact of social structure upon individual lives. In addition, however, it involves looking at how women have come to see and manipulate their social surroundings, seeing the woman's agency in that she is not merely a passive pawn of social forces. As Hunt (1984) puts it, even gender is an "ongoing accomplishment," not simply a given fact. In her view, many women resist role encapsulation, negotiating new role definitions in the process. By considering the woman as an active participant in the process of social construction, we come to appreciate the resourcefulness of women in dealing with their unfavorable social conditions and discover previously unrecognized activities and accomplishments. And sifting the evidence for outlines of coherent strategies suggest new directions for our social process.

In thinking about what our work world lacks because women's influence has been excluded, consider what women might contribute, what these workplace differences might be. Before doing so, however, I must point out this whole notion of difference is quite controversial, partly because it has become intertwined with that of competence in the minds of some. Because of this, I present an exhaustive review of the research that has been done on the topic of women managing at work, attempting to tease out what we know so far about "difference" and "competence."

Finding clarity on these issues is often complicated by the taken-for-granted assumption that women are less competent at work, especially when they are in leadership positions. Even when women *do* function competently, the social perception is often that they do not. For example, Wiley and Eskilson (1982) found men managers to be rated as more powerful and effective in experimental situations, even when women had greater actual impact. Many other studies find women managers to be rated as less effective even when they can be shown to be quite effective and influential (Martin, 1985; Tarvis and Wade, 1984; Dubno, 1983; Nieva and Gutek, 1982; Larwood and Lockheed, 1979; Rosen and Jerdue, 1978; Garland and Price, 1977), even in multinational corporation subsidiaries (Izraeli, Banai and Zeira, 1980) and in other countries such as Japan (Adler, 1988). Our population, in general, perceives managers to be more like men than women (Schein, 1975;1973) and supervisors seem to value subordinates with masculine traits (Cann and Siegfried, 1987). Small wonder women in leadership positions are less confident of their own abilities (*The Administrator*, 1990; Nicholson and West, 1988; Grant, 1983; Deaux, 1979) and perceived to be less confident by men (Carr-Ruffino, 1985). They are less often given credit for their successes, encouraging their tendency to ascribe those successes to external factors beyond their control (Deaux, 1979). Kay Forest (1988) argues that such vulnerabilities -- a lack of control in the workplace -- have led to higher rates of depression among women.

Managerial effectiveness is in large part a subjective assessment; there are few concrete outcomes to use as indicators. Hence, external characteristics, such as race and gender, may be more important than actual task skills in establishing one's leadership position (Ridgeway and Berger, 1986; Cohen and Zhow, 1991). Certainly, preferences for a certain type of manager, coupled with expectations and stereotypes about women in general, may be among the most formidable barriers women managers face (Riger and Gilligan, 1980). Group norms are important in determining group dynamics and perceptions of legitimate, preferred behavior; in general, male and female groups tend to have distinctive norms (Martin, 1985). As Ghilani (1987: 34) says, "When men see the work women do as different from their own, they are not likely to move women into positions involving discretion or uncertainty." This echoes Zweigenhaft's (1987) notion of management's attempts to maintain a closed circle, keeping control in the hands of those who are known and familiar. Hence, a different style used by women may contribute to perceptions of incompetence.

The difficulty women have surmounting these barriers is compounded by the disagreement about their contributions. Many observers do not agree with my assessment that women, as a group, have different strengths to bring to the managing enterprise. Some believe "difference" equals deficiency with respect to management and urge women to adopt styles more like men's, called a "male-identified" approach in the feminist literature.

Assuming deficiencies in women's socialization leads one to urge re-socialization (c.f Terborg, 1977), preferably *before* promotion (Harley and Koff, 1980). In some cases, women are urged to adopt masculine traits they supposedly do not have. These needed characteristics include styles of dressing (Molloy, 1978), team sport skills (Karsten and Kleisath, 1986; Brown, 1979; Hennig and Jardim, 1977), financial and decision making skills (Sargaria, 1985), knowledge of the structural and behavioral dimensions of power (Smith and Grenier, 1982), achievement expectations (Herbert and Yost, 1978), the willingness to take risks (Morrison et al, 1987), willingness to delegate (*The Administrator*, 1989), assertiveness (Gendron, 1977), and adopting hierarchical leadership dynamics (Freeman, 1972). Others urge women managers to give up feminine characteristics seen as detrimental, including smiling (Rogers, 1989), "chit-chatting" (Harlan and Weiss, 1981), a concern with details (Sitterly and Duke, 1988; Smith, 1985; Fogarty et al, 1971), and the tendency to be too accessible to subordinates (Powell, 1988; Josefowitz, 1980). A 1984 UPI story reported a study that concluded beauty and feminine appearance put corporate women at a disadvantage (UPI, Evansville Press, December 4, 1984). The perceived disadvantages of not using the male-typed style were summed up quite succinctly by a man in a Fogarty et al. (1971) study who said:

> Women often get things done by coaxing. I don't think this is the way. I think it's very difficult to take a woman seriously...Women can give nice little presentations, but they don't turn the knife...They don't leave the impression that they're going to make no concessions...p. 41).

Just a few years ago, a man said something very similar to me.

_____ would get on the phone and instead of spending a minute...she would spend two minutes. She knew everybody's wife or husband's name; she knew if they had kids and sometimes the kids' names...She was not placing her priorities in the right place. She was here to do a job...You can't go out to lunch with them and get chummy and then come back at 1:00 and say "Okay, you've got to do this job," and chew them out...

The issue here is not with the woman's ability to accomplish the task, but with the style in which it is accomplished. The man in my study was concerned that the woman who talked with subordinates about family *may* not be able to do the job ("You can't...get chummy with them...and then...chew them out..."), but he had no evidence she was not able to do so. Another man said:

...How women relate to others...[being] more sensitive...can affect their performance...makes them less willing to confront the problem and solve it.

Neither of these men had any particularly conclusive evidence that these women were not functioning well. They did not mention lower output or other negative results. They just seemed to feel uneasy about the women's style, *assuming* it would not yield acceptable results.

Perhaps because style is such an issue in the field of management, other researchers have tried to refute the claims that women are inadequate managers by focusing on the extent to which there are no differences in their approaches. They maintain there are simply no true differences, that what must happen is a correction of men's perceptions, since women are managing as effectively as men, by using the same methods; these facts, they claim, have simply not been recognized (cf. Freeman, 1990; Powell, 1990). To the extent there are gender differences in work motivation, dedication, etc., these researchers believe it reflects structural differences in men and women's work situations. For one thing, men tend to have the more challenging jobs. Men in jobs resembling typical female jobs behave much like women do (Kanter, 1977b), and it seems that women's tendency to be in these jobs more often reflects employers' decisions than women's individual choices and experiences (Wolf and Fligstein, 1979). Others point to the lack of actual differences between men and women managers in their dedication to career, indicated by such things as task orientation (Green,

1988; Winther and Green, 1987; Mirides and Cote, 1980), motivation to pursue their career (Lannon, 1977), career decision making (Keys, 1985), perceptions of promotion opportunities in the federal bureaucracy (Markham et. al., 1985), weighing family and career needs (Trost, 1990), and self actualization needs (Herrick, 1973).

Marilyn Machlowitz found no real gender differences in the young successes she studied for her book *Success at an Early Age* (1984). Generally, women and men managers are found to be similar on typical management assessment measures (Harriman, 1985; Massengill and DiMarco, 1979; Moses and Boehm, 1975). Specifically, they both have similar scores in negative imagery and anxiety toward success (Wood and Greenfield, 1976), influence strategies used (Rizzo and Mendez, 1988; Instone et. al., 1983), power use (Molm, 1986), decision task variables (Rizzo and Mendez, 1988; Muldrew and Bayton, 1979), conflict resolution (Stockard et. al., 1988; Watson, 1989; Watson and Kasten, 1987; Renwick, 1977), involvement in formal and informal networks (Moore, 1987), and reactions to resource cooperative dilemmas in experimental settings (Sell, Griffith and Wilson, 1993). Many of these findings were surprising, as differences had commonly been presumed to exist.

Some weak differences have been substantiated showing that women make fewer influence attempts (Powell, 1988; Instone et. al., 1983), initiate more structure (Harriman, 1985), take fewer risks (Muldrew and Bayton, 1979), and show more concern with job variety and good relations with co-workers (Markham et. al., 1985). However, this evidence also suggests that many of these tendencies are accounted for by differences in self-confidence (Powell, 1988; Instone et. al., 1983). A lack of self-confidence seems to also be a factor in higher drop-out rates among female pre-med students (Fiorentine, 1988), where women rated themselves lower than men on various academic and social skills and in their ability to perform the role of physician, and as a result were significantly more likely to drop out of a pre-med program.

Others argue women can effectively use approaches men use without incurring resentment from subordinates and co-workers. Bartol (1974) presents evidence that need for dominance does not lower satisfaction among women's subordinates; Insel (1987) suggests ways in which women may "take charge -- nice lady style" -- without being threatening. And Colwill (1982) argues that this "woman's approach" has no advantage over the traditional masculine approach and will only delay women's entry and full acceptance into this arena.

These contradictions illuminate the contours of the debate. Many take exception to views like Colwill's. Based largely upon changes in perceptions of adequate or preferred management styles, some wonder if women are not being urged to adopt a passé style. They take the view that women may actually bring special strengths to management, approaches that ought to at least be examined for incorporation into the mainstream of management practices. Observers like Loden argue styles women bring into the workplace might actually be more applicable to current situations than those they are being urged to adopt. While women managers may be as dedicated to career success as men managers, they may use different styles to get there. Some have noted the woman manager's greater attunement to those around her, and her presentation of a sympathetic and understanding appearance, creating a relaxed, less authoritarian and less hierarchical setting (Peterson, 1984; Watson, 1989; Iaconetti, 1987; Kagan, 1983; Denmark, 1977).

Differences have also been reported in the popular press. For example, a propensity to use a less hierarchical approach that focuses on human interest elements has been noted about specific women: Nancy Woodhull, head of two major divisions at Gannett Company (*USA Today* -- Sandroff, 1989); Dorothy Roberts, CEO of Echo Scarves (O'Toole, 1990); and Gale Anne Hurd, movie producer (*The Alps, The Terminator, Aliens* -- Rosen, 1989). Robin Orr, national director of hospital projects at Planetree; Barbara Grogan, president of Western Industrial Contractors; and Paula Forman, management director at Saatchi and Saatchi advertizing agency all claimed to use this approach in a recent *Working Woman* article (Billard, 1992). They all said they used free-flowing information, flattened hierarchy approaches where worker participation is the key to their success. "I don't think command-and-control management is ever effective," Paula Forman said (p. 71).

In general, women managers are felt to be better communicators (Hyman, 1981), more open to others' participation (Schmidt, 1982), more willing to show their feelings, and more sociable, fulfilled, and optimistic (Nicholson and West, 1988). Rosener (1990) found widespread use of this approach among women managers in mid-sized companies, and Adler and Izraeli (1988) suggest this may be true worldwide. Women are also more interested in work that is creative and involves challenge (Nicholson and West, 1988; Billard, 1992). Loden (1985) directly makes the connection she claims Naisbitt and others had originally missed between needed changes in managerial practices and women's known strengths. As Steven Berghan, a Harvard Medical School psychologist, has put it:

> In an era when the need to motivate is so important, women will do better because they are nurturers and value-driven...At a time when the corporation needs restructuring, women will be able to do so because they operate in webs rather than pyramid-shaped hierarchies (Billard, 1992:70).

Swoboda and Vanderbosch (1983) argue that women administrators in higher education can and often do "keep their womanliness...and ...develop their own models." And Judi Marshall (1984) found that women managers use a very different approach than men, one that emphasizes communion, attunement with others, and cooperation. The women managers she interviewed were very dissatisfied with the domination inherent in the styles used by men. In fact, companies are now sending male executives to training seminars to learn some of the skills women have (Harrigan, 1989). As is true throughout this change process, contradictory findings emerge. For example, not all researchers agree women are developing unique strengths. Gordon (1991) reports the women she interviewed had abandoned this "women's approach" and sought instead to adopt the male approach as the only route to success.

In my original study of men and women managers, the differences described above were quite apparent. To validate that these were actual behavioral differences and not simply wishful reports, I also interviewed secretaries, so I could verify to some extent what the managers told me about their styles and also to see how some women reacted to these women in power.

These data suggested modifications to previous thinking. In the past, it was argued that men tend to play instrumental leadership roles, while women concentrate on the socio-emotional aspects of leadership -- to the exclusion of task accomplishment. My results suggested something else. The women managers I talked with were, in fact, oriented in both directions. For some, task orientation was more important than people orientation. In fact, half of them described themselves as task oriented only, and were all very focused on accomplishing the task at hand. As one of them put it:

> Efficiency is the most important thing. If people don't love me at the other end, that's ok.

Interestingly, it was sometimes their secretaries who described these women managers as people-oriented. As Sargent would put it, they had an androgynous approach, emphasizing both human relations *and* task accomplishment. Badaury (1978) had earlier reported *both* task and people concerns to be important to women managers. Pursuing their focus on task, when I asked them to tell me about their jobs, they immediately began describing the long (and exhausting) lists of tasks they must accomplish.

> I supervise ten programs...accounting and accounting clerk programs, clerk typist, secretarial science, court and conference reporting...cosmetology...radio broadcasting, banking and finance...word processing and word processing specialist and I have thirty full time instructors...and average fifty to seventy-five part time instructors in any one semester.

> I...run the checking department, transaction department, the retirement department, all of our trust accounts...overall customer service...with anything related to savings.

They were clearly concerned with doing the job as well as with being people oriented. They showed concern for their subordinates in their efforts at motivating them. "I know my people and use a different management style with each [of them] because each one is different," one woman said. These women believed this approach was successful. "If my people are happy, they are going to do a better job for me -- and they do."

The men, in contrast, did not emphasize people or task accomplishment but, instead, the *importance* of their jobs in their organizations. They seemed mainly concerned with image. "This is where the rubber hits the pavement," one man said to me several times during his interview. By this he meant, "This is where the real influence of the company is felt." Others expressed the same sentiment about their own jobs. "This is a big buck project for the company; its whole future may ride on it," another man said. And still another:

> You are moving a lot more dollars around...the smallest investment is typically a half million...it's nothing to put out 2 or 3 million...It's nice to go to parties and talk about that, "Well, how much are you dealing with?"

This difference between men and women is illustrated by Anne Wexler, senior advisor to the Dukakis campaign, quoted in a *MS Magazine* (Simpson, 1988) article about the women heading his campaign:

These women are not into establishing their macho turf...They're into answering their phone calls, bringing people into meetings, working together to get things done.

Women's concern with the individual, with co-workers, is also seen in gender differences revolving around delegation. Here, we see men valuing autonomy, as Gilligan found to be true in the area of moral decision-making, and others have found to be true about work (Miller, 1980; Jurik and Halemba, 1984). While most women described themselves as delegators (and their secretaries confirmed this), many also said they liked to "stay involved" in the projects they delegated. One woman said she liked "to have time lines," although her secretary insisted that she

...follows up without making you feel that she's checking up on you...She's an *excellent* delegator.

Reasons for staying in touch often included showing concern for subordinates:

I delegate and make them very accountable for what they're doing, but I guess the people side of me says make sure you see them once in a while, know what they're doing...so they know you care...

Note that the women do not report *doing* the work of subordinates, but establishing time lines and check points. Men do not always understand this distinction. I remember talking to a group of academics about these findings, when an elderly man said, "That happens with my women graduate students. They expect me to do the work for them." He seemed to be interpreting requests for frequent consultations as attempts to "get me to do the work."

In stark contrast is the style described by the male managers. A predominant theme, mentioned by the majority, is independence -- both for themselves and for their subordinates. Delegation meant something very different to them; they were much less involved or invested in their subordinates. While women stressed the need for involvement with subordinates, the men believed it was necessary to "give people responsibility and let them be responsible for their actions." They also believed they should:

> ...give people the flexibility to do their jobs...assume the job is getting done unless I get complaints.

For the men, good management entails *not* being involved in what their subordinates are doing. The basic strategy is to:

> ...hire people with personalities that fit your needs and let them go...They'll work like crazy...

> ...hire people who take pride in their work...and get out of their way...back off and let them do it.

> ...search for good people and stay out of their way. And be certain they know what's expected.

The women seemed to be using a style different than men's, but one still focused on accomplishing the task. Men and women went about this differently, however. Men focused on their own sense of importance and gave subordinates complete autonomy. Women focused on organizing the work and motivating their subordinates to perform. They seemed to see themselves as part of the process, rather than apart from or above it. They used their interpersonal skills, a major resource they drew upon, to accomplish the tasks at hand. Their preference for team-work, for less hierarchical relations, was apparent. Their secretaries concurred that they used this approach.

I have found these same patterns in studies I have done since my original study, including the one of women who received advanced degrees from a major midwestern university between 1964 and 1974 and had become administrators. They reported themselves to be hard working managers who set high standards, yet were considerate and effective team workers who gave subordinates autonomy and helped them develop skills of their own.

This was also true of the women administrators from Wisconsin I studied, who were somewhat more likely than the men to stress giving subordinates credit, considering their needs, showing appreciation, encouraging teamwork, and establishing checkpoints. The men were somewhat more likely to stress giving autonomy and letting subordinates set their own pace.

Many of these same patterns also appeared in other of my samples; women supervisors were more often than men described as working hard, encouraging teamwork, listening to problems, and less often being too emotional or pushing their work onto others (highly educated administrators) or less hierarchical and more likely to show appreciation and give credit for their work (secretaries).

Several studies allowed me to compare differences in how men and women perceived men and women supervisors. Here, major differences appeared. In many cases, the two genders perceived the *opposite* to be true of female supervisors. Women were more likely to see their female supervisors as more considerate, sensitive, likely to give credit, while men tended to believe women managers were more difficult to work with. (See Appendix I for more details on these findings.)

These differences between men and women seem to involve process more than outcome; men and women may use different means to get to the same end. The goal of all managers is to effectively and efficiently complete the assigned task. Women may use different tactics, a point made in a recent article in *Working Woman* entitled "Tough deals, tender tactics." (See Calano and Salzman, 1988.) Lynn Zimmer (1987) also demonstrates this point in her study of women prison guards. She shows that the women were constrained from playing their role, unlike male guards, by their relative lack of physical strength. To compensate, the women formed certain types of relationships with the prisoners (mother and sister relationships, for example) that they used to obtain the prisoners' compliance voluntarily. In the end, they were as effective in controlling the prisoners, but still they did not receive positive evaluations from their superiors because their behavior (approach) deviated from the men's.

This situation mirrors that of the women managers. Shakeshaft finds that women school administrators are not as highly evaluated as their male counterparts, partly because they obtain compliance in very different ways than men do (much as women prison guards do) and, so, are judged less competent -- because of their *style*, not their results. Reed and Garvin (1983) report similar reactions among social workers. For these researchers, however, these reactions represent more than simply failing to notice or appreciate women's approach. They argue that strong negative reactions occur because of archetypal fears aroused in both sexes when women are put in leadership positions. Mayes (1979) had earlier noted the tendency of both sexes to panic and begin scapegoating assertive women leaders in group situations. Hence, the emergence of a "new model" may well be followed by or interspersed with backlash efforts to reinforce the "old model."

Some researchers have suggested moves to counter this backlash. For example, Navari (1988) has called for a move to "de-sex" managerial skills, to incorporate aspects of both feminine and masculine approaches into the models we use and teach. She argues that by re-conceptualizing management as an interactive activity, where feedback must be received, processed, and acted upon in a constructive manner, we will incorporate the strengths women bring to this endeavor, by virtue of their experience in our society, into the already male-dominated model. Evidence exists that such understandings are spreading. A recent Cooperative Extension publication aimed at women entrepreneurs in Wisconsin makes many of these same points, arguing women managers may be more organized because of their life experiences of juggling many roles at once; may be more intuitive and, so, better problem-solvers; may be better at managing people because of parenting and volunteer activities; and may be less likely to "think too big," a common mistake made by new entrepreneurs (Gassman, 1988). The power and skill that comes to women through their family roles has been noted by Native American women who write of the power of the grandmother, the clan mother, the women of the tribe who choose the chief. And this power is based upon connection and commitment to the community, not external signs we ordinarily think of as legitimating those in authority positions -- signs such as degrees, clothes, or money (see Rayna Green, 1988).

In arguing that women may bring valued differences to management in the workplace, we may ask about perceptions of women's competence by those who have experienced women as leaders or managers. Margaret Thatcher of Great Britain is said to have declared, "In politics, if you want anything said, ask a man; if you want anything done, ask a woman."

The women I interviewed unanimously agreed women's approach was best. Two features of women's style most appreciated were organization and hard work. They believed males performed poorly in these areas. The women's secretaries said things like:

The men can get away with dumping their work onto someone else and walking out the door. _____ works twice as hard as any man I worked for, and so does ___, one of her direct reports. Women strive to get the job done immediately. Men look to see who they can get to do the job for them. Women are the motivators and organizers, the ones with the organization and energy to come up with new ideas and carry it through, and prioritize.

A man doesn't understand that it's all the little problems underneath the big ones that cause the problem, like a woman does. Women are more conscious of doing it right.

And the women managers agreed:

You don't see the men counterparts doing the same amount of homework that women managers do. Women carry a project through a little better; they can see other alternatives. Men have ideas but don't always implement support areas or details that have to go with it. That way they need others to bounce their ideas off of.

In short, these women felt women managers did more work, were better at motivating and organizing, were more responsible and self-sufficient.

Other research suggests this may be more than perceptual, particularly with regard to hard work. Bielby and Bielby (1988) found that women allocate more effort to work than men, a difference that is *particularly* marked when comparing males and females with similar family situations. This tendency is at least partly the result of the formidable barriers women face in the labor force. Frankl (1985) reported the perception to be widespread that women managers who make it are "twice as good," and Symons (1984) comments upon her sample's perceptions that women work harder to get ahead, are more motivated and competent. Morrison et al, (1987) asserts that women often *have* to outdo men to make it to the top. Surveys of women managers themselves show they also perceive this to be the case, as they did in a study reported in the *Milwaukee Journal* January 9, 1983, and in an article in the *Chicago Tribune* May 18, 1987. This undoubtedly creates pressures for men, who may even feel threatened by such motivated and active coworkers or subordinates (Serlen, 1983).

While several studies suggest a growing preference for sex neutral traits among managers (Cann and Siegfried, 1987), I have found that many workers perceive and appreciate women's approaches. In several of my studies, I asked respondents to rate the ability or performance of their supervisors on a five-point scale, ranging from excellent to poor. (See Table 1.)

TABLE 1
Overall evaluation of supervisor

	Secretaries*		Highly Educated Women*	
	Woman Supervisor	Man Supervisor	Woman Supervisor	Man Supervisor
Excellent	38.5%	22.8%	32.5%	19.3%
Good	28.5%	50.5%	32.5%	37.5%
Average	19.2%	16.8%	15.6%	20.7%
Fair	3.0%	3.0%	10.4%	12.4%
Poor	4.0%	6.9%	9.1%	10.2%
N	147		352	

Supervisor's Ability:	Women Respondents*		Men Respondents	
Excellent	30.4%	32.2%	24.8%	23.1%
Good	26.5%	28.9%	32.5%	38.5%
Average	24.5%	13.3%	23.3%	30.8%
Fair	8.8%	17.8%	9.8%	0
Poor	9.8%	7.8%	9.8%	7.7%
N	190		273	

*Chi-squares significant at .05, .10 levels

I was surprised by the extent to which women supervisors were rated significantly higher than men. Especially among other women, women managers are perceived as being quite effective, sometimes more so than men. The lower level of this panel shows the same tendency to be much less pronounced among a general population of women (in southeastern Wisconsin) and to be absent altogether among male workers (no statistically significant difference).

Overall, these findings suggest women, as a group, have a certain approach to management they prefer to encounter in their supervisors. While I used a very general evaluative measure, we know from findings already presented that their supervisors were conforming to the woman-typed model they preferred and were themselves using. This was especially true of the secretaries and the highly educated women.

If women are somewhat more enthusiastic about their women supervisors than men are, this might mean that the different approaches men and women use lead to misunderstandings between them. This could be crucial for women, as they attempt to deal with potentially misunderstanding peers, subordinates, and supervisors. Cohen (1985) asserts men often see new women managers as not taking their jobs seriously. Could this be partly because women are using different approaches that men do not perceive, leading to a low evaluation? Christie Williams (1989) argues that men at work display a strong need to distinguish themselves from feminine qualities, as a means of preserving their own masculine identity. So, possibly even if they recognized that women were using a different approach, they would not be comfortable adopting it. Stead (1985) discusses the discomfort men feel when encountering women managers who use different approaches, devaluing them rather than simply seeing them as different. And Johnson (1993) notes the social tension that often exists in mixed-sex groups, perhaps around these issues.

The argument I am making for the existence of gender based models is, of course, a generalization; exceptions do occur. Such is usually the case when one is considering social patterns, as we humans are incredibly creative, capable of fashioning our own responses to social situations. It is true, then, some men manage in a way more like the style characteristic of women and, conversely, some women use the style that is more characteristic of men. This usually does not happen without some kind of repercussion, however, given the strong expectations most of us seem to have concerning male and female behavior. In a study I co-authored of university professors (Statham, Richardson, and Cook, 1991), where each sex tended to use clearly distinct teaching strategies, students disapproved of those men and women who did not use sex-appropriate strategies. Because of the importance of feedback from significant others in our environment, individuals tend to change their behaviors depending upon their audience.

In my own data, I explored resentment and/or misunderstanding among men because of the woman manager's unique approach. First, I considered the consequences for those who did *not* conform to gender-appropriate approaches.   Then, I directly considered cross-sex resentment.

In my original interview study, there were some men and women who used cross-gendered styles. Two of the women managers reported little investment in the people who worked for them, and their subordinates agreed; they were, instead, focused on giving autonomy. One of these women was also the only woman to make self-aggrandizing statements about the "importance of her operation" for the company during the interview. She also delegated much of the time-consuming activities -- and responsibility for them -- to her subordinates. She reported shorter working days, spending several days at ball games with men managers. Both were women whose style was resented by their female subordinates. A female managerial subordinate of one of these women complained bitterly, saying:

> She doesn't treat me as a person...She second-guesses me...never shows any personal interest in me...has only asked me to lunch once.

She was obviously expecting much different treatment from her woman manager. None of the men managers, rarely reported to have asked their subordinates to lunch, received this type of criticism.

The other exception to the female model was the only woman whose secretary felt working with her had been a very negative experience. The secretary complained about her supervisor's "superior airs" and unfriendly behaviors. She felt her supervisor was "too demanding." Not surprisingly, this manager reported difficulties with subordinates in general, claiming she was second-guessed and resisted by them when she made decisions in an undemocratic fashion. She also claimed to prefer participatory decision-making, but insisted that the constraints "around here" made it impossible.

> I suspect that others as well as myself aren't given the leisure to make decisions in a rational manner. We make them out of desperation.

Time lines, she said, were such that she did "...not have the time...maybe a year...to get everyone up to a certain level of understanding" where they could effectively participate in decision-making. She reported challenges and long sessions with subordinates who were refusing to comply with her directives, something the other women managers seemed not to experience. In one of these situation she felt compelled to issue an ultimatum, largely because her subordinates were taken by surprise, since they had not been included in the decision-making process:

> I gave her some alternatives and asked her to decide, with a deadline...She could move to another job...or a number of other things. But that group was moving [to another location, the source of the controversy].

In contrast to this woman, most of the female managers said they involved subordinates in decision-making, partly for the purpose of insuring compliance:

> If everyone's part of the decision, they feel more like carrying it out. I get a lot of input from the staff...and by the time we make decisions, they accept it, and I don't have a lot of problems with them.

For women, deviations from the style typically used by women seemed to create problems with female subordinates. Perhaps the subordinates were troubled by their failure to behave "like women," though none of them consciously articulated this. Since neither of these women had male subordinates, I have no idea how they reacted to their approaches.

The implications were not the same for men who deviated from their typical style, at least where female subordinates were concerned. One interesting case involved a man manager who had adopted the model commonly used by the women. He was the only manager who made no self-aggrandizing statements during the course of the interview. A women manager who reported to him described him as people oriented as well.

> I really liked working for him...He spent a lot of time training me; I feel he invested a lot of time discussing different issues with me...He always had time for me as far as teaching me the ropes or showing me different angles on certain problems...I felt a real deep devotion to him...He's very non-threatening...He doesn't use force at all...He gives you a lot of positive control.

She obviously appreciated his people oriented approach. She went on to describe this supervisor as "very unusual" in other parts of his life as well.

His wife is very intelligent...active...She has a job. He'd have to go home [leave early] sometimes from meetings. They take turns taking care of their daughter, like if she's sick...I wouldn't say a lot of executives in his position would.

Perhaps this man would have been resented by a male subordinate. But the woman, preferring the person-invested approach, appreciated his style.

In general, there was a wide-spread preference for the sex-appropriate style. For one thing, most of the sample conformed; the vast majority used gender-specific styles. Not only did men and women tend to conform to these sex-differentiated styles, they perceived them to be normatively preferable. I do not have data to test the assertion that either approach is "better" than the other. At the point when I did this study, I could only say that both approaches exist and must be recognized and dealt with in the workplace, although, as a woman socialized in this culture, I found myself drawn to the style used by the women. Now, I see contours of a more generalized model emerging.

Concluding Comments

These findings suggest that women are often enthusiastic about being managers and perceived, at least by women, to be effective managers. While some controversy exists about gender differences in managerial style, much data suggest that women do tend to use an approach that is different from men's. Other of my (unreported) findings suggest that women managers are more satisfied with their jobs than men managers and more highly value the intrinsic aspects of the management enterprise. The differences were quite remarkable, given the lower salaries and supervisory levels these women managers held. They remained much more enthusiastic about their jobs, even though their rewards were fewer. In fact, they were more likely than men to perceive their earnings as fair. For awhile, it seems women have been anxious to move into management positions, enjoying it a great deal when they have. All women, however, may not be anxious to become managers; the professional women I studied were not any happier with their lives and jobs if they are managers. (See Appendix I for elaboration.) These women managers simply reported different determinants of satisfaction than women who did not manage.

Of course, there is always the danger that just as women gain entry into a new field, the importance of the field itself will decline. Nicholson and West (1988) note that women are entering the management ranks just as the number of people who are managers has grown tremendously and the scope and variety of what managers do has greatly expanded. At the same time, a great deal of uncertainty exists about job security, since companies no longer make lifetime commitments to their workers. The question, then, becomes whether women are being recruited into a less desirable job situation. Others note that jobs often become feminized as they decline in status, compensation, and/or position on mobility tracts. Others wonder whether women will automatically become more accepted as they become more numerous in these positions (Blum and Smith, 1988). Another relevant question is whether women are being segregated into only certain types of managerial jobs. This question has not been explored systematically as yet. However, a key point here is that these positions, at least ostensibly, give occupants some power to make decisions that affect others, and so offer the potential for occupants to significantly impact workplace processes and structures.

CHAPTER 4

The Problem of Difference:
Remnants and Transformations

> How do we come to terms with some of the ways in which feminist ideas
> have been received, with all of the distortions, omissions and co-opting
> strategies that this has entailed? And how do we discuss these matters
> among ourselves, honestly and constructively, without having the feeling
> that we are washing our dirty linen in public...?
> Hester Eisenstein, 1991.

Several dangers are inherent in this enterprise, in this attempt to
valorize women's strengths and use them to build new "female-
inclusive" models for our institutions. For one, they are often
misunderstood by men, as the exchange with my cousin demonstrated
(Chapter 3). As is true in relationships with people of color, women
are also quite aware that two separate realities or cultures are operating,
but men -- not having the same incentive for awareness -- know much
less about the realities of women's lives. Hence, they tend to translate
our behaviors back into their own framework, and judge us
accordingly.

Because of this danger, the enterprise I am advocating is sometimes
strenuously resisted or at the least viewed ambiguously by feminists
themselves. These dangers have been much debated by academic
feminists. They worry, as the exchange between my cousin, me, and
our audience suggests, that *any* attempt to spell out women's unique

contributions will be reframed and trivialized by those in the old order. This is a real danger of our time. As Segal has warned:

> A potential essentialism, or the assertion of fixed, unified, and opposed "male" and "female" natures [is] always present in such a project (1987:xii).

Her concern is that any admission of true gender differences will ultimately be twisted and used against women, partly because all the differences we do extol so proudly can be traced back to that original stereotypical model of gender differences, that old time religion of patriarchy. Patriarchy, after all, rests upon the sanctioned split between the private and public realms of life, trivializing women's concerns and giving men control of the public realm they value more highly. Segal argues that the dangers of essentialist thinking have grown as the feminist movement has become more fragmented. Certainly, many of us have experienced our findings of gender differences being used out of context to support right wing propositions oppressive to women with no clear consistent defense by feminist forces. In my own case, for example, jointly authored work (Houseknecht, Vaughan, and Statham, 1984; Statham, Vaughan, and Houseknecht, 1987) showing some of the strains women experience obtaining advanced degrees was used by certain groups to argue that women simply should not try to obtain these degrees.

In the model of change I am developing, such resistance may actually be seen as part of the process that slows the adaption of new perspectives, in this case new attempts to re-define the feminine in a more balanced, less negative way. Despite these misgivings, however, the call for incorporating "women's voice" has grown increasingly common and forceful. It is not a call easily dismissed. While not without its dangers, this incorporation is an immensely appealing idea to many in the women's movement. And it may be vitally important for all of society. As Jean Lipman-Blumen has said:

> The women's movement is an example of...a re-visioning of social reality. We have developed meaningful answers to some of the issues that the dominant ideologies have failed to resolve. We are in the process of envisioning personal relationships, institutional arrangements, and public policies that will make more sense in the 21st century (1985:2).

I cannot help but believe that women will play a crucial role in moving us in the needed direction. The first step in examining this possibility has been to explore what it means to be "out of balance" in terms of "male" and "female" qualities on both the levels of individual lives *and* social principles. This first step must be accompanied by sorting through prevailing notions of gender differences, a process some call "deconstruction." In considering what women potentially have to contribute, how the work world might change because we are increasingly influential there, I am careful *not* to reinforce the stereotypical views based upon assumptions of female inferiority. Rather, I am engaged in a re-visioning of gender differences, creating a more reality-based view incorporating assumptions of feminine competence and potential contribution. While not all women have been active in the women's movement, it is still the case that women, as a class, have experienced society differently from men, given the patriarchal structure that has and continues to exist. Thus, I believe that incorporating women into segments of society where they have been virtually absent will ultimately result in new approaches being brought to bear, new realities being expressed and acted upon. The very fact that women are entering spheres formerly open only to men has tremendous implications for society, since an essential feature of patriarchy in our time is the separateness of spheres maintained between men and women. While women's influence has so far been contained, I believe fundamental change is inevitable as these trends continue.

In later parts of this book, I go beyond this to ask how the push to include women might be related to other movements currently gaining momentum, in particular those of race, class, and gender. I connect the increase in numbers of women managers with a class issue, the worker participation movement. I believe the changes being called for in management practice open a window of opportunity for women, since women may be especially adept at implementing these "new" strategies. However, recognition for such contributions will not follow automatically. As the exchange with my cousin recounted in the last chapter demonstrates, those committed to the male model have a tremendous capacity to reinterpret and discount what women are doing.

In taking the first basic step of examining difference, I am essentially asking this question: will women change the workplace or will the workplace change women? Evidence in other fields suggests that women will retain their unique viewpoint and function accordingly. See, for example, Eleanor Miller's *Street Women* and Gary Jensen's essay in *Changing Our Minds* which show that women, even when drawn into such all-encompassing groups as criminal subcultures, tend to function very differently from the men also involved. And a recent *Harvard Business Review* article (Rosener, 1990) titled, "Ways Women Lead," suggests this may be true of women managers, as well.

According to Kuhn's notion of paradigm shift, ideas radically different from the established framework are typically resisted strongly, even by those who stand to benefit from the change. Those committed to the status quo, for whatever reason, busily try to make existing evidence fit. If in our society, a new paradigm espousing greater equality and dignity for the individual, greater inclusion of women, people of color, other excluded groups, and of the "feminine" is truly dawning, the paradigm shift model suggests we would see strong resistance to these ideas. And indeed we do.

We might conceptualize sensitivity about talking of "difference" in light of this resistance. It is ironic that the intensity of this controversy, this hesitancy to talk about women's strengths, has been especially strong within feminist circles. This seeming anomaly suggests an important extension to the current understanding of paradigm shift. Resistance to new information is not only characteristic of those supportive of the working paradigm. Even those who oppose it may resist accepting emerging information in part because the old perspective provides the only framework for interpretation. It simply takes time for a coherent alternative paradigm to be integrated and accepted, working through the feedback loops discussed earlier.

Look at how many feminists have reacted to the notion -- and data -- that gender differences in approaches to management may result in women bringing *strengths* to that endeavor, not deficits. As I see it, there are three basic premises for objections to the project I am proposing here. First, there are those individuals, many feminists among them (perhaps what Suzanne Gordon would call "equal opportunity feminists") who do not believe the system can be transformed as I am suggesting. Janet Chafetz (1990), for example, a well-known feminist writer, says:

> Many radical feminists reject the entire notion of power and elites as part of a future society based on feminist values. They define such inequality as the product of male dominance (patriarchy) and, therefore, as a central

target to be eliminated. I might wish to agree with them ideologically, but sociologically I see no chance that human societies will return to substantial social egalitarianism...short of a holocaust that returns us to subsistence living...Elites will exist for the foreseeable future. The issues are then: Who composes the elites and what kind of policies do they pursue? (1990: 227-228).

For Chafetz, such transformation is simply not practical. Camile Paglia, in a recent debate with Suzanne Gordon for *Working Woman* magazine (Aguilera-Hellwig, 1992), agrees. She says:

Women are not going to be able to radically change the managerial style. We maybe can humanize it slightly, with a sense of humor and psychological insight. But ultimately, leadership is leadership; it means efficiency, stripping away feelings down to mechanization (1992: 78).

Both Chafetz and Paglia seem to believe that the current predominant style of corporate and political leadership *is* leadership, not simply one *type* of leadership.

Paglia adds yet another wrinkle, the idea that men will not give up their advantage easily, particularly in hard economic times:

When you shrink the employment pie, then competition becomes ruthless. No one is going to say to women, "Here, take it. It's yours. We're sorry. We've been bad boys for eons." (1992: 78).

These women are, in essence, asserting we waste our time advocating for such naive, impractical changes. One anonymous reviewer of this manuscript concurred when she said:

Let me make a final comment...I have some trouble with the thesis that women will transform organizations. From a personal perspective, I'd like to believe that. But I think this is an overly simplistic conclusion. What Statham really documents is that...some women...have a set of skills...that...are particularly suited to the types of...managerial tasks that many organizational theorists believe we need to meet...the future. Does that mean patriarchy is dead? I doubt it. Men continue to co-opt women's ideas and contributions.

I believe, however, that dramatic changes *can* occur, but only if prior visions are clearly articulated. If we can see clearly what we have done (or have allowed to be done), then we have the option of consciously crafting another approach. As human beings, we do create our own social systems. In the past, not all of us have had a voice in those creations.

A second adverse reaction to claiming and revering women's unique or special qualities comes from feminists concerned it may be dangerous, that all difference, no matter how positive, may ultimately be devalued and used against women. "If we cannot have separate but equal in race relations, we cannot have it in gender relations," one anonymous reviewer wrote in reaction to one of my earlier articles from this work.

In this view, there are no true differences between men and women, only socially constructed ones, so we should all be working toward the elimination of separate spheres, for a world where men and women are not distinct. Therefore, we should not be emphasizing the differences that do exist. As Epstein argues, the "separate but equal," two culture theory of the genders is "always hierarchical" (1988, 233). Bologh (1985) argues for a need to transform the public world to be more in accordance with "feminine values." For her, masculinity, as currently defined, reproduces the political economy and femininity reproduces the domestic sphere. For such theorists, the basic problem with the current social order *is* this separation -- or dualism. If these separate spheres could be merged, they believe, both women's oppression and the system of traditional gender identities would end. This is possible, she argues, as gender identity is an ongoing social construction, so it is within our power to change it. She combines what she calls a dialectical and phenomonological perspective to show only from active struggle and opposition against the political economy will a new arrangement emerge.

Many others have criticized the separate spheres as they currently exist. Rosenberg (1982) traces the painful, growing recognition such a distinction existed that was *socially* constructed, not biologically innate. She places Jessie Taft, an early student of George Herbert Mead, as the first of a long line of women thinkers who reconstructed our vision of the origin of sex differences, a line that, according to her, culminated dramatically with Margaret Mead. Others have followed Margaret Mead's lead in arguing for the social rather than biological origin of gender differences. Goffman, for example, argued this in a 1977 article in which he also pointed to the dilemma women face as a disadvantaged group who seemingly are thought well of. He argued that this deception constantly undermines our ability to confront our social position. Certainly for Rosenberg, the separate female sphere was a source of oppression for women, something Schur (1984) argues even more pointedly in his treatment of the labeling and stigmatization of the feminine. For him, women's position in their separate sphere directly resulted in objectification, restricting women's opportunities. As a result, women were not seen as individuals with a wide range of competencies and abilities. This effect was magnified by the power men had not only to restrict movement but also to define or name women's character. For him, both stigma *and* subordination were necessary for creating women's current predicament.

In some ways these writers seem to be arguing for the end of separate spheres, for the creation of a social order in which men and women are seen as virtually indistinguishable, capable of a wide range of activities. There are certainly ways in which common feminist formulations point to a merging of the personal and the public, against the standard gendered division of spheres under the current version of patriarchy. These concerns include understanding how the personal is part of a woman's public dilemma, an attempt to move concern for the personal into the public arena -- so it is important to both men and women (see, for example, Gould, 1983; Risman, 1985). In that sense, the two spheres would become much less distinct. And certainly, if women brought their unique contributions to the workplace and were able to truly transform it, that might well be the result -- greater similarities between men and women, more integrated lives for us all.

Actually, in our search for difference, in our attempt to document the differences as they truly exist, not through the distorting and devaluing lens of male bias, perhaps *fewer* differences will ultimately come to exist. If women reject the male model that focuses on the public realm while leaving the private to a less valued other, but also refuse to remain confined in the private (home) realm, the only alternative is integration of those two realms. In many ways, work never *became* separated for women as it did for men. Much of women's work has remained in the home and, even with work outside of the home, we see a recent trend for much of that work to move back to the home, a move exacerbated by telecommunication innovations. Many of these at-home workers are women.

Do we *want* women to adopt the approaches men have used (thereby eliminating any gender differences) or would we all be better off if women refused, but instead demanded more balance and integration in their lives, transforming the work (public) realm in the process? Can we have a true merger before re-asserting the *value* of those characteristics we call "feminine"?

A third line of thought argues that the spheres have never really been entirely separate, but instead have been joined by boundaries that are more or less permeable at certain junctures. In this view, the important questions become when are the boundaries permeable, under what conditions, by which types of individuals. Gerson and Peiss (1985) argued gender was not a dichotomous variable but a continuous one and, also according to Gerson and Peiss (1985), our concept of separate spheres should be replaced with a boundary that is more permeable, flexible, with territorial markings. Several individuals have observed children to discover specific features of the "border work" necessary to maintain these boundaries. Thorne (1986) provides rich detail of interactions which affirm gender boundaries and those in which the distinctions tend to break down, occasions when the two sexes are comfortable in the same sphere. Cahill (1987) looks also at children to discover how taken-for-granted gender norms are learned and enforced. In his work, the concept of border work is also important, as children sometimes distinguish what is male from what is female and sometimes do not. And Pleck (1976) wrote about "the myth of the separate spheres," saying they have only recently developed for those outside of the middle class where both spouses have worked and thus, were not caused by industrialization at all. Rather, she says, home production has declined quite gradually.

For these researchers, and for my purposes, the notion of separate spheres is useful in that it provides a mechanism for expanding our understanding of the dynamics of gender distinctions. Seeing women as "different" does not necessarily imply that they are inferior or incompetent. In thinking about the interactions of race, class, and gender -- as I will attempt to do here -- Jaggar and Rothenberg (1993) argue it is important for us to start from the proper standpoint, women's perspectives. Jaggar (1983) earlier asserted women have a world view less distorted, more reliable than capitalist or working class men because of our special class/social position. We have less vested interest in the current social structure and have suffered more severely because of it. MacKinnon (1982) noted socialist advances made thus far in western society, in the absence of a conscious concern with gender also, have not served women well. We are freed to work outside of the home but not in an equal capacity. The feminist emphasis upon internal redefinition and the individual's perspective could well be incorporated into the Marxist perspective.

Difference as stereotype?

Some feminists follow the lead of writers like Jaggar and Rothenberg, valorizing women's approaches, seeing the recognition of possible differences not as a source of oppression for women but as ways for identifying women's potential contributions to society, to our models of change.

According to Lipman-Blumen (1984), we are in the process of transcending traditional control myths that women are always or only altruistic, nurturant, manipulative, and so on and, instead, coming to appreciate women's true nature or strengths. Hence, we find others calling for an appreciation of women's intellectual strategies and cognitive styles (Swoboda and Vanderbosch, 1984), use of power (Baker-Miller, 1982; Gordon, 1985), perceptions of childbirth (Oakley, 1976), unique work experiences (Berk, 1985), and central core imageries or perspectives (Kimball, 1981). There has also been renewed interest in female historical figures, such as Elizabeth Cady Stanton, and new methodologies are being developed to more clearly illustrate their contributions (see, for example, Jacobson and Kendrick, 1986). Even in the more traditional literature, a willingness to consider such topics as emotions as valid areas of inquiry (Stryker, 1987; Thoits, 1985; Hochschild, 1983) may well stem from this impetus.

Some argue approaches peculiar to women may actually have a biological basis, as suggested by neuropsychologist Helen Hughes in a recent *Chicago Tribune* article (1988). She discussed findings which suggest women are more:

> bilaterally effective...have a more fluid way of going from the left to right [brain] hemisphere...[M]ore fluidity in terms of functioning left to right and right to left...should be an advantage in creativity.

In their book *Brain Sex,* Moir and Jessel (1991) also argue women's brains function differently in many ways, underlying many gender differences we commonly think of as socially constructed. This idea is something many feminists reject as "essentialist" thinking, that women are inherently or biologically different from men. However, it is not necessary to believe gender differences are biologically determined to believe they exist. Social influence is another likely source.

To do the kind of analysis where women's strengths are appreciated, the old negative stereotypes about women long existing in our culture must be confronted. The differences I wish to explore are *not* those negative stereotypes about women. Such stereotypes do exist, views that are inflexible, exaggerated, usually entailing negative beliefs or expectations about certain groups. Unfortunately, stereotypes are usually based upon an element of truth. Thus, they seem to receive confirmation in daily living and, so, are very resistant to change. They are also imbued with a great deal of emotional energy, often insulating the holder from facing some unpleasant reality of life, such as economies are simply unpredictable, emotions and sexuality do exist, etc. Stereotypes provide convenient scapegoats to blame when these simplistic fantasies are contradicted by experience. Hitler's holocaust is an example of an extremely skillful and sinister use of stereotypes; the Jews were not responsible for Germany's problems, though many were easily convinced this was so. It is, instead, the fact that economies are unpredictable and other countries put Germany in an unfavorable position. In recent times in the U.S., the use of the term "liberal" as connoting an irresponsible, bleeding-heart spendthrift, is a less extreme use of a stereotype. George Bush used it quite effectively in his first presidential campaign.

Stereotypes about women often function to protect men from facing the vulnerability and emotional sensitivity they may feel yet may not want to admit. Men can project these characteristics onto women, freeing themselves from the need to claim any of these tendencies for themselves. As a result, perceptions of how women managers actually behave are often quite distorted. Thus, Josefowitz (1980) contends women's behavior, even when the same as men's, is often interpreted differently. (See Figure 1). According to these stereotypes, women are too disorganized, emotional, and undependable to be good managers. With such perceptions, no matter how well women do in management positions, their expertise will not be recognized by society. Their behaviors can often be distorted to fit into and reinforce this negative stereotype.

Figure 1

His desk is cluttered; He's obviously a hard worker and busy man.
Her desk is cluttered; She's obviously a disorganized scatterbrain...
He's not in the office; He's meeting customers.
She's not in the office; She must be out shopping...
He got an unfair deal; Did he get angry?
She got an unfair deal; Did she cry?...
He's leaving for a better job; He knows how to recognize...opportunity
She's leaving for a better job; Women are undependable.

The tendency to distort women's behavior seems to be quite widespread. One of the secretaries I interviewed handed me a list at the beginning of our conversation. (See Figure 2). Again, when the

---

Figure 2

A businessMAN is aggressive; a businessWOMAN is pushy.
A businessMAN is good on details; a businessWOMAN is picky.
HE loses his temper because HE is so involved in his job; SHE is bitchy.
When HE is depressed, (or hungover), everyone tiptoes past his office;
SHE is moody, so it must be her time of month.
HE follows through; SHE doesn't know when to quit.
HE is confident; SHE is conceited.
HE stands firm; SHE is hard.
HIS judgments are HER prejudices.
HE is a man of the world; SHE has been around.
HE drinks because of the excessive job pressure; SHE is a lush.
HE isn't afraid to say what HE thinks; SHE is mouthy.
HE exercises authority diligently; SHE is power mad.
HE is close-mouthed; SHE is secretive.
HE climbed the ladder of success; SHE slept HER way to the top.
HE is a stern taskmaster; SHE is hard to work for.

---

woman conforms to expectations, that is bad.   When she fails to conform, that is also bad. As Swoboda (1988) has said, when women rise further to the top, they encounter an increasingly smaller band of acceptable behaviors that are both feminine and managerial.   And Swoboda provides a long list of stereotypical beliefs about women managers which she argues are not true: women are not more impulsive, not more humanitarian, not more suspicious, and not more tricky; they are neither less dominant in leadership positions, nor less self-disciplined, insightful,   even-tempered, goal-oriented, or able to cope with stress.

Stereotypes exist about men as well as women managers. Heller (1982) shows how managers in business, education, and social services hold stereotypes of men and women managers, namely men are too product-oriented and women too people-oriented.   She finds these beliefs to be strongly entrenched, despite evidence to the contrary.

In the course of doing my interviews and surveys, I came to see two distinct views of differences between men and women managers among those with whom I talked. One view, borne of lack of exposure, held that women were too demanding, emotional, and controlling to be good managers.   This view incorporated many elements of stereotypical beliefs described above. It is based upon the image of the emotionally unstable woman (especially during her monthly "time"), vindictively misusing her power on petty jealousies and personal relationships. This view leads to the conclusion that leadership positions are best left to men, who are capable of separating the personal from the professional and of working amicably enough with individuals they may not care for personally.

It goes without saying this is a stereotyped perception, based upon the age-old fear of what the oppressed female would do if suddenly delivered from bondage -- or allowed to exercise any degree of power. Many archetypes in our culture -- witches, moon phases, mother of darkness, Lady Macbeth -- represent this fear.   With this set of expectations at some level of consciousness, many of those I spoke with and surveyed expressed a preference for male bosses. Women, I was told, would be too difficult to work for. Other researchers have also found this perception to be widespread (Harriman, 1985; Ferber et. al., 1979; Kanter, 1977), although Kanter and Harriman suggest the preference for male bosses may reflect the woman manager's relative lack of power (hence, less status for the subordinate) as much as any real problems a subordinate may have in dealing with her. Many workers would prefer to work for more powerful managers. For example, the secretaries I surveyed found the higher positions of their men supervisors affected their own situation as well; if they had a male supervisor, they perceived their chances for advancement to be greater and reported higher levels of pay and benefits.

On the other hand, the secretaries answering my first survey who worked for women were just as happy with their jobs -- but for very different reasons. They more often felt included in decisions and appreciated for their contributions. They were more likely to say they were consulted about decisions, treated as equals, shown appreciation and given credit for their work than were the secretaries who worked for men. They were also more likely to say their women supervisors had given them tasks and other opportunities that would help them along their own career paths. As they came to *know* about women managers, they changed their perceptions, coming to see them as more considerate, appreciative, thorough, organized, and hard working than many men managers. They came to believe they were just as good, if not better than the men. Hence, they came to perceive more reality-based differences between men and women managers and discarded the common stereotypical perceptions.

Over time, I developed a scale to measure this shift in perception. The items are given below (Figure 3). Being a woman manager

FIGURE 3

Stereotyped and Reality-Based Views of Women Managers

Compared to men, women managers are:*

Reality-Based	*Stereotypes*
1. More considerate	1. More demanding
2. More appreciative	2. Having a harder time delegating
3. Harder working	3. Harder to work for
4. More thorough	4. More emotional

* For each item, respondents answered on a scale of 1 to 5, representing strongly agree to strongly disagree.

affected perceptions. I found evidence that those experienced with
women managers came to adopt the more reality based view. This was
true of the highly educated women I studied; those who *were* managers
more often ascribed to the reality-based view and rejected the
stereotypical one. (See Table 2.) They more often believed women
managers were more considerate, appreciative, harder working, and
thorough -- and less often believed women managers were too
demanding or unlikely to delegate. While many of them remained
neutral on these items, reflecting comments they made about no
perceived gender differences, significant gender differences appeared
when asked to describe their own supervisors on these same
dimensions. For these women, the experience of having *been* a
manager had a much more powerful effect on perceptions than having
worked for a woman. (See additional information in the Appendix.)
Likewise, the female Wisconsin administrators more often ascribed to
the reality-based view than their male counterparts (Table 3), more
often believing women managers were more appreciative and
considerate, harder working and more thorough, though they were also
more likely to believe women managers had a harder time delegating.

TABLE 2

Highly Educated Women's Perception of
Women Managers

Women supervisors are:	Strongly Agree	Agree	Neutral	Disagree	Strongly Disagree
1. More Considerate*	6.0%	19.3%	54.0%	16.7%	3.8%
2. More appreciative of secretary's skill/abilities**	8.9%	29.8%	40.4%	17.6%	3.3%
3. More Demanding**	2.7%	20.9%	51.7%	22.0%	2.7%
4. Harder working**	13.1%	37.7%	35.7%	12.2%	1.3%
5. Less likely to delegate**	3.8%	25.1%	43.3%	24.0%	3.8%
6. More thorough**	8.6%	30.2%	46.8%	12.9%	1.6%
7. Harder to work for	3.3%	9.6%	50.2%	29.1%	7.8%
8. More emotional	2.5%	17.0%	38.2%	29.3%	12.6%

*Significant difference if currently have a woman supervisor
**Significant differences if currently a supervisor

TABLE 3

Wisconsin Administrator's
Perceptions of Women Managers

Women Managers are:

	Men					Women				
	Strongly Agree	Agree	Neutral	Disagree	Strongly Disagree	Strongly Agree	Agree	Neutral 1	Disagree	Strongly Disagree
More Considerate*	0	11.9%	47.5%	35.6%	5.1%	2.0%	31.4%	45.1%	19.6%	2.0%
More Appreciative*	1.7%	10.2%	35.6%	45.8%	6.8%	5.8%	34.6%	38.5%	19.2%	1.9%
More Demanding	0	3.4%	50.8%	40.7%	5.1%	5.8%	13.5%	48.1%	30.8%	1.9%
Harder Working*	0	6.8%	30.5%	50.8%	11.9%	15.4%	42.3%	30.8%	9.6%	1.9%
Less Likely to Delegate*	0	3.4%	42.4%	47.5%	6.8%	0	30.8%	40.4%	23.1%	5.8%
More Thorough*	0	5.1%	42.4%	45.8%	6.8%	5.8%	40.4%	38.5%	11.5%	3.8%
Harder to Work For	0	5.1%	27.1%	54.2%	13.6%	0	7.7%	42.3%	34.6%	15.4%
More Emotional	0	6.8%	35.6%	49.2%	8.5%	0	15.4%	28.8%	38.5%	17.3%

*Significant gender difference

It seems that in distinguishing the *type* of difference -- reality-based vs. stereotypical -- we can address many of the concerns raised by feminists who worry that to admit difference invites further put-downs of women as incompetent and ineffective. We must control the terms of the debate, being careful to emphasize the differences to which we are referring. We must work toward a change in society's view of difference. Must those who use different approaches continue to be judged negatively? Or can we allow for a diversity of approaches? With projected changes in the make-up of our workforce, the anticipation that workers will become increasingly diverse, such flexibility in managerial styles may not only become desirable but necessary!

In looking at this evolution in perceptions of women managers, the movement from stereotypical to reality-based views, I also uncovered information about the process through which that evolution occurred. As I have intimated, a basic aspect of this process is actually encountering a woman manager, rather than simply imagining the experience. This was clear in my own studies. Time after time, in study after study, the experience of having a woman supervisor changed perceptions from stereotyped to reality-based. And the effect seemed to be strongest for the men who initially held the most stereotyped views and, therefore, could have made greater changes.

Other researchers have also found perceptions of women managers to change once an individual has had a woman boss, and these changes usually take the form of rejecting stereotypical perceptions and incorporating new perceptions of women managers as more effective because of their interpersonal and organizational skills. Ferber et. al. (1979) reported the experience of working for women markedly lowered the common preference for a male boss. Kagan and Malveaux (1986) reported having a good relationship with a woman boss resulted in secretaries preferring to work for women. As for men, Baron and Abrahamsen (1981) reported men who worked for or with women managers were more accepting and more likely to reject many of the stereotypical beliefs about women managers discussed above. Cussler, as early as 1958, had discovered this to be true among men executives. Gordon and Strober (1975) reported men who had worked with women were more likely to favor putting women in managerial positions.

Some literature suggests otherwise, that women working with women, in particular, leads to disastrous consequences -- re-affirming common stereotypes rather than calling them into question. For example, Ann

Harriman (1985:28) asserts the "petty, childish bickering often associated with female behavior [in the workplace]...may result from the similarity between women...[that] exacerbates the feeling children generally have that their parents can read their minds." Or, she says, it may result from transferring the hostility between mother and daughter to workplace relationships. And Tara Roth Madden (1987) asserts in a chapter of her book titled "Men's Reserved Seating -- Ringside at the Office Catfight," women "consistently function as their own worst enemies" (p.34), essentially keeping each other out of higher management levels.

> Why do women want to defeat their own cause? Trained from infancy to view other women as rivals, they'd rather give up everything than take the chance of allowing other women to do better than them (p. 68).

The interviews I originally did with managers and secretaries belie these expectations. They suggest a transformation of attitudes, rather than disaster, results from women working for women, especially among the secretaries. I was unprepared for the nearly unanimous positive acclaim the secretaries gave their women managers. Only one of these secretaries described her manager in the harsh terms found in the literature, and this secretary worked for a second woman manager whom she really appreciated. Several of the secretaries admitted to having misgivings before working for these women, but now a majority wondered if they could "ever go back to working for men again." All but one now felt women were not difficult to work for. While there were several misogynist comments made by the women in this study, ranging from describing women as more vicious and emotional than men and more likely to take things personally or "run to the boss" with a problem, no such comments were made by secretaries to women. All were made by secretaries to men.

First, opinions began to change as secretaries realized the overall relationships women managers established with them were more positive. The women managers were seen as being more considerate. One woman manager said:

> I tried not to make them do things (like, make coffee) that I wouldn't want to do myself.

Several secretaries elaborated with such remarks:

> I think women are much more respectful of their secretaries, more
> sensitive to them, appreciate more the things they do. Just simple things
> like saying thank you for tasks that are completed. So many men just say
> good morning and good night to their secretaries and that's about it. I've
> watched a lot of these men interacting with their secretaries and thought,
> "I don't think I could ever work for him!"

The secretaries reported reciprocating, trying to be considerate of the
manager also. The kind of interpersonal relationships that developed
between manager and secretary set the stage for further change. The
secretaries came to believe their women managers appreciated and
respected their skills and capabilities more than men.

> Most men think every girl who sits at a desk with a typewriter is a
> secretary. Women don't. Also, they don't understand what a secretary
> really is. Women understand the responsibility that comes with being a
> secretary.

> I prefer working with women. They are more respectful of me and my
> opinions.

Contrast these comments with that of a man supervisor, complaining
about all the paperwork involved in his job, "Sometimes I could be a
secretary and do the work I do."

While most of the men who discussed secretaries did not make such
disparaging remarks (with most of the men the subject simply never
came up), their remarks suggested that they saw secretaries as
"helpmates," often taking over functions they disliked. "I really need
a good secretary to take care of me. They take the air of responsibility
off your mind, organizing yourself," said one manager who recently lost
his secretary to budget cuts. And a secretary said of her boss:

> I don't think he knows what I'm doing half the time. Once he gets it off
> his mind, he forgets about it.

Another secretary gave even more compelling evidence that
secretaries were not taken seriously by male managers; she told of when
she wanted to hire a male clerk and was told by a superior, "We want
to see some women around here; we want to see legs."

The men's secretaries usually offered different positive remarks about their superiors than did the women's secretaries; they described them as "relaxed and easy to work for" or "amazing in their intelligence and energy." Few mentioned consideration or appreciation as traits shown by their male supervisors. Eight out of thirteen complained that their bosses were disorganized and depended on them to "hold them together." One of these women said of her manager:

> He isn't over-expressive as far as he would like to show his gratitude for a job that you've done well...but he shows it in other ways...your performance appraisal...He may even say a nice comment to *someone else* ...[about] the nice job you do. (emphasis mine)

Perhaps even more important in the process of attitude change was the realization women managers were not only more considerate and appreciative, but perceived the secretary to have a career path of her own, and they were concerned to help her develop along those lines. The literature on this topic suggests secretaries are seen as extensions or helpmates of their bosses, and that they can progress only if their bosses progress (Kanter 1977). Since the literature deals mostly with male bosses and their secretaries, the situation may be very different with the woman boss, particularly if she makes an effort to encourage her secretary to advance on her own. And these data suggest she does.

The women managers I interviewed encouraged their secretaries in several ways. Some simply talked to their secretaries about their futures, helping them to plan for it. One secretary talked about her woman manager:

> ____ gives me lots of responsibility, more than [that given to] other secretaries here who have been here much longer, and she has been telling her boss what a good job I'm doing. I'm just thrilled. She told me that if I tell her what I want to do, she'll work to see that a position would be there for me when I'm ready for it. It's so wonderful to have a boss who looks out for you like that.

> My boss has encouraged me to think about my career, going to school. She's talked with me about it a lot. She's the one who got me thinking about it.

Others encouraged the secretary's career growth by incorporating tasks "beyond the scope of secretary" into their daily routines. These tasks fostered autonomous career growth in two ways: 1) by preparing the secretaries for a specific job; or 2) by challenging them to perform at levels they might never have attempted otherwise.

> Working for ___, I did things I've always wanted to do and never really had a chance to do before. She asked me what I liked and I told her writing, and she gave me lots of responsibilities like that. I got to use my interests, and now I notice things I never really did before...My new boss doesn't even seem to notice me. I had broken my engagement several weeks before he even knew I had been engaged!

> I was her secretary, but more than that. We were like a team, filling in where the other was weak. I felt I really found my niche working for her. It really broke my heart when they laid me off. I thought I would follow in her footsteps.

> She trusts me...She doesn't question what I do. She has confidence...that makes you feel good. I worked for the man that sat in here prior...and that was just a bad experience...He never let you do anything; he only told you what he wanted you to know...I enjoy doing [these things] because she gives you credit...Like with this book...she stepped out and she doesn't even look at it anymore.

The situations described by the secretaries who worked for men were *very* different. Some were given responsibility -- some even used similar words ("I'm more like his assistant"; "We're like a team") -- but there were crucial differences. For one thing, these secretaries frequently reported being delegated responsibility for tasks they felt they did not have the authority to perform -- for instance, managing their supervisor's subordinates. The result was not pleasure and challenge for the secretary but inordinate "hassles" as the secretary often felt "caught" between a demanding boss and a resentful subordinate. One of the secretaries talked about this explicitly:

> I'm like on an equal level with another office worker...then my supervisor would put me in the position...of I have to correct her or him...I'm not real comfortable with that...If there was a position as lead secretary...then it [would] be my responsibility...But when I'm...on the same level, I would feel maybe they would resent my telling them what to do or criticizing them...I really don't know why he feels I should do this kind of thing...I tell him I don't feel I should do that.

Several secretaries described having to persuade their boss's recalcitrant subordinates to deliver. But were these secretaries being given positive responsibility? One secretary thought not. "I don't think he gives me responsibility; I think he depends on me a lot." She was also expected to push subordinates to "deliver" and often ended up making decisions for her boss:

> Sometimes, I have to guess what my boss is going to say, and based on that I'll give decisions to people...He tells someone to do something, and I'm the one that's got to be sure the thing gets done...One of our [officers] in particular struggles...in making deadlines. And I have to very nicely push without becoming a pain in the ass...If I can't get anywhere...I just take it back to ___ and say, "This is what you wanted done, and I'm not getting anywhere with it," and then he goes and raises hell.

Men managers were also less likely to delegate a task on the basis of its benefit to the secretary (expanding her career horizon) than they were to delegate tasks they disliked doing:

> He doesn't like the detail...He doesn't want to see all that little itty-bitty stuff...He wants to know about it, but he doesn't want to do it, so he delegates it to me, to the managers...

Some of the men managers talked about their dislike for organizing, saying they relied on their secretaries for this. The secretaries concurred.

> I try to keep my boss on time and...organized...haul him out of one meeting to get to another on time and make sure all the materials are ready as he's flying out the door...and setting up appointments.

Among all of these secretaries to men, there was only one case where the manager was attempting to upgrade his secretary's position to be "more administrative," and this man was close to retirement. Another manager talked about a secretary he had helped to get such a promotion, but his view was that:

> ...now, she regrets it...It's boring there...She misses being here, knowing so much about what's going on. And it will be hard on her marriage.

Overall, helping secretaries develop their own careers did not seem to be of much importance to these men managers. They seemed to see them more in terms of their positions, how the secretary helped them, and less as people with independent careers to pursue.

The secretaries who had never worked for women tended to maintain their stereotypical views of women managers. The majority said they preferred to work for men, most of them believing women were simply too difficult to work for. It was only those secretaries who had actually worked for women whose attitudes had undergone an attitude transformation, now believing women might be even easier to work for, despite the fact that they had formerly preferred to work for men. As one secretary put it, "I've had such a wonderful experience working for this woman."

It is interesting all of the individuals in this particular interview study who had changed their minds were women; they shared the view of management their women supervisors had, believing managers should use participatory, person-oriented techniques for accomplishing the task. They appreciated their managers' organization and thoroughness because they believed managers should stay in touch with what is going on, should not delegate without check points. These preferences seemed to involve gender-specific models.

Are male subordinates similarly affected? Results from the community study suggest they are, in many ways. In that study, I was also exploring the possibility that better relationships between women than expected may represent a change in the situation of women managers. As Kanter (1977) pointed out, women managers in the past had been few in number and in token positions. This situation causes unusual responses on the part of those around them (including closely scrutinizing the token) *and* on the part of the token herself. Kanter points out power-sharing and interpersonal support may be difficult things for tokens to do or give since they feel their position is so vulnerable (which indeed it is!).

Hence during these last few years, when women's representation in the rank of managers has grown tremendously, structural pressures may have lessened, enabling the forming of more cordial workplace relationships. I found those who worked for women in the last five years -- both men *and* women -- reported much better relations than those who had done so previously. (See Table 4.)

Table 4

Rating of Experience with Last Women Supervisor by
Time Since Experience with Woman Supervisor

Had Woman Supervisor:	More Than 5 Years Ago	In Last Five Years	Currently
Experience with Woman Supervisors:			
Extremely Positive	6.9%	29.7%	30.8%
Positive	24.1%	37.8%	38.5%
Neutral	34.5%	21.6%	7.7%
Negative	20.7%	0.0%	5.8%
Extremely Negative	13.8%	10.8%	15.4%
N	29	37	52

Chi Square = 115.23, significant at .0001 level

Secretaries who had worked with women managers in the last five years reported their experiences with women managers to be considerably more positive than those who had done so more than five years ago. In fact, more than a third of those secretaries who had worked for women more than five years before reported it as a negative experience -- and another third rated the experience as neutral. In contrast, more than half of those with more recent exposure felt it had been a positive experience. A similar pattern exists among the men and women in the community survey, though not nearly as pronounced. (See Table 5.) It seems, then, there is a period or time effect operating here, where reaction to working for a woman manager depends to a large extent upon when the experience occurred.

For those with recent exposure, there seems to be a process through which stereotypical perceptions are transformed because of encountering the anomaly, the woman manager, and learning about her through first-hand experience. In part, it has become less possible to convince oneself of the "exceptional woman hypothesis," that this competent woman is unique, not like other women. As women become more common in the managerial ranks, this will become even less possible. In essence, this evidence suggests men *do* change their perceptions of women managers in similar ways, although they may not be quite as enthusiastic about their women managers' performance. These attitude shifts seem to represent changes in perceptions of women's behavior and changing feelings about that experience.

Table 5

Assessment of Experience with Women Managers by
Recency of Experience and Gender
Community Survey

	WOMEN			MEN		
Recency of Experience:						
Assessment of Experience:	5 years ago+	Within 5 years	Current	5 years ago+	Within 5 years	Current
Extremely Positive	11.1%	18.2%	27.8%	12.98%	21.7%	23.1%
Positive	61.1%	30.9%	45.6%	59.0%	46.7%	61.5%
Neutral	16.7%	30.9%	20.0%	15.4%	28.3%	7.7%
Negative	0	12.7%	5.6%	7.7%	1.7%	7.7%
Extremely Negative	11.1%	7.3%	1.1%	5.1%	1.7%	0

Friendships

Both the woman manager and her subordinates are transformed by the experience of women managing; together, they create a different management approach, one I would argue conforms to the new paradigm we see emerging in much of social life. One aspect of this new paradigm is holism, where formerly segmented parts of life are joined and produce more balanced approaches. In support of this, I found these women managers and secretaries to approach the issue of friendship at work more holistically. As with other topics, they seemed to work out this issue differently than men and their secretaries. Remember, this is part of the stereotype of women as poor managers -- not able to separate the personal from the professional, not able to work with people they may not care for personally.

The belief that one *should* keep the personal and professional sharply distinct is clearly a male-centered norm.   The men managers I interviewed were very careful to do so.   With few exceptions, they said they had no close friends at work.   They gave work-related reasons for this.   Quite a few of them cited the need to be objective.   "It's hard to fire a close friend," many of them said, and one man recounted an incident where he had had to do just that.   Friends allow "inefficiencies to enter in," said another man; "people get promoted who really shouldn't, but they're somebody's close friend."   Several other men said it was "better to keep personal things at home," that it is more difficult to supervise someone you have "just poured your guts out to."   Others said it was not practical to socialize with work associates, since they lived so far from each other and a few said they simply liked their privacy.   One man talked about the "rash of divorces" at work that had caused him and his wife to withdraw from the social network, lest they be pressured to "take sides."   It was interesting to me that nearly all of the comments the men made about friendships at work were of a negative nature.

A few men said they did have personal friends at work, but they were careful to distinguish between "close, intimate" friendships and "friendly work relations."   And they were mainly talking about the latter.   These men might play golf or go to ball games with co-workers, but they did not confide in them.   Another man said he refused to see his subordinates as "employees" but instead developed "friend" relationships that did not extend beyond the office.   In general, these men were careful to keep the two realms distinct.

The women supervisors handled friendships very differently.   Most of them said they had personal friends among co-workers, and they mostly mentioned the positive aspect of friendships.   Some of them talked about the personal satisfaction that comes with working in a "friendly" atmosphere, saying they had friends at "all levels" in the organization.   One woman said she chose her friends by intelligence, not job type and another that she preferred to form friendships with women who were not managers, though she was not sure she would want to work directly with any of these women or others might begin to "identify me too closely with them."

In these patterns, we also see evidence of people-involvement enhancing task accomplishment.   More frequent were comments that these friendships actually improved their work performance.   Several women said they and their friends traded information on what was happening in the organization that helped them do their jobs more effectively, and one woman said her friends gave her a different viewpoint on work dilemmas from a more objective, yet informed perspective. Several other women said they could get what they needed more readily from strategically-placed friends in the organization. And several women said they could work more easily with people they were close to since they had some insight into their emotional make-up.

These women were, however, very careful about who they became friends with, and a few of them avoided personal friendships in the workplace. Their reasons were often image-related. One woman said she was careful "not to let my slip show" and others said it simply didn't pay to let work associates know too much about their personal lives. They seemed to worry this might somehow be used against them. Others cited work-related reasons. Several women, especially those at the manufacturing firm, said there was so much "confidential" material they couldn't talk about at work, it was better to not "develop a situation where you would be tempted to or might forget." Several others said it was difficult to maintain a boss/employee relationship if they became close to their subordinates. One woman said she simply lived too far away to form close friendships with co-workers and preferred to spend her time with other people anyway. "I see the people I work with eight hours a day, as it is!" she said.

The secretaries to these women supervisors echoed their bosses' concern about close relationships developing from a slightly different perspective, and it is here we see further evolution in their transformation of perspective. While most of these women said they had friendships with other secretaries, their comments were more consistently directed toward possible friendships with their supervisors. They had evidently thought a great deal about this and had decided it was "hard to work for a best friend," and it was "too easy to get your feelings hurt when they criticize you." These women saw as much reason to keep some distance in their relationships as did the women who supervised them. Hence, on both sides, the women in these new relationships find themselves tentatively evolving new guidelines for the nature of the relationship itself. As previous material in this chapter shows, they did have closer, more holistic relationships with each other than men managers did with their secretaries. However, they still were concerned about keeping some emotional distance. Many seemed to feel that under other circumstances, they might have been close friends.

These secretaries also mentioned some problems with peer friendships. "The other women gossip a lot," some of them said, "so you have to be careful what you say at work." And other secretaries mentioned problems the supervisors had about time "wasted" talking to their friends. However, their concern about the type of relationship they had with their women managers was paramount.

Contrast these concerns with comments made by the secretaries to men. For them, forming close relationships with their bosses was not an issue. It was never mentioned, save a few comments about sexual harassment by former bosses. These women concentrated on their friendships with other secretaries, and they were quite positive about these relationships. They saw these friendships as lifelines that "Let me blow off steam," as one woman put it. "I can say things to her [a colleague] I would be better off not saying to him [her boss]." Several other women mentioned the opportunity to discuss confidential matters with other secretaries who were privy to the same information.

Some of these women did give work-related benefits of these friendships. "A friendship can bear much more stress than simple business relationships," said one woman recounting an office incident where a friend had been offended by something she had done. "We talked about it and it was over," she said. "If we hadn't been motivated to do that because of the friendship, it could have built into something bigger." Several of these women claimed it was easier to get things done if they were friendly with other secretaries. "After all," one woman said, "so many offices communicate secretary to secretary."

These women did mention problems with workplace friendships -- criticisms for "wasting time" with friends, problems about confidential information they might have (mostly in the manufacturing firm), and the need for privacy. But these problems seemed to be more than offset by the benefits these friendships provided. Several of these women did mention problems with personal friendships with people *they* had supervised. Said one woman, "I will say this, though; I don't think I could be friends with someone that I supervised. After I supervised and had to criticize others, I saw the need for distance that men see. It's just too hard to criticize someone you're friends with." These women accepted the male standard to some extent when it came to friendships across status lines, although overall, women tended to see friendships as more helpful than hurtful in the workplace. This is especially interesting, given that women are often excluded from male-dominated networks where favors and benefits are exchanged.

Concluding Comments

In summary, it seems individuals who work for women managers undergo a transformation of perception in terms of women's capabilities. Many find themselves giving up their preferences for men bosses, most of them no longer preferring one or the other. The majority no longer hold negative stereotypes of women managers but have come to understand and appreciate the particular strengths many women bring to managing, developing a more reality-based perspective. (Recall also the strong approval ratings given to women managers, shown in Chapter 3.)

The relationship between the woman manager and her secretary illustrates something of this transformation process. In the interaction between the two, the secretary comes to realize benefits for herself, benefits such as greater appreciation, credit for work done, and attention to her own career needs. The secretary also struggles toward a new type of relationship with another woman, one that involves mutual respect, often admiration, but short of close friendship, as they feel they would be too vulnerable when criticized.

For both men and women, working for a woman manager may not change attitudes overnight (though it does in come cases), but may be more likely to gradually alter consciousness about gender differences. Given sufficient time, this experience -- and the model of management demonstrated and learned -- has the potential for modifying the workplace in the ways consistent with those suggested by "new paradigm" writers. And, as I have suggested, there is certainly much congruence between the model these women are using and the newer management styles being advocated (a point developed further in chapter 6).

Perhaps as those involved on the practical level of dealing with women managers begin to think of women managers differently -- and management itself -- society as a whole will come to adopt a new stance. Appreciation of what women and other left-out groups can contribute may grow, increasing the possibility that we can truly change our social structures. A new paradigm, a new way of conceiving and structuring our reality, may gain a foothold through the process seen here, where some individuals first experience reality differently, begin to articulate that experience, then communicate this to others. These are particular aspects of the process Kuhn did not explicitly consider.

These results show the difficulty of sorting through the idea of "difference," of understanding how we assess the possibility outside the influence of our current social systems. Many feminists warn we will be swept into dangerous territory, unwittingly supporting the very order assaulted by the valorizing of women's strengths. In the end, we will simply affirm the reign of patriarchy by reinforcing the notion of separate spheres.

Others point to more practical problems. For example, Jenny Chapman (1993), a political scientist, says:

> The celebration of difference - of motherhood and its values, and of the unique learning and insights that women's bodily and nurturing experience yields - is the most politically dangerous path that women can take. The only way to minimize the aggressiveness of men, either towards each other or against women, is to renounce the difference that they value. p. 227

As we carefully sort through accuracy from misperceptions in this terrain of difference and sameness, we must keept these dangers in mind.

Chapter 5

The Female as Problematic

The fact that change is possible, of course, does not mean that it automatically happens -- at least not in the specific way we might wish. I would appear to be Polyannaish if I were not to acknowledge that serious problems exist yet in our society for women, continued resistance and cycles of backlash toward women's advancement. There is a deep-seated hatred for women and the feminine, something feminists have been calling misogyny. This points to the need to laud or valorize the "feminine," to underscore women's actual strengths or differences, as a critical step in the change we hope to see. Understanding existing hatred for women in our culture will help us to understand something about how it may be changing, and how to encourage change along a certain line.

Many of us have directly experienced this hatred for women in our society. I have a personal experience to share that is relevant. I was beginning a new revision of these chapters and had the whole day to reconstitute chapters, breaking them into chunks and piecing them back together on my computer. As I was getting engrossed in the prospect, the phone rang and a strange male voice asked for a name I didn't recognize (I later realized that he was saying "Annie," the way people sometimes say my name when they first see it). I insisted that he must have the wrong number, until he said, "Then who is this?" Not liking the way that sounded, I hung up. Ten minutes later, he called back to say he had seen me in the shower and was coming right over to rape me. Thinking he had probably gotten my name from the phone book, therefore he knew my address, I decided not to respond. I simply hung up. But I was terrified. We never know when these threats are real or "only" meant to terrorize. I called my husband, a contractor, who was working in a friend's home 20 minutes away. Before I knew it, both he and a County Sheriff's Duputy were in our country home (a solar, earthberm house we have built with our own hands), with the officer giving me advice on protecting and arming myself. (The deputy advised that I not even go out to work in the garden without a handgun in my belt!) Since those phone calls, I've taken extra precautions to protect myself. Where we live, country or city, doesn't exempt us from violence or threats of violence in these times. Later that evening, I suggested to my husband the irony of having my beginning work on a project dealing with male dominance, the slighting of the "feminine," marred by such an incident. This was not life as I would choose to live it. I spent the next several days alternating between fear at various things that have happened and anger that I cannot have more control over the tone of my life. And wondering how people cope who actually have these things *happen* to them.

This incidence illustrates the hatred of women that runs through our social order. Some would term this the force of the patriarchy, a system that places men in dominantion over women. It is tightly woven into our social fabric, as Sylvia Walby points out in her discussion of the "six key patriarchal structures":

> These are the patriarchal mode of production; patriarchal relations at work; patriarchal relations in the state; male violence; patriarchal relations in sexuality; and patriarchal relations in institutions including religion, media, education. (1990, 177)

Clearly, we continue to live with patriarchy, even if it is undergoing modification. And, as I emphasize in the next part of the book, patriarchy is closely entertwined with other aspects of our culture. Male violence against women, as was threatened against me, is the ultimate weapon used to enforce the patriarchy.

Another method of keeping women "in their place" involves forces which make it difficult for women to support each other. This "divide and conquer" strategy posited by many social scientists acts to keep suppressed groups in their positions because if the majority of citizens worked together to change the system, radicial change would no doubt result. The "divide and conquer" process serves to maintain the status quo.

Judith Briles, for one, discusses one aspect of this in her book *Woman to Woman: From Sabotage to Support*, where she writes about women who present road blocks to other women. Tokenism, she says is used to pit women against one another. By making it clear that only a token woman or two will be allowed to enter, those in power ensure that women will act as one anothers' gatekeepers, working to keep others out so they will not be displaced. Also operating is a tendency for men to see the token as exceptional ("not like those other women") and for the woman herself to deny discrimination, blaming other women who have not made it for their incompetence.

The influence of patriarchy operates in other ways. Consider the evidence that women are disliked or resented in the workplace -- by men as well as by other women. Christine Williams (1989) demonstrates the extremely high levels of resentment men show toward women, even when working in female-dominated jobs like nursing, but most especially in male-typed jobs such as marines. She takes a fairly pessimistic view of the possibilities for change:

> The roots of this social organization are lodged deeply and securely in our current system of gender identity formation. As long as men feel a psychological need to separate and distinguish themselves from women -- as long as their own adult gender identity is premised upon denying and denigrating whatever they conceive to be feminine -- they will continue to desire that certain activities remain "for men only" (p. 142).

The preference for male coworkers is apparently widespread. Linda Brown and Julia Kagan in a 1982 *Working Woman* survey reported that only a minority of those in the workplace would like more women coworkers. James Baron and William Bielby (1983) find organizational barriers to gender equality. They conclude that these barriers and resistance are problematic, in that women are segregated into jobs that prevent them from getting the experience they need to advance in their firms. This, they argue, is a key factor in occupational segregation.

Thus, women are prevented from moving up into managerial or other leadership positions. Sokoloff (1985) decries the appalling lack of both black *and* white women in the professions. Chase and Bell (1990) document the continued existence of gatekeepers who block women's advancement into the male dominated-occupation of the public school superintendency. Ost and Turale (1989) show the overall lack of women in upper management levels in higher education. The extremely slow increase of female senior administrators (Boganno, 1987), for example college presidents (Touchton, 1988), has also been documented. In the federal civil service, Di Prete and Soule (1988) found that women experienced the greatest disadvantage in making the first initial moves up the promotion ladder. After the first move, the male advantage seemed to disappear. Others have documented women's difficulties making it into top management positions (Edson, 1988; Zweigenhaft, 1987; Korn and Ferry, 1982).

The resistance to women in leadership positions, in particular, remains strong. Kimmel (1987) found the resistance to be long-term. In examining texts from the 1800's and early 1900's, he discovered three themes that are still with us today. One line of thought blamed women for men's loss of masculinity and used biological determinism to try and get women back into the home (*The Total Woman?*). Another tried to dislodge women from the home, in order to remove them from parenting, shrilly and hysterically pointing to the extreme feminization of young boys by their mothers (Momism?). A third line of thinking was pro-feminist, calling for social changes that would include economic and workplace transformation. How long these debates and issues have been before us! How long before they are settled, before the cycle of change is completed? If there is this much resistance to women simply being *in* the workplace, how much more to having women in leadership positions, actually in charge of things!

Reactions to a Different Model

Part of the resistance arises from the different approaches women bring to supervisory positions. My own experience illustrates how higher level women can be reacted to in a very competitive, hierarchical institution -- academia. My original confusion about what was happening was greatly resolved when I analyzed my experiences with my model of change, seeing what had happened as a mixing of paradigms -- the old and the new -- and how women using "new" aproaches are reacted to. In doing this, I hope ultimately to shed some light upon the question of how best to proceed in creating change, in part by illustrating exactly what the problems are.

I realize I risk some misunderstanding in doing this, both by the individuals involved, who may not wish to have their stories told, even in an anonymous manner, *and* by the scientific community, who are prone to reject personal experience as biased, inappropriate data. In taking a feminist approach, however, I find myself compelled to take these risks. For one thing, I believe it is our silence that allows old patterns to continue. I do not *blame* any of the participants, but find that they and myself were responding, mostly unconsciously, to the social processes I have been discussing. A second, and related reason for telling this story, is to live by the feminist maxim, "The personal *is* political," in a very real way. By seeing in personal experience the possibility of real insight, we allow input from a substantial part of social life that has been more or less ignored by many social scientists.

I want to further preface my remarks by saying that much in women's early training prepares us to lead in a cooperative way, an approach I was using that I am convinced caused me great difficulty. Donna Eder (1988) finds that even young (adolescent) women build cohesion through "collaborative narration." This conversational tactic, in which previous statements of others are supported or ratified in some way, increase feelings of group solidarity among group members. Apparently, women learn this skill at a very early age, getting encouragement in their own gender group for using it.

The basis for my comments is from the first part of a diary, an accounting I have made of my first attempts at management, that runs roughly through the period 1984 to 1990. In reviewing this record, I can see clearly that my use of an approach comfortable to me landed me in some hot water in my first managerial position. Let me give you some background. As with many women managers (like the highly educated women I studied and discussed earlier), I had not *planned* to be an administrator. Rather, circumstances seemed to push me in that direction. In fact, I was a most *un*likely candidate. I had come to that particular university, a small regional campus of a large, statewide system, directly from a large research institution. I had moved to the state where the university was for several reasons. One, which I found difficult to admit to anyone, was to pursue a new relationship -- one that did lead to marriage, though I was not at all certain at the time it would work out that way.

But there were other reasons as well. As I said, I had been working in a large midwestern research university, where classes were large and the pressures to publish in particular outlets were great. I had a growing sense that I could not continue to thrive in a system that robbed me of my own personal voice. I had been overwhelmed by the two universities where I had done my doctoral work and started as an assistant professor, and found myself suffering from an increasing sense of inauthenticity. I had learned to play the game quite well and was being *most* productive -- though my work was *not* appearing in what was considered to be the "very best" places by my academic peers and mentors. Though I was beginning to feel confident about myself, a crisis nonetheless forced itself upon me, and I began making a midlife transition even before I had reached the age of 40. By the time this transition ended, I was teaching part time at my new institution and hoping for a full time job. My dreams of being only partly connected to the system seemed impractical. There seemed no way to support myself teaching part time, and the flexibility of academic life to pursue my own ideas was very attractive. I *liked* that part of it.

I arrived in the summer and met the chair. He was very impressed with my vita. At that time, I was getting a real lift from going to different places, showing it to people and getting that kind of reaction. My husband-to-be was being very supportive, also. The chair said they had nothing for that fall but could give me several courses that next spring. I went to the local technical institute and got several courses to teach that fall. (They *loved* me there, thought I was exceptionally qualified!) And with that, scared to death, I moved to a small apartment in a medium-sized town in the new state. I obtained another part time job at the technical institute writing a five-year plan. Altogether, it was *almost* a full-time job. For the next year and a half, I pieced together part time and some temporary full time work, always teaching at my new institution, at least part of the time. During my second year, a permanent position became available; the institution was seeking someone with my areas of expertise. I interviewed with them on my birthday and received a tenured appointment.

So I started a regular appointment that fall after several years of complete freedom from committees, institutional politics, anything but teaching and my own research. I had begun a new project, interviewing men and women managers and their secretaries. I remember it was quite time-consuming and caused me to miss several Executive Committee and Department meetings called at the last minute. The chair was not always pleased with me about this. I began to offer suggestions for improving several aspects of our collective life. Sometimes they were acted on, sometimes not. But I did produce several small departmental reports on these issues during that first year.

Toward the end of that year, the chair announced that he was leaving office. No one seemed interested in the job. Going home one day, I suddenly felt that I should do it, it would be good experience and no one else seemed interested, but *certainly* not the next year. After all, I had only been a regular faculty member for one year at that institution. However, I talked to the chair and offered to do a lower level administrative job that next year (for experience, if he would agree to stay on as chair) and then take the chair the year after that. After much discussion within the department, we decided that this is what we would do.

Things did not go quite as we all had hoped. Several problems immediately arose. I worked franticallty to finish other obligations before taking over the postion from the outgoing chair. I heard from others that he was displeased I was not working more closely with him through the transition. He was out of town and asked me to handle a hiring interview before I was actually in office. Members of the search committee pressed me to make an immediate offer to the candidate before our Executive Committee met, which angered Executive Committee members who had been excluded. Then, an Assistant Professor was denied tenure by an all-campus committee, some said because of material I had unnecessarily included in his file. I had initially failed to give another Assistant Professor a written 30 days notice of a contract renewal, which caused some problems that quickly were resolved. I had assumed office in July and by December, another faculty member (female) had decided to run agianst me for Chair. I won by one vote, but the factions were formed. I was angry and frustrated throughout much of this time.

These are my recollections of how I was thinking and feeling at the time. Since I began reviewing my notes and writing this manuscript, I have come to see my experiences more dispassionately and analytically. For one thing, I have come to realize that my experiences as chair, and later as director of the Women's Studies Program, exemplified the distinction between the competitive or dominator style and the cooperative or partnership style being discussed so much today. It seems more and more to me that my departmental colleagues and myself were operating at cross-purposes. I was, almost unconsciously, using the cooperative style and they seemed to be expecting the more traditional, competitive mode. Here, again, "difference" was important. I was using a model some ascribe to women, while my colleagues were using the more male-typed competitive model. This tendency toward competition and autonomous functioning is, admittedly, highly exacerbated in an institution like higher education.

Such misunderstandings mean that moving from a competitive mode to a cooperative one is not easy, particularly when the competitive mode still prevails. I believe this underlies many of the difficulties I had as a manager. Use of the competitive model is implicit *and* highly expected. In an academic institution, managers/administrators are expected to compete for scarce resources. We would not be doing our jobs if we did not. I continuously encountered two dilemmas around this. One issue was the perception that this was a zero-sum game, so if I "got something" for my department or unit, others "lost something." It never seemed to occur to anyone that if we all got behind each other's efforts, the entire institution might get a whole new set of resources. I have found that individuals outside of my department remember with a surprising degree of accuracy what I "got" for my department many years ago. As Kanter (1977) noted, the actions of token women managers are given careful scrutiny by others and, certainly, I felt that what I was doing was reacted to much more strongly because I was a woman. This issue was troubling enough when I was chairing my department. When I became Director of the Women's Studies Program, it became almost impossible to sort out reactions to me from reactions to the program, but the reaction to women "getting things" intensified greatly.

A second, sometimes even more troubling issue, was the manager/administrator's role in *distributing* resources. Here, those *within* one's unit can become quite nervous. Often I was operating from a cooperator model while my actions were judged from a competitor or dominator model. Previously, in my department, battle lines had been pretty clearly drawn; there were those "in power" and those "out of power." I felt that since we had a small department, we could not afford the luxury of non-participants. The more contributors we had, the better off we would be. So, I deliberately set about trying to bring those who had been alienated back in. I tried to see their side of an issue or find ways to encourage them in their own work, and so on. I meant to reach out to *everyone*. However, those who *had* been the powerful ones seemed to immediately assume that if I was "for those others," I must be "against them." Several issues arose when I did not do exactly what the powerful ones wanted me to do. My competence was immediately called into question; they wondered if I knew what I was doing. One of them (ironically, a woman), laughed when I spoke with her about this, and said, "Societies always have factions and cliques fighting with each other, trying to get the other out of power." It had apparently never occurred to her that we could *all* have power. She was saying very clearly to me that she identified me with "the other" group and was working to get "us" out of power.

I was unable to win her over. She persisted in carrying news about what I was "doing wrong" over my head to the administration for the next several years until I finally decided to step down from my position (at which point, *she* decided to leave the institution!). She was joined in her efforts to discredit me by several others (mostly women) who had seen themselves as power brokers in the department and were close associates of the "power figures" in our area.

A particularly telling example about the mix-up in models occurred at the end of my term in that particular position. We actually had two disciplines within our department, two vigorous programs with good students. At the end of each year, we were asked to nominate *one* outstanding graduate. We had been rotating the honor from discipline to discipline every year, and this procedure had been working well. However, that particular year, each discipline had what it considered to be a truly outstanding graduate. The students were very different. One had a much higher GPA and had been admitted to a competitive graduate program but had done very little outside of the classroom to contribute to the institution. The opposite was the case for the other student, where the GPA was not quite as high (though very good) but contributions to the institution had been very great. At least one of the faculty members involved very clearly expected me to rank these two students and choose the "best" one (the competitor/dominator model), using "the criterion" of GPA. ("How could you *not* choose this student?" this faculty member wanted to know at one point in these discussions.) And most department chairs had their Executive Committees choose only one student -- or they did so themselves. That year, however, two of us sent two names to the faculty committee in charge of awards. "It is impossible to choose between these two," we said. The committee told us that we had to make a choice; they would not accept two names from us. The other chair did as instructed.

I still felt reluctant and sought, instead, a way where both students could "win." There were actually two possible awards, one an outstanding senior award from each department and also an overall Chancellor's award that they all competed for. I felt the student with the excellent service record had a very good chance to get the Chancellor's award. So, I nominated that student for the Chancellor's Award and the other student for the departmental award. It worked out that way; both won awards! I was pleased; it was not *necessarily* a zero-sum situation. However, the disgruntled faculty member persisted in being dissatisfied. I believe this individual felt I was simply failing to do my duty by not choosing. When I approached that person saying, "It worked out pretty well, didn't it?" the retort was, "I just can't be happy with the way things worked out."

The presence of these two models certainly made things confusing and difficult. Perhaps we could have talked about the two approaches as a department and arrived at some consensus about our approach. I must admit that I did not communicate about things as well or as often as I now wish I had. However, I was not as conscious as I am now about why I was proceeding as I was -- or why others were reacting as they were. This has only became clear to me in the years that have followed, particularly as I began to analyze my diary. So, there are certain aspects of the situation it would simply have been impossible to talk about because none of us had the awareness or the concepts articulated. Even if that had been possible, if we had all realized what was going on, the group would most likely not have agreed with my approach. I remember discussing consensus decision-making and the need to bring alienated members into the group (not just out-vote them) with one of the departmental power brokers (a man) who found the whole idea unfathomable. I believe he -- and the group -- viewed this approach as "inappropriate" in a hierarchical, competitive institution of higher learning. In many ways, the model the total institution was operating with over-rode individual initiatives.

Many influences toward conformity exist. If the surrounding organization is using the dominator approach, it is hard to use the cooperative one. My department, a fairly weak one in the institution to begin with, was constantly concerned about the image of the department -- how "this would look" to others. Members of the department worried about us being the "laughing stock" of the institution. Thus, the larger organization can bring conformity pressures to bear upon individual units. Attempts to avoid such pressure is why the well-known cooperative-based community in Mondragon, Spain formed many support organizations that were cooperative (Chapter 6). These units enhanced their cooperative workplace, reducing the disjunctions and hassles that resulted.

However, there are still some very big obstacles to overcome before women can make great inroads in this transformation. It seems women are punished severely for not fitting into the "male club." We also are not allowed much leeway for mistakes. When I look back over my own diary, I see a whole series of episodes with a common element: I mishandled certain key people, badly miscalculating *who* had to be "handled" and *how*. But it is also true that my colleagues were not at all forgiving. Some incidents were small things, like not informally telling the former chair his annual merit evaluation (established by our Executive Committee) *before* it was published, as he had always done for those of us who participated in doing the ratings. It just never occurred to me. I did not realize he had done this systematically, for one thing, and, so, had always felt a bit uncomfortable by what might seem as a breach of the committee's confidentiality. In fact, there had been an incident the year before when he had told a faculty member how (anonymous) *individuals* had rated her and she had wanted to appeal her score on that basis. However, other department members were not upset with *him* for revealing that information but with *her* for reacting as she did. I found it curious that when the former chair came back into office after my term, confusions and mistakes on his part were treated much more kindly by those involved. There was *not* the immediate presumption of his incompetence. In fact, there were several problems we both had around the same issues -- implementing a new merit review system, for example, where a complex series of voting in stages was necessary, and we had both caused confusion in this. Yet, reactions were drastically different; certain departmental members were *extremely* critical of me and very forgiving of him.

In reviewing my journal from this period, I found eleven critical incidents that stood out as major turning points, events that set relations with the key departmental power-holders on a negative course that I was never able to correct. The majority of these incidents occurred during my first year as chair, or shortly after I was elected (before assuming office). Nearly all of the incidents that stood out for me as turning points involved power-brokers who ultimately opposed me, and were serious offenses within the framework of the competitor model. These incidents included:

1) my vote in favor of several (out-of-favor) faculty members' requests that we hear an appeal concerning their annual merit ratings (something we had never done before);

2) my assertion to some faculty that the administration saw us as a "weak" department;

3) a hiring effort (before I was actually chair, but serving for a week as acting chair) in which I was pressured by several (in-favor) faculty to hastily call an Executive Committee meeting so we could offer a candidate the job before she left campus;

4) a dispute over the scheduling of a contract renewal for an (in-favor) faculty member;

5) a difficulty with the case of an (out-of-favor) faculty member who was turned down for tenure by a campus-wide committee;

6) my initiations of dialogue with (in-favor) faculty who voted against my continuing as chair for a second year.

Many of these events involved confrontations that I was not able to resolve to anyone's satisfaction. Since we were not in fact working cooperatively, I often was not told directly that I had offended anyone, only to find out much later. With regard to the sixth point, for example, in my conversations with individuals in the aftermath of the election during my first year, I *tried* to reach out to people, to say that I realized that they had not supported me but hoped we could work together, that I had not been aware of their unhappiness but nevertheless hoped in the future they would come and talk directly with me about any problems they saw. One faculty member decided that I had violated their faculty rights by talking directly with them about the vote, and proceeded to go from Vice Chancellor to Chancellor to faculty committees trying to file a grievance and have disciplinary action taken against me without my even knowing there was a problem. When I heard this person and a senior member of our faculty had visited the Vice Chancellor and I asked about the nature of the visit, the Vice Chancellor told me that it was about me but that he was not at liberty to discuss it! It was several *months* before I even knew what it was about. This struck me as the ultimate in being frozen out of the informal network!

Often, our very humanness can be overlooked. I remember a particularly telling moment when I was having a discussion about temporarily sharing equipment between the two disciplines in our department. I was in the hallway outside of my office with another faculty member. That morning, I had cut my hand doing dishes and had gone to the emergency room to get six stitches. My hand was wrapped with a bandage. The discussion was becoming somewhat heated. Suddenly, another faculty member walked by and asked what had happened to my hand. The person I was talking to looked at my hand with a startled expression and said, "I hadn't even noticed."

Incidents like these declined in number during my second year in office. The person who had run against me in the election moved to another department. Things quieted down considerably. Each of the incidents that occurred during my first year in and of itself might not have been disastrous. But added together, it meant a very difficult time for me and, ultimately, for the department. I believe in looking at the series of events, I can see elements of my own inexperience and insensitivities and the personalities of others in the department, but I think most important was the systematic reaction to a woman in power, and, related to that, a mix-up in ideas of how power is handled. The reactions were to both my alternative power strategies *and* to having a woman in a male-typed position. The setting in which we were functioning, academia, with its highly competitive norms and practices, also contributed greatly to the problems I was having.

The literature suggests that women tend to approach power differently than men, and that men often misunderstand women's approaches. Here was a situation where the structure was based on the male-typed competitor model and most of the participants had adopted that model. The difference in our approaches, combined with my lack of experience and understanding of the power process (itself embedded in gender relations) produced a series of events that seemed disastrous to many department members and extremely painful for me. The entire experience has reinforced my belief that there are certainly many problems to solve before women truly have equal opportunities to succeed in management positions. I offer these experiences in the hope of making the way easier for others who follow, hopefully hastening the change process.

Who is to Blame?

Others have experienced similar problems. During this same period, I read an account in *MS Magazine* about Bess Myerson entitled "A Woman Undone" by Shana Alexander (1986). Many points here are relevant for women in power more generally. This article described Myerson's rise to fame as the 1945 Miss America, her eventual entry into New York City politics, then her indictment for conspiracy, bribery, and mail fraud on charges that she attempted to influence the judge presiding over her lover's divorce case by putting the judge's emotionally damaged (perhaps unemployable) daughter on the city payroll. (On top of this, Myerson had recently been arrested for shoplifting in a small Pennsylvania town.) This article did not argue that Bess Myerson had been unfairly accused. Instead, the author asked:

> Why does a person of great calculation and control, at this late point in her life suddenly throw caution to the winds?...[O]ne has an incredible sense of a person unraveling before one's eyes...What was once a spectacular...public success story increasingly resembles a slow-motion public suicide. (p. 43)

In answering her own question, Alexander concludes that a disjuncture between "female" and "professional" is causing this type of behavior in Bess Myerson.

> These acts seem somehow female...perverted love-gifts to [her lover]...[W]omen of some accomplishment...who have "made it" in a man's world -- which woman among us does *not* have great dependency needs? (p. 43)...As for the Women's Movement...We wanted to be equal. We did it. But we forgot we were in a man's world; everything we saw and felt, and raged against was seen through that perspective. We were like Eskimos who don't see snow...So when we decided to become equals, we meant...equals *in a man's world*...We forgot that we are different from men; we are *other*; we have different sensibilities (p. 44)

Alexander seems to believe that Bess Myerson has become emotionally ill from the strain of her life. She cites a list of betrayals, mostly by men, but beginning with her mother. There were two failed marriages, several disastrous love affairs, and Mayor Ed Koch's refusal to give her anything but a belated ceremonial political post in return for her tremendous influence in his successful mayoral campaign. This article, then, points to many of the societal pressures women in power feel, pressures that may ultimately prevent them from being as successful and creating as much change as they might. It also traces some of the possible ways in which the woman's own behaviors can contribute to her downfall -- and how these different factors are woven together.

I was reminded of the secretary at the manufacturing firm I visited who believed the company had so few women managers because women, in general, could simply not handle the strain of the job. She told me about a woman buyer who had a nervous breakdown and had to be re-assigned as a secretary. She believed that women just "can't handle" the strain of these positions. It just so happened that I had interviewed the woman she was describing. She did seem to be having some difficulty coping and staying focused, showing some degree of psychological distress, but she also complained bitterly about the lack of support -- downright harassment -- she had received in her position as buyer.

In this kind of situation, whom do we blame? The woman or the situation? Both? Where should our efforts go toward correcting the situation? Certainly, improving the climate for women, changing attitudes toward them, would make a tremendous difference. As part of this, articulating women's contributions, orientations, special insights by virtue of our position in society might be helpful. My own managerial experiences show the difficulties of executing a new approach within the old order. When I discuss my later experiences in Part III of this book, I show how consensus within a small subgroup of an organization can help this new approach flourish. And the larger organization may end up providing support, despite itself, if it needs this subunit to appeal to new markets, something being said about all of our companies and organizations in general.

My hope is that, by looking at the darker underside of the feedback loops, where resistance arises to women's advancement, we will all become more conscious about how we are acting and why. From the resulting dialogue, meaningful change might come. And finally, connecting women's contributions with needed workplace changes would also be helpful. Perhaps by seeing these issues in broader social context, we can see more clearly how to proceed.

In ending this part of the book, I am struck by how "stuck" we seem to be. We cannot ignore difference, yet we cannot talk about it. We still encounter strong hatred of women. We have been talking a long time about these issues, yet some feel we have made very little progress. By better understanding the total process through which change occurs, perhaps we will become better positioned to take larger steps. The last two parts of the book are devoted to furthering this effort by clarifying the process of change, the patterns of altered perceptions.

PART II

GENDER AND INTERTWINING OPPRESSIONS

To this point, I have talked about the impact of gender independent of its inter-relationship with other factors such as race and class. Part I ended on a fairly pessimistic note, largely I believe because the broader view was not taken. Many feminists today feel very discouraged as they look at all of the problems that remain for women, despite the greater understanding in our society as a whole. Because we have been taking a fairly narrow view of oppression and change, we fail to appreciate the breadth of the transformation potentially afoot.

In this section of the book, I offer three chapters that deal with the simultaneous or multiple impact of gender combined with class and race. Using this wider lens shifts our focus just enough to expose hidden or implied assumptions about management and leadership almost endemic in an analysis based on evidence collected mostly from white, middle-class males and females. Seeing even more of our errors or biases moves us from a strategy of only correcting biases against women or making women's experiences visible to reformulating the fundamental theories and concepts of our existing knowledge base, thereby potentially transforming our entire social order. This goal is lauded by Schwartz-Shea in an entry for the International Encyclopedia of Public Policy and Administration on how organizations are gendered (1995).

As Patricia Hill Collins (1994) says in her review of bell hooks and Cornell West's *Breaking Bread*, this attention to multiple perspectives follows the postmodern sensibility of allowing several voices to speak at once. Here, the shift is from finding one "true" perspective to the notion of multiple realities, particularly incorporating those voices kept on the margins of our society.

This development in my own thinking offers a model for how change might occur on a larger scale. Individuals first realize a basic fact, previously hidden -- in this case, the idea the "feminine" or women have something vital to contribute. Then, that idea cycles through other understandings to create a more integrated version of the original insight.

In this case, a wealth of thinking about difference suggests the factors that will provide a new vision. In feminist circles, white middle-class women have been criticized for assuming their experiences have been true for all women. Race and class, combined with gender, strongly influence experiences, as shown in recent writings by and about women of color and working/lower class women. These groups seem to give even stronger credence to the impact of personal relationships. For example, Phil Brown and Faith Ferguson (1995) show that among mostly working class women organizing grass roots environmental actions, the power for action comes from community ties, giving a personal context for knowledge. Patricia Ticineto Clough (1994) shows the same to be true for African-American women writers. The following chapters pursue insights drawn from examining interactive effects of gender with race and class, giving us a greater understanding of the transformation we are witnessing.

CHAPTER 6

A FOCUS ON WORK

This chapter integrates a concern for women's place in the workplace -- and how that may be changing -- with the understandings we have obtained from other approaches to studying the workplace. This has been the site of much pressure for change around the issue of gender, since women's progress (or lack thereof) is often measured around workplace indicators.

Another integral issue in this regard is that of class. Many feminist theorists are increasingly arguing that race, class, and gender issues are closely intertwined -- that oppression or exploitation of these various groups springs from a common propensity toward oppression in our social system. If so, it is likely developments in one area may be inter-related with those in another, even though it may not seem so on the surface. This is what I will argue in these next several chapters, that movements for change in the workplace on the surface seem to be only about class, yet have close connections to our ongoing gender revolution.

Before considering the interactions between class and gender, I would first like to examine the progression of social class analysis, involving issues of distinctions between those who own, manage, and labor. Social scientists have long been concerned with class issues at work; Karl Marx was one of the first to articulate the problems workers encounter. His model is still the standard by which others are judged. He focused on the worker's loss of control and increasing exploitation.

While many of his predictions about the capitalist system have not come to pass in our country, particularly his forecast of mass uprisings, his claim about the "alienated worker" continues to influence our thinking.

Sociologists have expanded Marx's notion of individual alienation beyond that of separation from (loss of control over) the means of production to a broader concept of self/society relations. While these researchers disagreed among themselves about some of the specifics, they did agree about several key things: many individuals in our society experience a sense of normlessness, powerlessness, isolation, alienation from social processes, lack of commitment to values, and a meaninglessness in life (Dean, 1961; Schacht, 1970; Scott, 1963; Seeman, 1959; Srole, 1956). While some of these researchers, such as Schacht, viewed alienation as a natural, neutral outcome of our attempt to create unity with one another by objectifying the human spirit, most of them were troubled by the feelings they discovered.

This concern about individual worker alienation has expanded, as authors have begun characterizing entire societies as alienating. Daniel Bell, in his influential book *The End of Ideology* (1960), saw widespread alienation to be the result of our social system, which isolated individuals and dampened the ideological fervor that empowered many of the social critics of the nineteenth century. Others have lamented the anxiety or stress brought on by the "loss of identity" (Stein, Vidich, and White, 1960), excessive and competing role demands (Holroyd and Lazarus, 1982), or blocks to effective political action (Thompson and Horton, 1960) endemic in modern life.

The problems that Marx wrote about in the last century are still with us in later stage capitalism. Some researchers have written about related workplace trends, as well as those more society-wide. Bell (1960), for example, emphasized the unmet need of workers to have control of work process and products as a critical cause of the crisis he saw looming on the horizon. A study by Aiken, Ferman, and Shepard (1968) found alienation to be strongly related to economic insecurity, a growing condition in our society, caused by the increase of part-time jobs with no benefits. Losing control of the work process was an additional factor in a study of Parisian workers by Melvin Seeman (1972). Others focused on the impact of control over one's work situation (Rushing, 1972, and Shephard, 1971). For example, Jon Shephard found workers in mechanized situations (again, those with less control) to be the most alienated. Among small businessmen, marginality in the professional context seemed to be the determining factor (Photiadis and Schweiber, 1971).

Later, Harry Braverman (1975), in his highly influential *Labor and Monopoly Capital*, showed specific developments (de-skilling and narrowing of jobs) that were bringing this crisis into existence. He believed capitalism's inherent tendency toward job segmentation and de-skilling would create an increasingly large group of alienated and ineffectual individuals, totally incapable of mounting any type of political action. Instead of a conscious mass uprising, we may see individualized actions of sabotage and apathy that may ultimately be serious enough to stop the system. T.R. Young, in talking about capitalism's tendency to create national social problems, and increasing levels of personal distress, noted:

> As class relations arise, new problems of production and distribution are created and move into the public sphere...largely because capitalism tends to separate more and more people from both production (in order to cut wage costs) and from distribution (in order to sell at the highest possible cost). p. 71

Lembcke (1986) believes, as did Marx, these tendencies will ultimately force some type of "collective struggle of workers for the social ownership and control of capital." In the meantime, he chronicles the painful disintegration of "social individualism" brought about by the dictates of capitalism. These writers are concerned about the dehumanizing characteristics of capitalism, the drive toward profits that eschews all concern for the worker. Marjorie Kelly, editor of *Business Ethics*, places the blame not on individual greed, but on the free-market system many believe will ultimately work for everyone's benefit. As she puts it:

> ...over half of the income generated between 1977 and 1989 went...to the top 1 percent...In roughly the same period...the number of people who worked full-time...and still fell below the poverty line climbed by an embarrassing 43 percent...We're not talking about welfare recipients...about street people. We're talking about people who work forty hours a week and still can't feed their families...How can we possibly allow this to happen? (1991b, 7)

And Segal (1987) adds:

> In our intensely individualistic, competitive, capitalistic society, love and concern for others become inappropriate outside our very own small family groupings. (p.5)

Marx thought these tendencies of capitalism would be the downfall of the system, that workers, as a class, would be pushed to the point where they *would* ultimately rebel.

While these critiques of our economic system are often characterized as coming from a radical left perspective, certain elements are seen in more mainstream analyses. Critics of our current business practices, such as Kanter (1983), point to many of the same factors that dehumanize workers: lack of control or input and no chance for creativity. In her scenario, indeed, also in Braverman's, the workers do not revolt. Instead, a conscious, calculated decision is made to change the system, to factor in the human element because of an even more basic contradiction in the system; as it currently operates, profits cannot continue to be generated. The workers have not actively revolted; they have passively rebelled. According to Kanter they have not left the system, but have sabotaged it by slowing down production, damaging products, etc.

Other critical theorists (Howard, 1977) have further refined the Marxian critique, positing various stages of capitalism: liberal market capitalism (where all believe the free market will ultimately solve all problems) and late capitalism (where inherent instabilities in the capitalist system have required heavy state intervention and control). Habermas proposed four types of crises that may manifest themselves, all with the potential of destroying -- or badly damaging -- the current system: "as system crises of the economy or of the rationality of administration, and as identity or social crises in the form of legitimation or motivation failures" (Howard, 1977: 121). Put more simply, many argue that crises with the management process of our economic system and worker alienation loom large on our horizon.

Telling examples of exploitation of workers endemic to economic system are numerous. Consider, for example, a particularly gruesome example I read about a few years ago in a pamphlet called *Food and Justice* (1990) in which migrant farm workers were reported to live in shacks in fields with only chemically laced irrigation water for bathing and drinking, forced to work over time for no additional pay, with no breaks or lunch. Basic amenities were often missing.   One woman reported having to use the toilet:

> Like always [employer] hadn't put any toilet paper in the bathroom...I took some papers that we had used to pack grapes...[and] I cleaned myself with the papers...Immediately I felt something wrong with me, an itching in my vagina and all over my body...After five days, bleeding [I] visited the doctor...[I] was six months pregnant...The doctor said it would be better for me to go to Bakersfield and get an abortion, because if I didn't, I would have very serious complications.   The doctor's recommendation was devastating (p. 5).

Other workers reported having no toilet facilities at all, but having to relieve themselves in the fields and having no opportunity to wash their hands before returning to work. Other women reported being sexually harassed by Anglo male owners.

Data on Everyday Problems

Some of these examples are quite dramatic. However, problems for workers also add up in less dramatic, more everyday kinds of situations found in many work sites. In my own research, I found elements of systematic exploitation that give rise to the feelings of being exploited and alienated. I believe what I found comes largely from how our firms, as capitalistic enterprises with profit as the sole motive and power concentrated in the hands of the few, tend to operate. The victims, often, though not always, were women. In my original study, I received reports of difficulties encountered by managers and secretaries in the three work settings in southeastern Wisconsin: a bank, a durable goods manufacturing multi-national firm, and a technical institute. Here, we see detailed examples of various problems existing in traditionally organized work sites. By focusing my analysis on issue of class rather than gender, different insights emerged.

Although the work settings themselves were quite different, I found common themes across these settings. All three, particularly the bank and the manufacturing firm, operated with traditional capitalistic impulses. "The bottom line" was said to be of utmost importance by many workers, even to the detriment of long term quality and/or customer satisfaction. Also, those running these organizations were reported to show little regard for the health or well-being of the workers per se, but rather with getting "as much work as possible out of us" [the workers].

I began my study at the bank and was immediately impressed by stories of overwork, exhaustion, physical break-downs in some cases, recounted by all of these workers. They were clearly workers under stress. They had been going through a "computer conversion," the bringing of formerly purchased computer services "in house." The process had been tremendously stressful for many involved.

As the bank grew, the company had opted to both reduce costs and gain more control by running and maintaining its own computerized programs. However, plans for this "conversion" were made without considering input from those individuals who had to do the work, a common complaint in this organization. Many workers mentioned total reorganizations taking place frequently, always "behind closed doors." This lack of upward influence is not unusual, but typical of capitalistic free-market firms, where power is concentrated in the hands of owners or high level managers.

Several workers reported one troubling aspect of this top-down control structure, with its lack of felt powerlessness; it often resulted in overwork:

> They have no idea what needs to be done to accomplish something they want. They're totally removed from the situation so they think they're objective.

> We have senior managers here who are very goal-oriented and the paramount thing to them is completing their goal. Whether the place starts on fire or not, if they have a goal to complete at this particular time, they are going to do that no matter what it takes to get that.

The problem of "too much work" became acutely apparent in this situation of completing a computer conversion. The process of assembling the machinery, the network, and the software for users had been exhausting, particularly for those engaged in preparing documentation for the actual users -- the tellers. A feasibility study done previously by the implementors suggested a conversion date, but higher management, in keeping with its top-down predilection, had ignored this advice and selected instead a date nearly a year earlier. Attempts to meet the deadline had required enormous amounts of overtime on the part of certain women managers and branch workers below the level of vice president. Most of these managers reported they had not been able to schedule vacations during this period and had suffered from stress. Their morale was low, and there was no respite in the consistency of problems, even though the new system was now running fairly smoothly. As one manager put it:

> We were concentrating our efforts in two areas; we were putting on new products, writing new procedures for new things that needed to be started right now, plus working on the computer...I was getting timelines from four different [supervisors]...and my primary responsibility is [still] to make sure my people are doing their jobs...so my customers are happy...So, I've really got five lords and masters.

Since there was little influence from below in the company, upper level managers did not learn how they might be useful in this process from their more technically advanced subordinates. They reported feeling "helpless" during the conversion process. "There was very little I could contribute to that entire process," one of them said.

Here, we see one result of a hierarchical, top-down control structure. The advice of lower management was sought, then ignored. Upper management discovered, however, that it *was* effectively up to the lower managers to execute the task. They felt helpless when the attempt failed. Rather than communicating with lower level managers throughout the process, they chose a timetable deemed untenable by lower level managers, turned things over to them, and then seemed shocked when things did not go according to their schedule.

The results for the workers were devastating. This deadline problem was mentioned with great concern by virtually all of the bank employees I interviewed. The majority of managers reported feeling over-worked, and several had been in the hospital, a direct result, several said, of the stress they had been experiencing at work. One of the affected workers said:

> There is just too much pressure...Eighteen months of gearing up for the conversion has given me a lot of gray hairs and sleepless nights. It's not unusual for me to spend 55 to 60 hours a week...here in my office...since October of last year...that's a long time to keep going like that...I'm suffering from burnout because of the hours and the pressure and the constant problems...

The situation at the manufacturing firm had similar elements. Although all employees had been facing no single crisis, top-down influence was evident in several ways. First, in response to a recession, the company began a program of massive layoffs, with little input from below, despite the fact that drastic reorganization of both clerical and managerial work was often deemed necessary. The result was increased work demands for the individual. As one secretary, who had to process paperwork for those targeted for lay-off put it, "We think after each layoff we can't possibly do it with less, and then they ask us to lay more off." The secretaries had been particularly hard-hit by this policy; many had lost jobs altogether. Others (the "fortunate" ones) had been called back after periods of lay-off. "They seem to be pulling names out of a hat" for lay-offs, one secretary said. Even engineering was being pushed to produce a new product in a "compressed period of time" in an effort to "keep up with the competition." As one engineer put it, "We've been asked to do in three or four years what would normally take eight." As a result, these employees were also feeling tense and overworked, a general feeling throughout the company.

Directives often originated from the very top, concerning such diverse issues as memo format (from which secretaries were hesitant to deviate), budgets (which were invariably "rewritten" by upper management, leaving department heads to "rethink all our plans for the year"), changes in parts or products (which resulted in large paperwork requirements). However, few channels existed for upward communication, and several managers reported being very frustrated by their efforts to "convince" their superiors to adopt certain policies:

> We go ahead and do what they say and then spend the next six months feeding them information that says they should be doing it another way.

In general, managers felt communication was good only "up to the level of vice president." Many felt their advice was sought but not heeded. Some managers reported feeling they were "advisors" to certain parts of the company, with no one compelled to act on their advice. The same feelings existed among the secretaries. For instance, one of them said ideas were continually being sought from her and others in her division but never acted upon.

The managers were frustrated by their inability to communicate their own "real life" perspectives to upper management -- or the perspectives of those in the field. "We used to get input from the field on a regular basis," said one, "but now, with the way things have changed, we don't get that anymore." The general feeling was "they don't take advantage of the experience they do have." One manager cited a competitor company doing better largely, he felt, because their "president had worked his way up from the assembly line into the office." About their own managers, it was felt they were "out of touch" with the market the company faced:

> Few of them have come up through the ranks, and it shows in their decisions. Our dealers are constantly throwing up their hands and saying, "What the...?"

The fact that management trainees had been brought into the company directly from graduate school was a particular irritation.

> Fast trackers just really don't understand the contingencies of the marketplace. We spend a lot of our time trying to convince upper management that what one of them has suggested just isn't going to work. They try to get information in 200 phone calls that it takes us years to gather from the field. Their information just isn't as good.

The current managers were seen as "financial people" who were mainly concerned with the immediate "bottom line figures," not with future concerns.

> If they can save a few bucks today and make our stockholders happy, they will, even if it means our [product] will fall apart five years down the line. And that will cost us thousands of dollars in the long run.

> They put off paying bills until the next month so we look better to the stockholders, but then we start out each month behind.

These features of the control structure and process were reflected in general supervisory styles. Because the managers were so busy, they felt attempts at "long range planning and thinking" were made difficult by day-to-day demands on their time. "I feel like I'm running around putting out fires all the time," one of them said. One manager who reported close communications with upper management experienced the style as "crisis management," with effects spilling over into the departments, while the managers attempted to buffer or protect their subordinates. These same complaints were also made by managers at the bank. It seems the system exploits not only lower level workers, but also higher level workers who suffer from stress and overwork on a regular basis.

Here, a problem of overwork also arose in relation to technology. One massive computer conversion was undertaken with only one female employee who could type. That employee was required to enter all of a large amount of data, though some plans were being made to add more typists to that work pool. Again, a critical factor was a lack of participation in setting the time frames for these conversions. "They're (deadlines) just handed down to us," one worker complained, adding that these deadlines were often not realistic.

We should not be surprised to find the introduction of new technology posing special problems. We have long known that new technology can have negative implications for factory workers (cf. Boyle et. al., 1984; Braverman, 1975) or professionals in manufacturing firms (Perrow, 1972). We now also know that new technology has had a negligible impact on the satisfaction of office workers, basically because it generates both positive and negative effects (Silverstone and Towler, 1984; Cassedy and Nussbaum, 1983). On one hand, innovations like word processors have greatly simplified many tasks; on the other hand, it has caused many health problems (e.g., eye and muscle strain) and the de-skilling of many jobs (Boyle et al., 1984; Feldberg and Glenn, 1983; Kleeman, 1982; Makower, 1983).

At the technical institute, somewhat different problems emerged. Here, the structure was also very hierarchical in theory, but much less effectively so in practice. This was largely the result of historical accident. The style of management in the institute reflected structural constraints. Most supervisors expressed a desire for participatory decision-making, but found such efforts hampered by institutional pressures or by the incompetencies of those below them. ("Sometimes they just can't handle it.") Because of "strict accountability" to those above them, most of these managers felt constraints were imposed on their management styles, on how much they could involve those below them. Several supervisors complained external time constraints on decisions prevented them from doing so. (These constraints, "external" to their own positions, sometimes arose from within the institution, sometimes from outside the institution.) "We often don't have enough time to discuss it with everyone," said one supervisor. Others specifically mentioned guidelines set by those above them as constraining factors.

Because of the "accountability model" of the downward control operating in the institute, most supervisors perceived themselves as delegators, discussing issues with "those affected," but retaining ultimate control, often "checking back" on tasks that had been delegated. So, statements such as "I try to brainstorm with my staff" were often followed by contradictory statements like "I am authoritarian."

Since the technical institute was much less effective in its top-down control structure, problems involving technology were very different. Though a computer was on the main campus, very few of the internal operations were computerized. The computer staff responded it could not be done; "It is impossible," was said to any computer requests that came their way. No one seemed to be in charge enough to demand the staff produce the needed work. Certainly there were tasks that needed computerization. Yet surprisingly, registration was still handled manually. A high ratio of part-time teaching staff in a perpetually marginal position left many clerical workers with the task of signing several hundred pay cards every two weeks, something that easily could have been computerized. Secretaries staggered under the weight of keeping up with the personnel and course-related workload for all of these individuals. Because no system was available, they found themselves doing many time-consuming tasks manually when the same work could be done "so much more quickly" with a computer. "The administrators here just don't seem willing to move on this," one of the secretaries said. "They just don't seem to have the push."

All three of these work settings, though different in some details, have a great deal in common. Many workers complained about feeling powerless to affect the direction of these organizations. They expended a great deal of energy trying to anticipate and influence the thinking of those at the top. Such upward influence or communication is not an ongoing, normal part of these organizations. Two are explicitly set up to make a profit, while in the third, these concerns are more implicit. But for all three, concern about the bottom-line underlies most decisions, often regardless of the impact on employees, one of the important factors determining how these organizations function. Such concerns about over-all employee well-being are externalized in their calculations, as are environmental considerations. As a result, many workers, even fairly high level ones, feel exploited in some way -- overworked, under-rewarded, bypassed, and, sometimes, out of work.

These are precisely the problems many economists and other social observers have been pointing to in our workplace, problems that can easily lead to an apathetic, cynical, angry work force. Suzanne Gordon (1991), in her book *Prisoners of Men's Dreams*, has written about the growing demands on workers, which create stress and anxiety for all. In reference to women workers, specifically, she sees only two possibilities as things are currently structured -- pain (staying and suffering) or flight (leaving the work force).

In the three work sites discussed in this chapter, we see some of the specific features of our workplace that cause problems. Certain management practices troubled these workers. In all three settings, bureaucratic structure and process coupled with strict top-down control -- with some appearance of seeking worker input -- frustrated the workers. This reliance on bureaucratic control is not surprising, as Baron, Jennings, and Dobbin (1988) report industries such as these to be highly bureaucratic. That the manufacturing firm was the setting with the tightest control structure is also not surprising, as Baron et. al. (1988) report this type of industry most often uses a scientific management approach, replete with time and motion studies and formal lay-off procedures.

Critiquing Organizational Structure and Process

As awareness has grown about these problems, certain organizational structures or processes have been identified as the culprits, leading to proposals for specific workplace changes. Most of these changes involve management style, focusing particularly on relations with workers. Friedman (1992), for example, wrote about *The Leadership Myth*, calling into question common notions of the "natural" leader who is good in all situations. He argues for dispersing that power, saying leadership is the responsibility of everyone in the workplace, and that workplaces ought to facilitate the contributions of all.

The development of this idea can be traced through the management literature. Earlier theories of management, termed *Theory X* by many researchers (cf., McGregor, 1960; Likert and Likert, 1976), were based upon the assumption that workers were primarily externally motivated, meaning managers must devote most of their time to control through punishment and reward. And influence is necessarily of the top-down variety. Subordinates spent a great deal of time avoiding external punishments, in time developing narrowly-defined fields of expertise, which served as power bases they guarded jealously (Kanter, 1983). This prototypical bureaucratic arrangement worked well during the nineteenth and early part of the twentieth century. However, with the development of a globally interdependent world economy (O'Hara-Devereaux and Johansen, 1994 and Fernandez-Kelly, 1987) -- and changes in worker expectations for more satisfying jobs (Yankelovich, 1981), fueled in part by rising expectations in society for greater freedom and satisfaction -- this approach has now become particularly counter-productive (Kanter, 1983).

In the last half of this century, theorists began rethinking these assumptions, moving away from the three basic assumptions of *Theory X*: that most persons dislike work, will not try to achieve organizational goals unless coerced, and wish to avoid responsibility (Carr-Ruffino, 1985). McGregor (1960) developed *Theory Y*, based on opposing assumptions. He posited that individuals find mental and physical work to be as intrinsically rewarding as play or rest. Because of this, many workers actually seek responsibility and commitment in the workplace and, therefore, are motivated not by external coercion, but by their intrinsic desire to make a positive contribution. Yankelovich (1981) has documented the prevalence of this worker outlook. The trick, McGregor argued, is to find ways of making use of each worker's potential, since traditional organizations tend to draw upon only a small fraction of what workers can contribute.

Managers ascribing to *Theory Y* were faced with a whole new set of issues. Aside from external coercion, what other motivators could be used? Were some workers different than others in this regard? To answer these questions, researchers began looking at managerial behaviors in a different light. With *Theory Y*, worker trust of superiors is now more important than worker fear. Interpersonal skills are no longer superfluous but central to the successful manager's repertoire. Stogdill (1974) asserted the most effective manager was one who employed the "golden mean," balancing task and people orientations. If a manager destroyed his/her subordinate's intrinsic motivation to do the job, productivity would undoubtedly suffer. Hence, attention to "people issues" is no longer seen as time away from the bottom line, from getting the job done, but an intrinsic part of doing so. Likert (1976) noted that while this realization was growing in the world of management, in practice the classical approach was far from gone, as can be seen in the three examples described above. He believed most managers could be divided into two basic groups: those who were authoritative or exploitative and those who were participative -- these distinctions in many ways mirroring *Theory X* and *Theory Y*.

Once it was recognized different styles existed, the idea emerged certain management styles work best in certain situations. Fiedlar and Garcia (1987) developed a contingency theory in which he argued group function ultimately depended upon the fit between the manager's style, the group, and the work situation, broadening the manager's concerns from only individual motivators to aspects of the work environment. Fiedlar argued, for example, the extent to which a task is or can be structured affects the extent to which a manager can exert control and hold workers accountable, and that quality of the worker/manager relationship was important. Others (cf, Lawrence and Lorsch, 1967) adopted this perspective, arguing perhaps top-down/authoritarian control was essential in certain situations.

The process of change is seen in the new models that began to emerge, models of organizational structure and process, generally incorporating notions of flexibility, worker autonomy, and responsibility. Based upon scores of data and consulting experiences, Paul Hersey and Kenneth Blanchard (1988) in their influential management text, set forth a model that emphasizes the people skills necessary for effective management in today's world. These include 1) three competencies of leadership: diagnosing, adapting, and communicating; 2) three necessary skills for leadership: technical, human, and conceptual; and 3) four managerial roles: producing, implementing, innovating, and integrating. They see the most critical dimensions as those involving human resources. Earlier, Michael Maccoby (1976) in a book called *The Gamesman: The New Corporate Leader* had noticed the emergence of a new type of manager, one who was less driven to preside over empires but who strived to organize winning teams, who was less security-seeking, less dependent, and more detached than successful managers had been to that point in time. He predicted this "new type" would soon be the predominant kind of manager. Leavitt (1986) asserts the need for organizations to encourage innovation, making room for the "impractical...stubborn...impulsive ...pathfinder."

Practical guides for managers also include these suggestions. Blanchard and Lorber's (1984) *One Minute Manager* is one of the more popular examples. Here, managers are given specific, practical rules for managing relationships and giving feedback in the most productive manner. McKenzie's *Time Trap* is another, where managers are encouraged to strike out in new directions, not simply repeating well-done tasks. Peter Russell and Roger Evans suggest creative ways to deal with modern turbulence in *The Creative Manager* (1992). Tom Peter's two books *In Search of Excellence* (1982) and *Thriving on Chaos* (1987) point to the fall of the rational model and the rising importance of interpersonal relationships and other qualitative approaches. As he puts it:

> Today's structures were designed for controlling turn-of-the-century mass production...They have become perverse, action-destroying devices, completely at odds with current competitive needs (1987).

He argues poignantly for the "empowerment of the workforce." Kamerman and Kahn also argue:

> ...for American industry to remain competitive in a world market, management *should* start paying more attention to employees...recognizing that today's labor force is not the same as yesterday's...[has]...new...needs and expectations (1987,18).

Kanter's (1983) work is perhaps the most exhaustive in chronicling the new emerging model -- in terms both of the industry trends examined and the specificity of practices proposed. She gathered detailed data from many different corporations and used these data to differentiate between what she called integrative and segmentalist organizations, arguing the former stance must be adopted before the United States can improve its position in the world market. In the traditional, segmental organization, managers set policy at the top with little or no input from below, bolster their power positions within narrow segments of the organization with little communication across organizational units, and encourage open competition among subordinates, hoping the best will survive. This is reminiscent of the *Theory X* approach, where control was seen as paramount because workers were viewed with suspicion. In these organizations, Kanter argues, innovation is stifled.

In contrast, the integrative organization is characterized by open communication, constantly fluctuating networks and work groups (often forming *across* traditional boundaries -- both horizontally and vertically), decentralized resources, and flatter hierarchies. This profile, drawn largely from new high tech companies, entails a different approach to management. Here, managers cannot rely upon tradition for a power base, but instead must use personal power, actual contributions, and the ability to identify with and motivate subordinates. In this model, it is assumed workers are intrinsically motivated and both the individuals and the company will profit by allowing workers to take the initiative. Interpersonal skills become essential, often determining if a manager will effectively accomplish the task. Thus, task and people orientations become even more closely linked.

In Kanter's view, the predominant control structures and managerial styles that have existed in corporations in our society are largely responsible for our faltering world economic position, even though some researchers view the culprit as both internal and external to the organizations (Useem, 1984). Kanter points to specific aspects of traditional managerial styles:

> ...firms with early and progressive human resource practices...have been significantly more profitable over the last twenty years (Kanter, 1983:353)

She believes a direct causal link exists between managerial structure and process and the overall functioning of the organization.

In her book *When Giants Learn to Dance* (1989), she makes the point that for corporations to effectively motivate today's worker in order to successfully compete in the current economy, managers must understand how to create an atmosphere where cooperation thrives. We must have a "more co-operative" corporation. Under the old system she calls "cowboy management," in which departments within a corporation compete for a single prize, fear of losing is the big motivator. People began acting as much from a desire to avoid punishment as from seeking rewards. This scenario can actually begin to hamper a corporation's performance, as the individual's sense of self and motivation are undermined. She argues instead that fostering cooperation is more effective in the longrun. To do this, rewards must be available for good performance, not just for "winning." Such a reward system must be built into the very fabric of the corporation. Evaluation and compensation systems, in particular, must be structured to reward these desirable behaviors. It is important, Kanter stresses, to set aside rewards for team *and* individual accomplishments, for concepts and ideas as well as "the right answer," and to encourage the development of networks and friendships.

Worker Participation

These ideas involving more worker participation have been explored elsewhere, as well, and re-connect to the literature discussed in the beginning of the chapter about alienation of the worker. The father/son team of Bluestone and Bluestone (1992) argue corporate America is in serious trouble in large part because of its tendency to exclude workers from sharing in the responsibility for growth, profits, and other aspects of the company. They present evidence showing, between 1983 and 1988, a growing erosion of trust among *all* workers, but especially hourly workers, in corporate decisions and ability. They discuss a 1989 *Fortune* magazine report of an Opinion Research Corporation survey which shows only a slight majority of managers in 1988 felt their company treated them with respect and consideration (down from 71%), while only 30% of hourly workers felt this (down from 39%). Both the Bluestones and Gary Miller (1992) believe corporations running on hierarchical, purely rational, classical economic principles will produce sub-optimal results in the future. Surely, many of the workers in the three settings I described above felt they had little upward influence, frequently feeling exploited and alienated.

These changes, of course, require new approaches to management, where managers must function more as coaches than controllers, "inspiring a willingness to cooperate, to take risks, to innovate, to go beyond the level of effort that a narrow self-interested analysis...would summon" (Miller, 1992, 2). Co-operation is essential in this world. A key feature of this new workplace is greater worker control, autonomy, and input.

Much has been written recently about this workplace democracy. Tausky and Chelte (1988), in a special issue of *Work and Occupations*, while noting the tremendous difficulty companies are having truly democratizing their workplace, argue that successfully implementing worker participation would be very worthwhile for companies, helping them to solve many of their current serious problems. Other researchers report successful outcomes of such experiments, ranging from enhanced job satisfaction (Neuman et al., 1989) to increased organizational commitment and worker productivity or effectiveness (Administrator, June 1988; Faxen, 1978; Gaertner and Nollen, 1989a, 1989b; Lincoln and Kalleberg, 1990; Zeitz, 1984). Others report these techniques must be accompanied by fundamental organizational support to work successfully -- a change in attitude throughout the company and support from the top echelons (*Business Week*, 1981), improved coordination (Faxen, 1978), ties to incentives for cooperating (Kanter, 1983), prior worker commitment (Levin, 1980), and inclusion of all types of workers (Alperson, 1988). Substantial shifts of power are apparently necessary. According to the 1981 *Business Week* special staff report "paying lip service to the concept is rarely enough" (p. 89). Changes in structure, process, and attitudes -- of both workers and managers -- is required before quality circles or worker participation can be effective. The extent of worker participation can range from temporary membership on planning groups to stock ownership by all employees (with full stockholder rights).

Evidence abounds that when such efforts are unsuccessful it is often because management hesitates to share control in significant ways (cf. Hancock, Logue, and Schiller, 1991; *Teamster Conway Express*, 1992; Chelte et al, 1989). Problems apparently result when such measures are used merely as a facade to make workers believe they have more input when, in fact, those at the very top are retaining their full control and are simply trying to manipulate their subordinates. According to Karl-Olof Faxen in the *American Economics Review*, changes in pay systems may even be necessary; group bonuses are frequently used to give workers a stake in the outcome, along with other measures. Both reports claim success with worker participation systems when these supporting changes have also been made.

The movement for workplace reform draws much from the pluralist tradition. The worker participation movement uses an essentially systemic model, extending the pluralist view, seeing participation as an effective antidote to the widespread alienation noted by those discussed in the first part of this chapter. Proponents believe individuals are motivated if they have control over key aspects of their lives. Consensus formation can be called authentic if real control is exerted in the upward direction. This control is possible if the various parts of organizations have this input. In other words, control depends upon the capacity of each group of individuals to make the entire system stop; functional interdependence must exist. Although some groups will be more capable of causing such a stoppage than others, authentic participation requires each group have the capacity to at least cause severe difficulties in the continued operation of the system. But for maximum performance of the organization as a whole, the groups ought not to have to exercise this power to have its influence felt. Input from all groups must be an ongoing process.

Since lack of worker participation has seemed to be a critical factor in producing workplace problems, increasing worker control has been a major emphasis around the world. Many countries are realizing the necessity for designing more efficient systems that foster more creative and productive employees, just to be competitive in the world market (Frost, 1988), with worker participation (control) as a key factor.

In our country, the Japanese system is given much attention. William Ouchi's *Theory Z* (1981) was aimed at helping U.S. businesses adopt appropriate Japanese practices. He argues the Japanese deal with their employees in holistic terms, offering them resources to solve family as well as work problems, non-specialized career paths, sometimes life-time jobs. In addition, workers at all levels are involved in collective decision-making and are given responsibility. This model involves not only working and communicating with workers but actually giving them some of the control, sharing the power. While other cultural factors are undoubtedly involved, one key factor may be that the Japanese seem to favor less hierarchical views of the relationship between management and workers. On January 8, 1989, the president of SONY was interviewed on *60 Minutes*. He said this about American and Japanese business practices:

> American managers need to change how they view workers...as tools in the process...When times are good, they hire them; when recession comes, they lay them off. The workers did not cause the recession.

Asked by Diane Sawyer if he thought American managers should not make such high salaries, he continued:

> In Japan, they only make $40,000 or so...the managers aren't the only ones responsible for the profit.

In the sense of income and employment security, workers are treated in a more egalitarian fashion. Just looking at the income factor alone, Kelly (1991b) in *Business Ethics* reported with apparent disgust that over the last decade, top executive pay in the U.S. climbed 212%, but employee pay has gone up only 54%.

We hear more often of experiments aimed at incorporating elements of the Japanese system, particularly the idea of quality circles, a system whereby all levels of workers are involved in planning and evaluating the company's performance. This idea has been used in a variety of industries, including service companies (Ingle and Ingle, 1983). Scholars have reported running entire research projects with this collaborative model, involving either graduate student assistants (Whyte, n.d.) or subjects (Marshall and McLean, 1988) as full partners.

In our own culture, utopian communities are those which have tended to use the principles of collective decision-making, effective communication, holistic concern, and egalitarian principles. Kanter, in her 1972 book, *Community and Commitment*, showed how these techniques were used by the more successful nineteenth century groups -- such as the Shaker and Oneida communities -- to retain membership. The more long-lived of these groups ran very successful businesses with cooperative principles. Perhaps the best known example today is the Mondragon community in the Basque region of Spain, a community-wide co-operative effort which includes industrial companies, support organizations such as a credit union, retirement fund, a technical institute, and several health clinics. Since all of these organizations are co-operatives, the principles of equality and self-determination are seen here in action. Economists claim that these businesses are as productive, perhaps more so, than conventional capitalistic concerns in similar types of settings (cf. Frost, 1988; Levin, 1980; Campbell, 1977).

Rothschild and Whitt (1986) have written extensively about five co-operative institutions in our country -- a food co-op, a legal aid society, a free health clinic, an alternative high school, a newspaper -- where consensus decision-making is practiced in non-hierarchical structures. While Rothschild and Whitt found many problems in these organizations, they felt they may offer a brief glimpse of the future. These types of organizations certainly address many of the problems with our "mass society" discussed by writers like Daniel Bell. They provide the means for individuals to become integrated into their cultural milieu, to feel they have some control over their lives, to shake the apathy and alienation of much concern to many social observers from Karl Marx to the present time. And they do so in a much more sophisticated and substantial way than the voluntary association route proposed by the early pluralists. They form a bridge between the private sector and Third Sector (the service sector) pointed to by Jeremy Rifkin as a growing area of engagement, a solution offered to many of our problems in his new book *The End of Work* (1995).

In 1979, a resource book listed nearly 400 co-operative organizations across the country that offer a variety of goods and services (Co-op America, 1988). While it may be argued that many of these companies, ranging from self-help agencies to energy producers to restaurants, food and clothing producers and distributors, do not represent the core of our industrial sector and so are of no consequence to our mainstream culture, they do represent a substantial number of individuals, and represent the types of changes called for by many futurists and seen to some extent in the newer, more flexible high tech companies.

Another model in achieving worker participation is worker ownership, something to this point most likely to happen in a plant shut-down situation. Some workers have prevented shut-downs by taking over the companies involved, turning them into participatory workplaces. William Foote Whyte (n.d.) at Cornell University has been involved in many of these endeavors, summarizing them in an undated manuscript. Individuals involved in his applied research program on New Systems of Work and Participation both studied and assisted workers faced with plant shutdowns. He reports, in the process, the research project itself became participatory, losing much of its original hierarchical structure and giving students real ownership of (shares in) the project.

These changes are already occurring in some of the more traditional segments of the workforce. Certain companies, such as Hallmark Cards, are known for their sensitivity to "people issues," particularly their willingness to empower employees (Roessing, 1990). Long established co-operatives attend to these issues as well. Examples are Co-op America, a confederation of co-operative organizations (Community Jobs, 1990) and The Moosewood Restaurant in Ithaca, New York (Taylor, 1990), the latter started by a woman. Instructions abound for helping companies and individuals move in these directions, including advice on creating a sense of comfort and control in one's own office (Yager, 1989), encouraging companies to meet women's family-related needs (Sandroff, 1989), managing careers over time (Farmaion, 1989), and criticizing one's boss (Weisinger, 1990). In each instance, the worker's initiative, sense of control, and responsibility are encouraged and/or rewarded.

The model we see women using in Part I of this book fits in remarkable ways with changes being called for in management practices, calls that, for the most part, completely ignore gender differences in leadership propensities or style. Even the less conventional literature on co-operatives has tended to ignore women's potential -- or women's continued oppression by such systems (Hacker,

1987). Likewise, the feminist literature valorizing women's potential pays scant attention to these other trends.

Obviously, the workplace is undergoing a tremendous transformation. The new social contract Yankelovich asserts is being written between workers and employers moves us in the direction of worker participation and integration between personal beliefs and values, family status and workplace practices.   These are the same preferences women are expressing in their approaches and ideas about management.   The convergence of these two areas suggest that we cannot fully understand what is happening with gender in this society without considering changes in the workplace, particularly the negotiations occurring across the class divide.   Nor can we understand workplace trends without considering what is happening with women.

Chapter 7

The Intertwining of Capitalism and Patriarchy:
Is Capitalism Particularly Cruel to Women?

> ...using...both a feminist and a woman's standpoint epistemology shifts the analysis of ideology from class to relationships of power/knowledge and therefore at least resonate with the conditions of late twentieth-century, postmodern capitalism...By the early 1980's, Marxist critics not only recognized a crisis in historical materialism brought on by changes in the relations of production and the meaning of labor; they also had begun to recognize the relation of feminism to this crisis.
> Patricia Ticineto Clough, 1994, p. 63

The last chapter showed a convergence of thinking in two apparently distinct areas of inquiry -- that of feminism and the worker participation movement. In both areas, we see an emphasis on individual dignity and control, calls for an end to domination in many forms that are constantly expanding -- of men over women, managers over workers, people over nature, white men over people of color, the young over the old, the physically well over the physically handicapped or differently-abled, straights over gays. The prevalent world view, the belief that hierarchies and dualistic distinctions are necessary, leads to the creation of social structures that engender exploitation. Through time, humans have confronted these social tendencies with demands for greater equality. In our own culture, we have moved toward greater depth in our preference for equality, coming to expect more in this regard *and* to become increasingly critical of conditions as they exist. However, the process through which we begin to perceive and embrace this new way of thinking is not always straight-forward. We resist seeing things in a fundamentally different way, even if this new way is a direction we might ultimately prefer. Part of this resistance comes from our failure to see the connections between trends moving in similar directions. This chapter will explore more fully the connection between recent advances in feminist thinking and critiques of capitalism, particularly those focusing on the role of workers.

As with many of these related trends, we can find a growing tendency in many areas which push us to reconceptualize our relations to the world and each other. The idea that participation at work, in community, in government, in every aspect of life is the order of the day is appearing in many guises. Many ideas have emerged about how to accomplish this goal. *Small Is Beautiful!*, a trend-setting book by Schumacher (1975), is becoming a common slogan, bolstering a belief our largeness must be transformed into systems small enough so the individual *can* participate and feel a certain amount of power. Also, our systems must incorporate concern for each other, for the earth and all living creatures, as immediate considerations, not externalities to be left for others to deal with or to be imposed upon us by the federal government or other outside entities. In essence, we must give up our heavy reliance upon hierarchies to provide us with social order.

Feminist thinking is only beginning to broach these broad questions, venturing out beyond the rather narrow focus on gender alone. However, the idea is growing that a focus on patriarchy must be supplemented with a concern with other issues, such as race and class, to truly transform our entire social order and restructure our organizations (Balsamo, 1985). A similar process is happening in other areas, where concern with gender issues is beginning to be incorporated into these inquiries, as well.

The connection between women's oppression and labor market trends seems obvious. Women's progress (or lack thereof) is often gauged by measuring women's workplace progress: male/female wage differentials, women's entrance into predominately male occupations, and women's movement up the corporate hierarchy. Hence workplace position, indeed conditions at work more generally, are of central importance in our current understandings.

As patriarchy involves distinctions between male and female spheres, with female spheres being clearly devalued (and market work has traditionally been a male preserve), women's movement into this realm promises to ultimately undermine the very basis of our patriarchal order. After all, the undoing of patriarchy follows from a reduction in the gulf separating our two gender-specific spheres, largely because of women's increased labor force participation. As "those who know society differently" enter the formerly male realm, particularly as leaders with the power to make changes, different perspectives are undoubtedly brought to bear. Hence, the potential for a major transformation of the work world is great, indeed.

It is also true that class distinctions (related to who has control in the workplace) are also very important. If race, class, and gender oppression spring from a common propensity in our social system, we must simultaneously consider various movements in response to these issues, if we want to truly understand what is happening. I believe movements for change in the workplace, on the surface seeming to be only about class, are in fact closely tied to our ongoing gender revolution.

Problems at Work

Let's first look closely at the problems with work. Workers without voice experience frustration, hardship, and eventually, alienation. This can be true for all types of workers. Kelly (1991), for example, in a study of Fortune 500 executives found half felt their lives were "empty and meaningless." Many moral philosophers, such as Christopher Lasch (1991) decry the pressures of competition and commodification running rampant throughout society. As Bellah et al (1991) have put it, "Americans have pushed the logic of exploitation about as far as it can go." Our institutions, they argue, compel us to compete with one another, rather than work cooperatively for the common good, which contributes greatly to chaos and trouble in our times. Even Bruyn's (1991) work, admittedly more of an apology for the current system, argues a new social order must be constructed, "one that shows how social factors are intertwined with economic factors."

Warning signs something was seriously amiss have long been among us. Our trade imbalance, plant closings, bitter management/labor relations, worker apathy, and poor production are but a few of the signs cited by experts. For awhile, we have ignored these signs pointing to a need for great change and have attempted, instead, to fix things within the old order. Eventually, writers began to give these problems center stage resulting in many authors bursting upon the scene with proposals for radically different approaches to workplace organization and management. These proposals have all been surprisingly similar.

The major culprit, many argue, concerns how we organize and run our organizations. Kelly (1991a) says that we are moving

> ...toward a higher synthesis...[seeing that] meetings are in fact more productive when they're less formal...goals are more apt to be reached when they harmonize with the natural growth course of a business...organization itself can be relaxing (1991a, 6).

In this movement to balance the need for control and order with the need to acknowledge human needs, she says,

> ...we [are] seeing bureaucracy give way to participative management. The era of the Organization Man is being followed by the era of the flattened hierarchy. Nine to five is maturing into flextime (1991a, 6).

In the many proposals for change, a major component is increased upward influence and a systemic view of how that influence is incorporated into self-organizing systems. In general, increased participation, lack of hierarchy, and holistic perspectives are seen more positively. Bateson (1979) presented a systems view of social life that ultimately argued for these ideas. In the past decade, many workplace reforms have been suggested that contain these elements at the core of the proposals. On the surface, developments here appear to have little connection with changes in our thinking about gender. However, careful examination reveals similar factors to be operating in growing feminist awareness, especially a common drive toward holistic, participatory, less hierarchical structures. I believe the changes being called for in the workplace represent a unique opportunity for women, a time when we can step forward and visibly lead the way in restructuring our workplace. The skills we have acquired through our particular socialization are becoming more highly valued.

Connections between Patriarchy and Capitalism

Other feminists argue problems for workers and women are not isolated phenomena but are, in fact, highly related, that the systems of patriarchy and capitalism are connected. Both intrinsically involve one-up/one-down, dominating, hierarchical types of relationships -- exploitation, in other words. Capitalism, the belief monetary benefits from a product rightfully belong to those who own the means of production and not to those who create the product, intrinsically drives toward exploitation of the worker. Similarly, patriarchy, the belief men are superior to women and women's sphere is separate (and inferior) from men's, intrinsically drives toward exploitation of women.

As Sylvia Walby has pointed out in her 1986 book *Patriarchy at Work*, these two systems are often intertwined, exploiting both men and women at the same time, though at specific times they have seemed to work at cross-purposes. One example of seeming cross-purposes would be historical periods when male labor movements acted to exclude women from the workplace, even though women were cheaper laborers (and more logical choices, according to the logic of capitalism). During these times, the logic of capitalism did not prevail, but was superseded by patriarchal urges. Also, the logic of capitalism may not always predominate in workplace changes supposedly aimed at protecting the worker. Both Walby and Graham Lowe (1987) make the point that changes such as worker protection legislation and the development of rational, bureaucratic administration which served to protect male workers from the excessive abuses of capitalism actually placed women at a disadvantage. Women were explicitly or implicitly excluded from the new structures, or ghettorized into specific job categories. At these points, women have been doubly disadvantaged, often excluded from protections male workers managed to acquire against capitalism's propensity toward exploitation.

To fully understand developments in our society, we must examine the ways in which class and gender interests operate in combination. The situation is quite complex and made even more so if we consider Walby's notion that the specific form patriarchy takes has varied across time, making it difficult to say anything universal about patriarchy, particularly without specific historical context. And it seems increasingly clear that we cannot solve issues in one area (gender) without considering related problems in the other (class, workplace).

Himmelweit (1984) argues that both systems are intertwined, that our capitalist system *requires* a separate sphere for women, offering them as objects for exploitation.

Walby argues the women's movements of this century have improved women's place in society, essentially moving the struggle from one centered in the home ("private patriarchy") to one also centered in the workplace and other social institutions ("public patriarchy"). Shere Hite in her newest book (1995), *The Hite Report on the Family* argues that neither quest has been successful, in that democracy is only belatedly coming to the "private" world of the family.

One way of exploring the interconnections between the thinking about gender and workplace trends is to look at the ways in which our capitalistic system is especially difficult for women. Several connections exist. First is the tendency toward exploitation, especially overwork, that has a special impact on women, largely because of traditional family responsibilities. Second, our work system allows (some would even say encourages) sexual harrassment. Third, exclusionary tactics make life difficult for many women in the workforce.

The classical approach to managing the work world does present *special* problems for individuals not part of the dominant group, as the last chapter demonstrated. I believe it is the responsibility of scholars to bear witness to such facts. Of those less privileged workers in general, T.R. Young (1988) has written:

> The immediate task of the radical scholar is to provide the American public with a comprehensive understanding of the Reagan administration [in order] to warn Americans away from fascism and to fashion a democratic socialism that fits well within the structure of human rights broadly conceived to include the good earth and all its life forms...American sociology has a special obligation to provide the data and analysis of justice and injustice...benefitting as we do from the special position of trust as the richest, most powerful nation...in the world capitalist system of exploitation. That trust is betrayed when we ignore the distress of the American workers whose labor feeds us, clothes us, houses us, and moves us about the land...(p. 75).

The last chapter documented the extent to which our hierarchical, segmentalist organizations and systems create distress for workers. Here, I argue this is especially true for women.

Exploitation and Overwork

In the literature on the anthropology of work a concern is raised women will replace men as the "primary focus of formative class struggle," that women's integration of work with family "at the interface of the natural economy" will provide a means of exploitation (Habben, 1988). In June Nash's (1989) terms, women are particularly vulnerable to the fallout of current labor market trends:

> When we include the noncapitalistic subsistence producers as an integral part of the analysis, we [see]...the broader basis for social movements (p.6). The presence of women changes the class struggle from one limited to the arena of production to a struggle for reproduction where moral persuasion based on the right to survive rather than the threat to withdraw labor becomes the imperative (p. 10).

Women may simply become the new underclass, especially given their large proportional representation in that position already. This general prediction, that class and gender lines will become merged in the future capitalistic system, suggests ways we might approach these two trends in a holistic fashion.

How does the capitalistic system's propensity for exploiting workers apply particularly to women? Given women's traditional family role commitments and resulting time constraints, capitalism's tendency to get as much work as possible for the least possible compensation becomes particularly problematic. For example, a 1984 Gallup Poll discussed in *The Wall Street Journal* showed our population overwhelmingly believes executive women have had to make "substantial sacrifices," and as a result, suffer a "lack of balance in their lives." A new term, "Type E Personality," refers to a tendency among successful women, analogous to but different from the "Type A Personality" often found among successful men. Type E women feel they must be "everything to everyone." Psychologist Harriet Braiker discussed this at a meeting of the Committee of 200, a group of women who run their own companies with at least $10 million in revenue or a corporate subsidiary with $40 million in revenue or are senior executives of major corporations (Solomon, 1989). Such women often find the stress levels to be very high as they attempt to do everything: succeed at work, earn money, keep a perfect house, raise wonderful children, be passionate wives, and so on. The capitalist system will not accommodate less than total dedication or involvement.

Suzanne Gordon in *Prisoners of Men's Dreams* (1991) argues women face tremendous pressures to perform -- over and above the exploding expectations of workers in general. She shows, for example, median hours at work have actually increased over the past several decades, the result, she asserts, of capabilities made possible by new technologies. As a result, workers face spiraling expectations for performance. One has done never quite enough. Many of the women she interviewed said it was impossible to achieve a good balance between work and family/personal life. These women reported work to "eat up all of their time."

Arlie Hochschild in a 1986 *New York Times Book Review* entitled "The Totaled Woman" also points to this imbalance. Reviewing three books that deal, in part, with the overload working women face, she notes the impossible struggle for mothers in our current system. One book, she argues:

> ...perpetuates the notion that if we just work things out in our heads, the problems of the working mother will basically be solved. In fact, much of [this] conflict is a reasonable response...to real conflicts between the way jobs are set up and what children need. Women are trying to squeeze themselves into jobs and careers originally designed for men who had someone else to care for their children...(p. 17).

She asks:

> Where is the fantastic workplace day care center to which your child would beg [to go]? Where are the well-paid regular part-time jobs? And where are the books about men who feel guilty about not being workaholics like their fathers? We need nothing short of total transformation of economy and family (p. 17).

Oftentimes, when women do take on the most challenging of jobs, they feel they must choose to have neither children nor marriages nor other stable relationships in their lives. This she sees from McBroom's (1986) study of top women in the financial worlds of New York and

San Francisco. Others note working women seem to experience much higher rates of stress than working men (Bird, 1986; Scott and Spooner, 1989).

Some of the women I interviewed reported feeling tremendous pressures for production. Recall the situation in the financial institution (Chapter 6) when workers (primarily women) were given a deadline to complete a computer conversion one year earlier than they themselves had estimated to be reasonable. They completed the work according to their own estimate, "one year late" according to the company. Several were hospitalized after a great deal of overtime and stress.

Other women in the financial institution believed that women had to work much harder than men to be successful. One woman said with all of her work and success, if she had been a man, she would have been promoted "long before now," and another woman flatly said, "They couldn't find a man to do what I do for the money I make."

A similar perception existed in the manufacturing firm, where both men and women believed that women managers had "to work a lot harder" to "prove themselves" than men did. One woman manager said her boss expected:

...lots of me. He expects me to be like a helpmate or something, not minding staying after work and such things.

The general consensus was these women had to be "really special people," persistent and confident in establishing "their value and not backing down," "very analytical," [with] "a lot of moxy."

It seems these problems are widespread. And the implications may be troubling. In 1986, a *Chicago Tribune* article titled "Office Madness" appeared in the Tempo-Woman section (Austin, 1986). The title continued in smaller print "In corporate America, sanity is often the price paid for success." The author began with the statement:

We have seen the best minds of our generation destroyed by a modern madness...They pass through universities on a fast track to financial bliss, slipping quietly and permanently into pre-formed niches, parlaying their MBA's into BMW's. They are the result of a society that accepts a mountain of consumer goods as adequate recompense for a lifetime of meaningless labor in a rigid corporate environment (p. 1).

This article is a review of a book by Douglas LaBier, about the young professionals he psychoanalyzes. Overtime, he came to believe the emotional problems they reported were caused not by "childhood trauma, but from conflicts between personal values and the demands of their careers" (p. 1). The article notes:

> Much of the pain is felt by women who are trying to hang onto the traditional values of love, marriage and family in a corporate environment that has long downplayed the importance of a happy and successful life outside the office (p. 6).

As LaBier says:

> The essential thing to emphasize is how much women have been sold a fake bill of goods...that's why these "pioneer women," the earlier ones who where the first ones to move up were like men...they've taken on the worst of the male characteristics. The younger women see that...they say "I don't want to be like that...I want a balanced life" (p. 6).

And he believes corporations will have to change.

> Organizations are having to realize that they need to cultivate their own human resources, that there's [sic] a lot of talented, educated career women that organizations are going to have to hire and support...[and then adapt] to their desires, to their attempt to combine a fuller emotional life with a career (p. 6).

While pressures toward corporate change may be transformative, much distress and anxiety still exists over the situation as it currently stands. For example, Thomas Harrel and Jane Baack (1989) found husbands in dual MBA couples to actually have more anxiety than their wives if they had children. The authors speculated men may be taking on more homemaker duties than they desired, and that no magazines or role models exist to give men advice on how to handle this situation. For both sexes, perhaps, pressures to fill both roles are becoming increasingly overwhelming. This depends, no doubt, on how the couple manages to work out the conflict. Schneer and Reitman (1993), for example, found what they called "post-traditional" two career couples to be more satisfied with their situations -- even though they made less money -- than those couples who tried to meet the demands of traditional careers *and* family role expectations.

Sexual Harassment

Pressures to perform were not the only issues raised by the women I interviewed. Another issue mentioned specifically by several women managers at the manufacturing firm was sexual harassment. Public forums such as Anita Hill's testimony at Clarence Thomas' Supreme Court Justice confirmation hearings, the William Kennedy Smith and Michael Tyson rape trials, and the controversy about Bob Packwood have heightened our awareness of this issues. Much evidence exists that this problem has long been with us (Stead, 1985).

The women I interviewed who had experienced sexual harrassment, before our collective consciousness raising, seemed to feel they had to deal with it on their own. They recounted personal comments made to them, "things men would never say to each other." One manager said:

> For instance, in the middle of a big business meeting, one of the guys I work with -- he had just noticed a new ring on my finger -- yelled across the table at me, "Hey, are you engaged?"

Another woman reported her supervisor's relief on hearing of her divorce, "Now are you available to be transferred?" he asked. "I *always* was," she replied. Another manager reported about a presentation she had made to her new colleagues.

> They started yelling filthy remarks at me during the presentation, suggesting what I might do to myself with various objects on the table. My general manager thought it was funny. They expected me to be used to it.

Several other women managers mentioned the "rough kidding" that goes on among the men, the importance of "knowing when to be one of the guys and when to excuse yourself." A 1986 letter to *MS Magazine* recounted a similar experience.

> I have recently been employed as a district manager of a Fortune 500 company...[O]nly after I started to work for this company did I...realize the many obstacles against women trying to break into the predominantly male business world...On the last day of a training session the director of learning services...told me that I had one big advantage...if I ever came close to losing a sale, I could always just lift up my skirt (p.16).

Such experiences represent added barriers in women's attempts to find a comfortable space in which to compete on equal footing. By most accounts, women managers find it difficult to function in this environment. However, among the people I talked with, there were two different views of why women encountered so many difficulties. Many respondents blamed the situation itself, saying the barriers to women's progress meant women had to be very astute at "figuring out how each person operates around here." A few, however, felt the individual women themselves were responsible for their own difficulties. For example, while waiting for an interview at the manufacturing firm, I spoke to a receptionist who intimated that it "isn't the company's fault there are so few women managers." She believed the company had tried very hard to "get women in those positions, but most are just not qualified." She told me about a woman buyer, an apparently well-known case in the company, who "just couldn't handle it. She got emotionally sick and had to take a leave of absence. She came back as a secretary." This woman receptionist, along with a few respondents, felt many women were simply "too emotional to be good managers"; they were "unable to take the pressures."

Advancement and Exclusion

Another, perhaps more basic issue, is the extent to which women are permitted into these positions in the first place. Judi Marshall (1992) has carefully outlined the extent to which women feel alien in:

> ...organizational cultures...pre-programmed with male values. They [women] do not share in the contexting that makes communication understandable....[so] they are not accepted as legitimate meaning-makers (p.8)...Women have a long history of having to read the dominant culture in order to survive as members of the subordinate group...But if they are trying to operate as members of the dominant group, they can never be sure of knowing fully the culture in which they must function...[so] many women managers feel precarious, as if they are impostors (p.9).

This situation, Marshall argues, affects how women perform as well as how they are perceived. "Living in this potentially hostile world," Marshall says, "women often describe themselves as struggling to survive rather than thriving." (p.9).

Outright attempts to exclude women are often referred to as the "glass ceiling," symbolizing women's problems breaking out of middle management into higher levels. Anne Morrison and her colleagues (1987) have explored this phenomenon more thoroughly than others, showing various ways women feel blocked from advancing. Some of it involves the strain of managing very complex impressions:

> Many of the pioneer women in our study felt terribly confined. They had to avoid being feminine *and* avoid being macho. They had to get the right kinds of help *and* succeed on their own. They had to take risks without making mistakes (p. 145).

The barriers were sometimes more explicit:

> Sometimes their bosses told them outright that they shouldn't have their jobs. Some of their colleagues had networked around them as if they didn't exist (p.147)...These executives are savvy. But many are also tired and a bit fed up with the extraordinary expectations that others have of them (p. 149).

Swoboda (1988) has defined this "glass ceiling" as a "collection of barriers women experience when attempting to move up one more rung on the ladder of success...[I]t...usually lies at the level above where merit no longer matters and politics [alone] does." Several sorts of factors -- role models, acceptance, pregnancy, and daycare policy -- are among the collection of barriers referred to by Swoboda. *Ms Magazine* asserted that few companies, maybe only twenty, could be listed as being particularly good for women (Starrett, 1987). These companies, cited for their records at "listening to women" were not perfect. For example, many of them were still treating pregnancy as a long term disability, although nineteen of them had at least one woman on their board of directors and fourteen had at least one woman senior vice president.

Other researchers have reported problems created for women by men's resentment. In a 1984 *MS Magazine* article, Anthony Astrachan reports hostility working class men feel in working with women. Evidence exists that senior male managers also feel threatened by successful women colleagues. In the course of doing my original interview study, I was given an undated anonymous mimeo entitled "The Hand That Rocks the Cradle." This four-page treatise began with the statement, "Frances Caircrose argues that being a mother is one of the best groundings in management, yet few women are top managers." It goes on to say:

> The main difference between running a division of say, United Biscuits [in Britain] and a family of two adults and two children is one of scale. And, of course, of social esteem...Professor Cary Cooper of the University of Manchester Institute of Science and Technology has been interested for some time in the fact that women make up a growing proportion of his undergraduate management students -- now nearly 40% -- and get just as many job offers as the men. But once companies take them on, they find they get no further than middle management; there they get stuck...He has just completed a survey of women managers in 3,000 companies. It drew furious inquiries from the top Tory MPs who wanted to know why the MSC was bothering its pretty head about women when there were so many men out of work. He found, predictably enough, that the root problem lay in the attitudes of senior managers...They often felt threatened by successful women...[who] were better educated and more assertive than their male counterparts...The way you start to change this is to give women more confidence in themselves.

As a result of this "glass ceiling", it is believed, women are establishing their own businesses at record rates. Tucker (1985) reports an increase in women with MBA's going into business for themselves because they realize they cannot make it into the highest levels of management, and this was also the preferred solution of the executives Morrison and her colleagues (1987) interviewed. Gordon (1991) found this also. This trend may present an expanded path to success, since women seem to be more successful entrepreneurs than men, *or* it may be yet another barrier to success, isolating women further from resources and contacts, the real sources of power in the workworld. Research is just beginning is explore this phenomenon (Young and Richards, 1987), but early evidence (Loscocco and Robinson, 1991) suggests, here again, women do less well than men, finding themselves concentrated in less successful businesses with lower average receipts, in markets relatively unattractive to men.

Other strategies proposed to women for coping with the glass ceiling include maintaining flexibility by developing "side lines" as well as a "core career"; continuously developing plans and resumes; and continuously working on the possibility of establishing a consulting firm (Sandroff, 1988). It seems women managers are not yet promised stability in promotion opportunities, at least not on a par with men. And they are urged to devote a considerable amount of energy to actively pursuing alternatives.

These concerns also surfaced among the women I interviewed. In my original interview study where I talked with every woman at the highest managerial levels in all three organizations, many said they were affected by the glass ceiling. In each setting -- the manufacturing firm, the financial institution, and the technical institute -- women's situations were similar. While specific titles differed across settings, as did the exact placement of the barrier to women's advancement (see Appendix I for more details), the glass ceiling clearly existed; there was a very clear perception women could "go only so far...It's hard for them [women] to get promoted past a certain point." The barrier was simply at a different place in the hierarchy in the three settings, but nonetheless virtually impenetrable wherever it was. Both men and women were acutely aware of that "point beyond which women could not go."

There was only one female senior vice president in all of the organizations (in the financial institution) and a great deal of variation in the number of women vice presidents across these organizations. In the manufacturing firm, for instance, there were no women vice presidents, only one highly visible woman who was a general manager, and the company itself was thought to be "a traditionally male chauvinist company" that caters to a "very conservative clientele" by many women and a few men.

Many employees perceived blocks to exist for women managers. Members of both sexes thought women were incapable of the technical expertise necessary to manufacture the product (though many women engineers were doing well with the company) and certainly "should not be in the field selling" (though, again, several women *were* successfully selling). Finally, the men at the top of the organization who did not support women's positions made it difficult, if not impossible, for women to break through the barriers that existed.

The atmosphere of the company was readily perceived as being unsupportive of women. It was commonly felt women could "go only so far" in the company. "I'm probably not going to get any higher than the position where I am right now," one of the women managers said. Both secretaries and supervisors alike believed they would not "see a woman vice president"; they also believed that women would have an easier time moving up in other industries, such as banking and consumer companies. "In a consumer company, I would have more of a competitive advantage," one woman manager said. "I would understand the customer a lot better than I do here." One manager stated, however, that "for a smoke-stack company, ours is doing O.K."

Those few women in managerial positions were often in meetings with "200 or 300 other managers" in which they were the only women. It was a hard situation for them, in one woman's words:

> It's very lonely when there's no other woman to talk to in your position. You just can't talk to men about the things that happen. With another woman, you could.

The small number of women managers created other complications, as well. Several women managers reported being excluded from important trips or meetings with the explanation the men managers would misunderstand and want to know "why they hadn't been allowed to bring their wives."

Even for women who had "made it" into the ranks of managers, the situation was not promising. Quite a few of these women were reporting directly to managers or general managers; thus, while their positions were ostensibly managerial, they were in fact but "advisory" in the company. They often were not directly supervising anyone; instead, they generated planning documents coworkers were free to adopt or not at their will. Several women managers I talked with reported conversations with bosses concerning the "ego problems" potential male subordinates would have if required to report to a woman. "They're really dragging their feet on this one [promoting women]," one of them said. It was perceived that only "3 to 5 honest-to-gosh" women managers existed in the entire company.

Another common perception in these settings concerned women's lack of inclusion in formal networks. Some felt that women themselves were responsible. One woman said:

> Women do less informal talking...stopping by the office to discuss things...and we've got to learn to do more of that.

Several of these women were concerned lack of informal communications, including golf games during the week, would prevent them from moving up in the future. A letter to *Ms Magazine* (1986) elaborated:

> [M]y employment...has been peppered with incidents...designed to discourage and demean women...One sales contest featured a Star Wars Theme; the ultimate goal was to become a "Jedi Knight." Another...was a pennant race...it was assumed that all players were familiar with the rules of baseball and would be motivated to score homeruns (p. 16,18).

In the financial institution, the culture seemed more open to women managers. It was perceived by these respondents women could do moderately well, at least to the level of vice president. Beyond that, "a bottle neck" was thought to exist here as well -- at the level of senior vice president.   This perceived "glass ceiling" was noted most consistently by the women managers and the secretaries who had worked for them. As one secretary put it:

> Branch manager is about as far as you can go. The chances for another senior officer that is female is [sic] nonexistent.

This was true, despite a general recognition that many talented women were vice presidents within the company.

The lone woman senior vice president was highly visible and mentioned with a great deal of respect by every woman manager I talked with, as well as by several secretaries and men managers. However, many of these individuals, especially the women managers, stressed that company loyalty had finally been rewarded, that this woman had been with the company a long time: "35" or "20" years. These women felt if a senior vice president position *did* become available, a woman would be as likely to get it as a man, although they believed that men moved up faster in the company. There *was* some evidence of men moving up faster than women; some senior vice presidents, both current and past, had gotten to their positions very quickly.

Despite the problems women encountered in the company--"the old chauvinist baggage," as one man put it -- most respondents felt women's chances to move up were as good here as elsewhere -- and thought by some to be better compared to industry or other areas. Several managers were quick to point out the gains women had made in the last several years (promotions, raises, etc.), with one manager pointing to a personnel manager who "protects women from potentially discriminatory actions."

The technical institute seemed to be on a middle ground in the perception it was open to women's advancement. Several women managers did refer to the atmosphere as "chauvinistic," in some instances referring to the voc/tech system in general as being a "macho" area. However, this feeling was not as widespread as it was in the manufacturing firm. On the other hand, the atmosphere was not perceived to be as supportive as in the financial institution. The source of the resistance to women was seen as both external and internal to the institute, owing to the "conservative types who teach trade and industry courses" as well as the clientele served by the institute. In fact, however, only a portion of the clientele in this situation was conservative; another sizeable portion (women who took various degree and non-degree courses) was probably very supportive of women managers.

As with the other two organizations, most respondents felt very definite limitations existed for women, that "they can only go so far." None had yet risen to the rank of vice president/supervisor, though many hoped a re-organization in process would result in "at least one woman" rising to that level. Here, there was external pressure (affirmative action guidelines) from top level administrators to improve women's positions. A new president had recently come to the institute and begun a re-organization. A woman in a higher-level position was sincerely hoped for by many respondents as an outcome of this effort. However, as in other aspects of the institute, it was difficult to take any real action, and most of the previous administrators were simply returned to their former posts. There were no women among them. Despite pressure from the top for women's advancement, the organization seemed unable to carry it out, due in large part to the hierarchical inefficiency noted in Chapter 6. Women remained at the same level as they did in the manufacturing firm, though proportionately more had risen to that level.

In all three organizations, women experienced barriers to achievement that were clearly perceived by both men and women. The specific point at which the barriers existed in each setting depended upon the combined impact of the organization's internal cultural acceptance of women managers and the effectiveness of the hierarchical control structure. The point in the hierarchy beyond which women had not risen was the same level in both the manufacturing firm and the technical institute. There, women were perceived as capable of managing only very specific functions, not the more general ones. However, women managers even at this level were much more common in the technical institute than in the manufacturing firm, and they had moved to much higher ranks in the financial institution.

These findings suggest if the culture of the organization included acceptance of women managers, women might more easily rise to the top. However, the effectiveness with which cultural dictates were enacted depended upon the characteristic organizational stances. In the manufacturing firm, women found it difficult to move into and function in powerful positions. There was no top-down dictate in this hierarchical organization that made it necessary for others to accept them. The "old boy culture" remained intact in so many parts of this large organization the women were not able to change the culture or functioning from below.

Where acceptance was low and control was high, women managers did not progress very far up the hierarchy (the manufacturing firm). Conversely, where acceptance was higher and control was high, women had progressed much further (the financial institute). However, when acceptance was moderate, but control was ineffectual, women had not progressed as far as they might have gone otherwise (the technical institute).

Prospects for Women

Despite the evidence of such widespread difficulty for women managers, there is growing evidence that women managers are becoming more accepted. Ridgeway and Diekema (1989) in an experimental setting found that when viewing confederates being attacked by bystanders in an experimental situation, experimental subjects did not react differently to males and females in dominant positions. Kushell and Newton (1986) found gender of leader did not affect satisfaction in an experimental group; all group members were happier with a democratically led group, *especially* if the leader was female. The conclusion they draw from this is that female subordinates will not sabotage female managers so long as they are able to participate in decisions. Chase and Bell (1990) found stereotypes of gate keepers against women school administrators are sometimes changed when women perform well. Scherbaum and Shephard (1987) found variations in dress presented pictorially to MBA students affected responses to male figures much more than to female figures and, in fact, women were generally given higher overall ratings. It seemed women actually were given more freedom and flexibility in what they could acceptably choose to wear. Men were more often bounded by the standard "corporate uniform": the three-piece suit.

However, the difficulties women face remain serious, overall. The problem is complex, multi-faceted, with a range of causes. My own respondents often came to believe in the meritrocracy of the system -- making them hesitant to advocate change -- and found their own aspirations to be blunted by watching their male counterparts. ("I wouldn't *want* the top position.") They failed to appreciate the transformative impact they might have on the situation.

Others point to the added complication that oppressed groups may turn on each other. Briles (1987) urges women to face the subtle pressure to put each other down, saying we cannot hope to resolve our problems of inequality with men until we confront our tendency to compete with one another. She specifically urges us to do more mentoring of each other, consciously seeking out promising young women to help along the way. Tara Roth Madden (1987) also discussed women's supposed tendency to sabotage one another:

> Almost every single corporation in the United States has a single, solitary spot for a woman on the traditionally all male team (p. 52)...[yet] women relieve men of the burden of doing anything much about them. Because of their unique approach to "success," women serve consistently as their own worst enemies (p. 54)...Despite evidence to the contrary, some people will continue to blame men for women's career stagnation (p. 56).

Concluding Comments

Whatever the source of the problem for women, and the sources are varied and complex, the dilemma is quite real. Women are needed, sometimes encouraged to enter these new realms. Many other women would like to do so. All of our lives would ultimately be richer and fuller if women were more integrated into all levels of the workplace -- because of women's initial contributions *and* because of the ultimate transformation of our institutions. Allowing women to bring their perspectives to bear, perspectives advocated in the worker participation literature, which ignores the fact that women tend to use the practices advocated, would solve many of the inter-related problems of patriarchy and capitalism. I believe such changes would produce an improvement in our current workplace.

It is only by looking at both patriarchy and capitalism simultaneously, that we can see clearly what is needed to solve the problems we face. This growing awareness happens gradually. The next chapter shows how considering race, in addition, clarifies the picture even more.

Chapter 8

THE LINK WITH RACE

> Men, especially seems to me the white men, are always..."This is what I want you to do, this is the way you're to do it." I think it's a part of...the mentality, they want to control and they want to rule...and, even if you have a good idea to offer...they...give you the impression they're the only one able to think constructively or capably...
>
> (Respondent)

The first section of this book, considered the idea that a greater balance of both "feminine" and "masculine" qualities is needed in society, that feminist critiques of our society could be re-cast in that light. In the last several chapters, we saw that problems around gender might be re-analyzed in the context of other related problems, such as issues of class or workplace exploitation. In this chapter, we extend this even further by considering how the simultaneous impact of race and gender affects these realities. Our understanding or awareness grows by taking this a step further.

In Part I we saw that developments in the women's movement have, over time, led to a call for a new type of society and that the notion we need a re-visioning of society has come from many sources simultaneously, from various groups which point to similar problems in our current society. However, the strong voice that might come from valorizing women's approaches has been silenced somewhat by concerns over essentialism. Looking at similar trends in different race and ethnic groups will help us move beyond this dilemma. By doing so, we can see that it is not only women who show a propensity to use a new approach. Other groups do so also.

What is the viewpoint or approach that is emerging? It grows from a widespread dissatisfaction with society as it is in all areas of life, for whatever reason. Corporations search for new management techniques, lovers struggle to find new relationship structures, governments and world organizations explore new types of power arrangements. Multinational corporations are changing our economic life. Technological change, particularly the information explosion, threatens to outpace our ability to comprehend it. Major changes in the way we live are moving us to the brink of a new era. Problems with social relationships, as they have existed in varying shades of difference from the beginning of the Judeo-Christian tradition through the Industrial Revolution to the present time, are seen increasingly as unacceptable. Families no longer function as they did; friendships take on new meaning; requirements for intimacy are in flux. Basic premises in our collective outlook on life are being challenged. Possibilities for a new order appear. The last two chapters showed how voices from the feminist movement might converge with those from the worker participation movement, offering many of the same insights and, in the end, calling for similar solutions.

Within an evolving feminist perspective, many of these disparate views are pulled together under a single umbrella, where many types of oppression, including worker exploitation, racism, sexism, even environmental degradation, are seen as arising from a common tendency toward exploitation in our current economic and social order. Such thinking sees these various systems of domination -- particularly but not exclusively, race, class, and gender -- as "interactive and interdependent" (Jaggar and Rothenberg, 1993, 124), and the goal of analyzing the interlocking effects of these systems is to create societies "without injustice at their core" (p. 125). Women of color, in particular, have made feminist scholars very aware of distortions that may arise when only one factor, such as gender, is considered in isolation from the others.

In keeping with the spirit of this new feminist direction, I consider various combinations of the impact of race, class, and gender. It seems core dilemmas exist that, if solved, could move us toward solving several of these problems simultaneously. For example, openness to change, flexibility, consideration of individual rights and needs, and participatory democracy are themes consistently appearing in pressures for change in various area of social life. Such widespread change, if it occurred uniformly across society, would improve the position of women, people of color, working *and* lower class citizens.

Additionally, it is not only women who stand ready to contribute a needed perspective at work. People of color are another excluded group that may have similar or complementary perspectives. In this chapter, the views of African-American managers illustrate this possibility.

Recall in Part I findings from my research suggesting how men and women managers might differ. Women seemed more engrossed in task completion, men in enhancing their image. They differed in how they thought subordinates should be managed. Men believed total autonomy should be given, women that involvement with subordinates was essential.

I replicated that original study with African-American managers (along with an African-American student on our campus) and found these gender differences to be drastically modified. With the African-Americans, the experience of racial discrimination was a compelling factor, in many ways over-riding the impact of gender. Nearly all believed that racism had affected their career progression in a profound way. Those working in predominantly Euro-American settings had more to say about this problem than those working in their own communities. One woman said:

Credibility is not automatically given to you based on your experience and your qualification...I have twenty-two years in the field...I have two degrees, and credits toward a third degree, organizational projects, successful history...People challenge small things that should be automatically understood. They don't do that to everybody...I believe a black professional, be it woman or man -- period -- we do not receive the credibility we deserve based on our experience...

The salience of race in their lives influenced how they approached their work, and this became a backdrop for how gender impacted their experiences.

Community

These individuals add a new dimension to the emerging paradigm. They emphasized the importance of community. Most of them talked at length about the importance of community support, with families cited most often. One woman illustrates:

> ...my father and my mother...worked with me very early in my life. I came from a very large, very strong, southern family...regular Southern Baptist people...the goals were always communicated very strongly that education was the answer. That we could do anything that we wanted to do as long as we believed in ourselves.

One of the men talked about his mother:

> [She] was my greatest mentor. She was my greatest pusher; my greatest backer; she was my inspiration. And I certainly appreciated that. And then my brothers who acted as my father, because they were much older...I sort of patterned after them.

He went on to say:

> And the church people in the community, we had the whole community that was your mentor. Whether you had a father or not, everybody seemed to be your father and your mother. If you were out of line, it might well have been your father or mother that saw you get out of line, because they did the same thing to you...they gave you the same inspirations...the same encouragement.

Wives were also mentioned as being supportive. One man said:

> There was a time when there was an intrusion...I think..we all have done that as a part of growing up. We are all excited, lots of opportunities...I remember...traveling while [child's name] was getting sick...I didn't even bother to call home...that really comes with growing up and becoming perhaps more established and secure.

But he asserted his wife was still supportive, "And now, my wife, who was angry with me at the time...understood why...I really had to work very hard to prove myself."

In contrast to many Euro-American women managers who report much family/work conflict, these women, especially those who worked within their communities (in predominantly African-American organizations), reported little conflict with but rather support from their families. One of them asserted, "I've got my priorities...the children understand...so it really hasn't been any conflict." Others reported high levels of support from their husbands:

> My husband always tells me..."You're never home." But then he's always telling me, "You've got to go for everything you can get in life," and he's very supportive of me. So, there has never, never been a conflict. In fact, when I meet with people, especially the ladies, and I tell them that my husband does all the cooking and all the cleaning and all the washing, and all I have to do is go home...it's like, "Where'd you find this guy?"

Support came not just from immediate family members but also from the broader community. The majority stressed the importance of giving back to the community in some way. One male president of a company operated by people of color put it this way:

> ...I never would have believed in 1990 that I would have been marching like I marched in 1960...not for the same exact things...that is, for only *fair* treatment for all human beings.

For that reason, this man said, he:

> ...put[s] in 12 hours a day, maybe a couple hours on Saturday...on Sunday...that makes about 60 to 68 hours a week...a lot of that has to do with outside activities that I get involved in...that have some type of leadership...in our community.

Two other men, presidents/CEO's of companies or agencies established explicitly to serve the African-American community also discussed how they worked for the good of the community in their jobs. One said:

> This is the only minority owned _____ in the state of Wisconsin. It really was founded because people felt that the minorities were not getting a fair shake from other institutions. So, its mission has always been to assist in the empowerment of minorities...of African-Americans in particular.

Those males who worked in Euro-American-dominated settings did not mention commitment to their community so explicitly, although a few of them did make a vague reference to the need to advocate for general community needs.

The women were more likely to express commitment to community, regardless of work setting. For example, one of the women in a Euro-American-dominated setting, a school administrator asserted that:

> In the area of educating black children, of which I think I am somewhat of an authority...I have a lot of experience with knowing the psychological development of black children [so] that I feel that I could really assist someone in assessing their own personal teaching style...I will point out an area that I think a teacher needs improvement in.

The women working in settings surrounded mostly by African-Americans or people of color -- or running programs designed to assist this clientele -- were more consistently explicit about the relationship between them and their community than the men who worked in similar settings had been. As one women put it:

> I am a minority and I am taking advantage of a number of programs available...to women and minorities, and I want to make certain that I do give something back to the community and not be just one taking. So, there's a real conscientious effort to seek minority employees...somebody that went to prison...[and was] rehabilitated or somebody who is on welfare...

These respondents' sense of involvement with and duty to their communities carried over into their approaches to work. They were conspicuously different from the Euro-American managers, discussed in Chapter 3. These African-American men and women seemed equally engrossed in task accomplishment and very similar in their desire for teamwork. The men rarely made comments about how important their operation was for the company or how many resources they controlled (as the men did in Chapter 3), and when they did, these comments were closely followed by statements about the importance of their work for the community and/or other individuals. Here are the two examples of a stance somewhat similar to that taken by the Euro-American men discussed in Chapter 3:

It's just like molding a baby, or molding something in your own image...being able to look back and say, "Yeah, I have accomplished a lot"...not to brag or anything, but that's the kind of thing or the satisfaction that I get. Yes, we have done the most important thing which is provided jobs for people in this community that I don't think would have been employed, had we not been here.

Another man discussed what has pleased him about his job:

It has really emerged as one of the finest [type of program] and for that, then, I would say there is a sense of satisfaction, that what I really came and was determined to accomplish, I was able to accomplish. I would say it was anywhere between a weak to an average program, and now it can really be classified as from a very strong to an excellent program, so that is a satisfaction I have felt...The part I still like is the fact that you are really able to shape the future...

The proportion of such comments was *markedly* lower than the incidence found among Euro-American males. And their comments were often conditioned by the notion success is important partly because it serves the wider community. This last man went on to say that:

...we were just talking before you came,...someone who graduated from the school and just called...to tell me that he has passed his exams...It's the thing that makes it all worth while when you...get that kind of personal connection, somebody who took the time to share with you the good news.

Teamwork

For most of these respondents, then, their personal level of success was seen in the context of what it might mean for the community. Related to this was a tendency for both genders to emphasize teamwork as their major means of accomplishing their work tasks. This was especially true of those individuals working primarily within their community, either in African- American companies or agencies designed to serve that community or those working in such units within larger bureaucracies.

The women nearly unanimously stressed teamwork as a crucial part of their approach. For the men, this preference was conditioned more heavily by the type of work setting, a conditioner for most of the gender differences we found. Collins (1990) argued that might be the case in her treatment of African- American men's attempts to resolve the contradictions between Afro-centric notions of masculinity (more likely to emphasize connection and responsibility to community) and those of the dominant group (which emphasize individual success). According to Collins, men working within the dominant group should experience those conflicts more intensely.

Women working primarily among members of their own community seemed to view management as an opportunity to help individuals develop. One woman owner said:

> We are a team...Even though they technically recognize that it's my company, it's still ours because we're all building for our future, and I absolutely intend to have some kind of employee stock ownership or something...I don't want to be a dictator...When you dictate, you stop people from thinking and you lose creativity, and there are a lot of good ideas and things that I can see flowing.

And another woman said:

> I believe everyone has an idea, everyone has something to say...to share. It's up to me to listen to that person. We work together as a group, as a team...I guess you could call it participatory.

Even a woman in the military expressed similar sentiments when discussing her philosophy of management.

> Basically, the give and take thing...You have to be willing to meet people at their own level and get people to work with you instead of making demands. If they can see the total picture, I believe you can get more response, good response.

And, further, about decision-making, she said, "If it's involving everybody, and it's concerning feelings...I have to make group decisions."

The men in the Euro-American-dominated settings more consistently and forcefully emphasized the importance of clearly establishing expectations, rules, and order, and expressed little preference or allowance for participatory decision-making. One of them put it quite explicitly:

I have a no-nonsense philosophy. I like to inform staff and students of our goals. I like to get staff input, let students and staff know that we have a few rules, but stick to them, and they're all responsible for their actions. And consequences follow immediately...right away.

A man in the military said:

I impress the importance of the mission, but I also impress the importance of respect to the rank structure...I think you have to have a respect for persons in order to get people to work for you, then they respect you. They don't necessarily have to like you, but I think when they're obedient and you're obedient, that's what gets the job done...Stick to the rules as much as possible...

Men working in African-American settings sounded, as a group, very different. Several described themselves as "working managers," saying they often worked along with their subordinates on projects. One man insisted he did "not expect my staff to do something I wouldn't do myself." This same man, who directed a program designed to serve people of color in a large bureaucracy, sounded very similar to many of the women:

I find out what the person's expertise is. I let them tell me what their expertise is and what they want to work at...There isn't a set way to do any one thing. There are a number of ways something can get done...If they couldn't be here to do something, I would take it over. Just like if I wasn't here, they would be able to fill in, too. So, I let them work with me just like I work with them.

Another man, a president of an African-American company, said he tried to manage his subordinates with "coaching":

I try to leave a certain amount of leeway to working among themselves. I do a lot of managing by roaming around...I try to set the overall direction and have my people work through situations...If someone were to approach me with a problem, I try to get them to figure out a solution rather than give them the answers by asking them questions and try to get them to think through the situation...

Another man stressed the autonomy he tried to provide his subordinates, something also evident among Euro-American males, although this man also stressed the need to work closely with subordinates.

> I think that people learn from examples and I like to think that I set some examples...As long as they stay within that budgeted plan, my managers are pretty much -- free. I give them a free hand to work it out...give them the means to carry out that responsibility...Sometimes a decision that would have been made has been sort of molded around what everybody agreed would be the best way to make a particular thing work.

Several of these men, however, expressed a sentiment mentioned by none of the women, "Sometimes...in business...there is equality but sometimes there is not. Because there is a man at the top that really has the final decision..." One man working in a predominately Euro-American setting put it plainly:

> I discovered in my career, that the more difficult the decision, the more lonely you become. People do not really want to share in [a] negative decision or adverse decision...[They think] "That's what you are paid to do," or "That's why you get the high salary."

This feeling, while not expressed by the majority of men, was expressed with equal likelihood by men in all settings. Perhaps the Afro-centric notion of masculinity, while allowing for more equality and team effort than that existing in the dominant society, still includes some preference for hierarchy and the notion of "a man in charge." For women, ideas of managing seem more uniformly to involve the notion of working together, "in community," although a few of them who worked in Euro-American-dominated settings, as the men who worked there, tended to emphasize the need for clear directions, for following rules and procedures, for control.

Double Binds

Both sexes reported race affected their success strivings in another way, saying they had to gingerly maneuver, taking care not to appear too "abrasive" or "aggressive," least they engender racist reactions. Several men said:

I don't have any problem going to...whoever it is I need to go to tell them how I feel. And, unfortunately, they don't appreciate it...because I come on to them in such an intellectual manner...They don't know how to handle it because they're expecting for me to act silly...

Given my leadership style, perhaps it's not compatible with the good old boys and having these meetings...because I will say my mind and I will say what I think is right...

Several of the women also mentioned this problem:

Being black, female, and intelligent is classified as three strikes against you, but you have to be pushy, you know, you have to be pushy.

It may be construed as being pushy, as being aggressive, and I'm categorized that way at [name of organization].

Here, we see both men and women dealing with the thorny issue of managing a double bind -- appearing competent while not simultaneously creating resentment -- an issue the literature (on mostly Euro-Americans) assumes to be faced only by women. However, one man believed African-American women actually had fewer problems with this.

I have seen a lot of cases where a black man has had more difficulty than a black female...I saw where black females got away with things that black males would not...They were allowed to do things and they were advanced quicker...I have seen black females that are aggressive and got their way...and the white male doesn't seem to know what to do.

Perceived Gender Differences

When asked directly about gender differences in work style, the men in predominantly Euro-American settings more often said they saw none. One of these men said:

I really don't think that there is a flat difference...It's really individual taste...I have seen females who are very productive, very conscientious and fantastic workers, I have also seen some who are not. It's the same with males.

And another man said:

> I don't look at it that way...I don't see any differences in their styles. As
> a matter of fact, my immediate supervisor is a woman, and she is the
> most talented person I can think of as a supervisor. It has nothing to do
> with gender. It has something to do with the person.

Several other men agreed, "No, it doesn't matter, as long as they're
going to do their work. It doesn't really matter who or what gender
they are," or "To me, if you have a good person, they can come in all
shades of color or gender."

Other men working predominantly with African-Americans, where
the two sexes may be working together more co-operatively for the
betterment of their community, emphasized differences that involved
women's strengths. Some differences involved integrity:

> Women seem to be...honest with you...they seem to think a lot more
> sensitive and they seem to be a lot more aware a lot of the times. Men,
> especially seems to me the white men, are always..."This is what I want
> you to do, this is the way you're to do it." I think it's a part of...the
> mentality, they want to control and they want to rule...and, even if you
> have a good idea to offer...they...give you the impression they're the only
> one able to think constructively or capably...

> Men seem to be a lot less compassionate to the needs of people, they're
> more bureaucratic, shall we say. I think men are probably more...I would
> have to say that I think they're more hind-sighted than fore-sighted.

Other differences had to do with efficiency:

> I have worked in several different industries...there are some women that
> may be a little more efficient...They may persist more and they are a little
> more meticulous than men, not being as detailed. Women, I do feel, have
> this intuitiveness disposition, and they can read situations better than a
> man would read it because of their detailed nature, and women pick up
> on more things that I would probably not be able to pick up on.

The women were more likely, overall, to see differences in each
gender's approach to their work, but were divided about whether those
differences were positive or negative. Some criticized women's
approaches, saying that women were "more touchy" than men, taking
things personally or procrastinating or being less competitive. "I would

rather work with guys," one woman said. "Guys keep me motivated, probably because I am competitive."

Some women, as well as a few men, were critical of men, noting a tendency for men to be less work motivated or less organized.

Men just...from what I've noticed...they are trying to find time to take a break...but women seem to be a little more diligent in what they're doing.

I would say...women have the tendency of rush, rush, "I've got to get it done, we've got to get it done right." Men on the other hand...they're pretty much laid back, and they're pretty much delegating.

I think women are very good when it comes to paying attention to those types of details and organization.

Women are a little bit more detail, follow through...If they make an appointment, they try to keep it. If not, they get in and let people know they can't...The men that I've been dealing with, if you have a 10:00 appointment, they don't care, they're there at 10:30, 11:00. Women seem to be a little bit more compassionate.

Decidedly so, especially in the ministry. This is one thing that I'll point out to my fellow male ministers...I don't have a wife...okay, that the wife takes care of all the creature comforts and whatnot...I've got to do that as well as the other...so there's a lot of difference in the way they work in that they consider themselves *busy* and really they're not....[about a specific minister] People will say, "He's so busy," but really he's not; he's disorganized, that's what it is...

Concluding Comments

Here, we see women's strengths being appreciated by men and women working in predominately African-American settings, where the two sexes may be working together more cooperatively than in predominately Euro-American settings. In the former situation, men and women are collaborating, often to serve those in their communities, using their leadership positions in part to help others achieve. In the predominately Euro-American settings, men tended to deny that gender differences existed or to be critical of the methods they observed women using, not really being aware that the women were using an alternative, organized model.

Among these African-American women, setting makes little difference. Most women believed differences existed, though they equally often mentioned women's weaknesses as well as strengths. Some felt women were harder to work with, while others felt women were much harder working. This latter perception has also been found in my own studies of predominately Euro-American managers.

These results show the importance of considering the influence of factors such as race and gender simultaneously. Looked at singly, one could easily draw an over-simplified conclusion, for example that most groups of men tend to use a more image-engrossed, autonomy-invested style of management, or all women more often experience the need to walk carefully between the double bind of appearing incompetent or too aggressive or to prefer a participatory team approach. Here, we see that African-American men may not conform to notions we have of Euro-American men, since their management styles have been significantly modified by their own experience of discrimination and a resulting commitment to improving the situation of other African-Americans in our society -- a trend especially true for men working in their own communities.

A strong determinant of this strategy appeared to be the belief that opportunities for management or leadership ought to be seen, at least in part, as a chance for uplifting the entire group. A sense one owes the community service, if at all possible, seemed to be a strong part of socialization patterns. Parents passed this sense on to their children. Others also report this aspect of the African-American professional (or middle) class. Sarah Lawrence Lightfoot (1994) found this tendency among all six of the professionals she interviewed in depth for her book *I've Known Rivers*. Bell hooks and Cornell West also show this strong tendency in their dialogues and interviews for their book *Breaking Bread* (1991).

Effects of race and gender in the workplace are being emphasized by many companies working to "manage diversity" in their workforces. Demographic trends suggest the majority of workers will soon be women and/or people of color (Cohen, 1991), so it is imperative companies institute policies making their workplaces more comfortable for such workers. As one observer puts it, "What is good for women and minorities is good for business" (Erkut, 1990).

To "unleash the power of...[the] total work force" (Thomas, 1991), organizations are being urged to make such changes as retraining managers and other workers, instituting more flexible work rules, examining corporate commitment to diversity, eliminating structural barriers to becoming a truly multi-cultural setting (where differences are valued, not simply tolerated), and modifying communication processes and reward systems to institutionalize the necessary changes, (Cohen, 1991; Cox, 1991; Loden and Rosener, 1991; Overman, 1991; Songer, 1991; Thomas, 1991; Erkut, 1990; Mandell and Kohler-Gray, 1990). The findings reported in this chapter suggest another key strategy would be moving women and people of color into leadership positions, as those currently in leadership positions seem more likely to already be using the managerial approaches deemed necessary to make the impending transition successfully.

Results such as these can markedly transformed our notions of "gender" and "difference." African-American women (and other women of color) have long complained the mainstream feminist movement in this country does not represent their interests. For example, some groups are suspicious of the women's movement great emphasis on abortion rights, since they view such birth control measures, coupled with involuntary sterilization of their people, as related to attempted genocide. Other groups grow tired of complaints about "forced" labor force participation, since they have never been able to "stay home and be a housewife."

In this case, we see race conditioning how gender sensibilities are enacted in managerial positions. The men in this group are much more aware of the model women are using, often using it themselves. They are also much more appreciative of the strengths women bring to leadership situations. Among these respondents, men often mentioned characteristics of women that only women mentioned in my original study.

Here, we have an apparent paradox: fewer actual differences, while at the same time greater regard and respect for the differences that do exist. The strain and resentment between the men and women in the workplace in my original study seemed to be greatly mitigated for this group. I am not trying to imply that no difficulties exist here. Certainly they do. In fact, one woman talked quite explicitly about the sexism she had experienced:

> There are places...churches that will not allow women in the pulpit. I can give you a for instance; I had joined a ministerial alliance here in town, and I had been invited to be a part of their alliance to do the opening prayer at this huge Martin Luther King program that they had...I'm sitting

there...they had me on the front row...Well, first off they did everything
they could so that I could not march in with them...When they came in,
there were men on either side of me, [and] as the program progressed,
they moved their chairs back...pretty soon I'm sitting there [alone]...I've
learned to mask my feelings, but I was so angry, I could have just slapped
everyone of them.

What I am suggesting is that by looking at gender in combination
with other features of oppression, we get a different impression about
how universal the differences are, how they can be adopted by one
group or the other given cultural pressures, and what future relations
between men and women may look like. We also get a clearer picture
of the type of changes needed to solve the problems facing us.

Part III of the book will greatly extend this examination of gender in
cultural context. Building upon what we have seen here, we will begin
to see gender difference in a much less centered way, much more as a
feature of the total cultural landscape. This further step enhances the
apparent importance of community as a powerful framework for
grounding our notions of gender, as conceived and executed. Perhaps
in building new versions of community, we will find the way to
construct new, more viable gender relations. It is only by incorporating
additional factors into our analysis of the situation that we can begin to
see the total process of change that is upon us.

PART III

GENDER IN BROADER CONTEXT

In Part I of this book, we saw that developments in the women's movement have, over time, led to a call for a new type of society. However, in Part II, we saw the idea we need a re-visioning of society has actually come from many sources simultaneously. The notion that many types of oppression, including worker exploitation, racism, sexism, and environmental degradation spring from a common thrust toward exploitation in our current economic and social order is dawning on many in those movements.

In this part of the book, we continue to decenter our focus on gender, adding more elements that move us further toward a more highly integrated perspective. The point here is when all types of oppression are given equal weight and when the lens of a different cultural perspective is used, a fuller, richer, more complex picture is obtained. This approach begins to uncover a commonality in perspectives among those affected, helping us move beyond resistance to valorizing "women's perspectives" as "essential". Patricia Ticineto Clough (1994) has traced the evolution of feminist thinking about "difference" from the first dawning of the idea of women's perspective through the impact of previously marginalized groups such as African American women and lesbians. She shows how the growing materialist grounding in these other viewpoints ought to push away from essentializing "women's" standpoint, as a unitary phenomenon, to a more valid perspective. For example, Patricia Hill Collins (1990) valorizes African American women's experiences and reactions, showing in the process how knowledge itself has been subjugated, adding more variety to that "other" perspective.

In making sense of the world, women of color offer an alternative viewpoint, one that might be helpful to our entire society in solving our pressing problems. One critical component of that worldview is the importance of community, its importance arising from the fact -- pointed out by Clough -- that women of color ascribe not so much to the white feminist phrase "the personal is political" but to the notion that "the public is personally political." This suggests the type of community we must envision, one which provides space and support for resisting the assaults coming from mainstream society. In these communities of color, solidarity between committed men and women is especially valued.

Others have also noted that incorporating other cultural perspectives opens our thinking to more diverse viewpoints. Teresa de Valle (1993), in her edited volume *Gendered Anthropology*, shows the importance of race and class issues in shaping our views of "difference" around gender. In her volume, "differences within" (i.e., societies, selves), loom as large as "differences between." For her, more valid notions of difference can be obtained by looking at that generated by race, class, *and* gender. For example, Brown and Fergeson's (1995) study of enviromental activists shows how class placement influences the process of knowledge creation among women -- and their resulting behaviors -- all part of standpoint. They describe a "remarkable transformation," arising largely from a "personal relation to knowledge" among mostly working class women. Clough and de Valle also make this point, that the standpoint taken ultimately depends upon the intricate interplay of gender, race, *and* class, leading to this thought: if there *is* a "woman's standpoint," it cannot be seen by looking only at white, middle-class women. At the very least, we must study other groups of women to clearly understand what viewpoints actually exist, before determining what direction we should take. And this may not be only a woman's standpoint; it may exist among marginalized groups more generally.

In this part of the book, I continue the process toward integration, a necessary step before deciding where we go from here, how we will solve our gender problem -- as it is related to a host of other problems.

We began this journey in the last section by looking at class and race variations in the issues I am considering. In this part, I begin with a look at leadership in Native American context, showing that by giving full weight to cultural context, we come to see this project is not just about leadership or management transformation, but about cultural or societal transformation. De Valle discusses "the indigenous concepts of personhood" and their importance. As we will see, such concepts are rooted in the sense of a community still alive, something also stressed by the African American managers who spoke in the last chapter. This strong preference for a democratic, participative, less autocratic approach was also found among ethnic women in Hawaii (Ramos, 1992), perhaps also true of the ethnic men there. These perspectives on life and leadership, I believe, are major components of the model we see emerging in greater detail. It is only by looking at diverse groups we come to see the importance of community, and community lost, as a highly related problem that is an intricate part of our solution.

Chapter 9

Leadership in Native American Context: Foregrounding Cultural Background

> ...I don't think that there's such a thing as a white way to lead and an Indian way to lead; I think that there are leadership strategies which have been developed by humans everywhere; different groups favor different strategies for lots of different reasons...There are many different strategies for leadership, and different cultures...optimize different...strategies...I think that Indian cultures tend to optimize cooperative modes, or non-authoritarian modes of leadership...
> (Respondent)

Several years ago I began a project to replicate the results I have discussed with yet another cultural group -- Native Americans living in Wisconsin. The state is home to eleven different tribal groups, many with their own reservations, a few still on their original lands. (See Appendix I for more information about this sample and study). I began driving around the state, accompanied by a Native American student at our university. I was focused specifically on gender differences, but this project quickly took a sharp turn, as those I was interviewing insisted I understand the entire cultural context in which leadership or management issues are framed.

Their voices were strong and clear, in many ways reflecting with great coherence the new approach I see emerging in so many places. While there are important differences between the various groups living in the state, there was remarkable consistency in the themes I describe below. Because their voices were so clear and forceful, I offer them as directly as I can, often unfiltered by my own interpretation. I believe they stand on their own, reflecting more clearly than in other groups the new paradigm we are struggling to discern.

Cultural Basics

Some of the cultural components these respondents described are clearly relevant when thinking about how leadership is provided for a community. They are also related to the "new paradigm" being described by people such as Capra (1982). The notion that all things are inter-dependent -- creatures with earth, spirit with material, person with person, culture with social functioning -- was mentioned in many ways. This is a strong theme Jane Oitzinger (1994) also found in her comprehensive review of Native American writing. One man said to me:

> ...You're thinking spiritually, you're thinking the animals, you're thinking the clouds, the sky and the creator...all important parts of the decision making process, how you look at things...You address them in decision making...the creation and all the levels of knowledge and the creator from every rock, to the tree, to the ant, to the bird...

Others talked about the interconnections among various aspects of human life. It was clear in these discussions that a strong preference existed to link things at work with cultural imperatives. One woman said:

> ...We had people that were coming in that were sober but weren't practicing healthy lifestyles; there were other issues in their lives that were affecting their performance on the job......

She continued:

> ...We do a talking circle before our staff meeting every week...we use...traditional medicines -- sweet grass, sage...before we start our meetings and then we give a time for people to talk...

Others talked about daily practices.

> ...As a Native woman who is trying to recover as much of the traditional practices...I'm someone who...has held the traditional values in my heart forever...I try to...do...things with...a conscious respect for the traditions

> ...the values...When I come in in the morning I burn the sage and try to cleanse myself so I'm real clear for the day...In the morning when I put my tobacco down...I'm getting better about remembering to do that...I...just pray that I do everything in a good way...

> ...I identify as an Oneida person; I try to live my life in the Native American values as much as I can...I get up...every morning and say the opening prayer in the Oneida language...

Another woman talked about some of these cultural components providing a foundation for human service programming:

> ...they have a cultural curriculum -- it's an AODA prevention program...to introduce them to some of those cultural...things that they can practice today because in the old days they never used alcohol and drugs...It's like a cultural approach to addressing that problem which is real prevalent here...

Equality

Closely related to the notion of inter-connection is that of essential equality. One woman talked about this as linking between human and non-human forms:

> ...All things are of equal importance...every experience that I have in life is important to me as an individual...I am not better than a squirrel or a blade of grass; I am given the gift of life by the Great Spirit in the same way that the rabbit or the squirrel or the grass...I'm seeking that, a balance and a sense of unity...

Belief in equality extended to relations between people. Two women said:

> ...I'm not prejudiced toward anybody...We're just alike. God created us that way; He gave you different skin color...

My grandfather always told me "People are people; color doesn't mean a thing"...that's...how I grew up...there was no difference between me and the next person...

This pre-disposition to treat all with equality extended to treatment at work; a woman said:

...They were always open to suggestions from the staff -- from anybody...I was sitting there taking notes at one meeting and one of them turned around and asked me what I thought and I was...just there to take notes...They said "Well we know you probably thought about this"...sometimes they encouraged me to give some input even though I was just an observer...and they always made everybody so important, like nobody's job was...more important than the next person...

This idea of equality was put in terms of the circle, sometimes explicitly opposed to a pyramid or hierarchy. A woman said:

...When I think of the value systems, I think of the difference between a hierarchy and a circle...That's probably the key...for me...In a circle all things are a part of the same thing...each point on that circle is important...To me the other thing, the hierarchy, means...some people are considered better than others because they have one thing or another and the two don't really work together real well...I think you do have to make choices about which value system you're going to live by...That hierarchy value system that I'm talking about is sort of a lie...

These values were strongly sustained by cultural functioning. Individuals had methods for using such approaches provided to them by cultural tradition.

Another way of granting respect to all individuals had to do with styles of inter-relating, which were based upon rhythms and cycles that honored natural processing time, rather than conforming to external constraints. A man said this:

My grandfather or my mother would say something to me or I would say something to them, there could be 30 seconds to 5 minutes or a whole day before a response from one or the other would happen, and the more important the question the longer the time...

He felt this affected his experiences at work:

> It wasn't that I thought "Well, I can't ask questions or I can't talk" I just didn't because of the way things were at home with my family and the idea of...silence...One of the reasons why I didn't participate very much and respond to different kinds of questions did not have to do with the fact that I didn't understand what they were talking about but they never would give me...silent time...

Decisions and responses *should* be carefully considered, since implications extended forward through time. Two women said:

> Yeah...it is...important for not just me, for our kids too, 'cause they're the future...It's just not that we're here today and let's do this...To me we should look ahead and see what we can do for our kids, even though we're gone...they'll be here to carry on...Preserving...many things are important to my people as well as what kind...of future they're gonna face...

> ...We're supposed to make decisions thinking about seven generations to come...It's true; we're living the results of seven generations ago...

Here, we see a strong preference for treating all creatures in certain ways. In general, a spiritual basis for life's directions and choices was stressed by many of these respondents, again a theme Oitzinger found to strongly permeate much writing by Native Americans. Here is what two men had to say:

> ...I like to lay down and look at, either the sky when it's real blue, and just lay there and look...or if you just sit there...in the nighttime...You're just part of this whole big universe...you can't imagine how small you are...But you...fit into that whole perspective...you...have access to...not just the five senses, but...a whole spirituality, intuition, that takes you to a further plane of understanding the world around you...

> My priority right now is to....progress...spiritually, physically, mentally, and emotionally...the communication with a major spiritual power...

From these basic beliefs flowed ideas about how people should be treated. Respect for others was mentioned as important by these two women:

...In the traditional way it's not what you have, it's how you use...and...respect what you have...how you respect others...being conscious and attuned to the needs and the wishes of the people that you lead...

...just a genuine caring about people, a respect for people...a focus on helping them find their strength, not creating dependency...the....element of equality as opposed to status differences...That's what my mom did, not just with me but with her staff...her approach to supervision...[was]... to...help them find their strength...

Several others also stressed the importance of allowing others their space and autonomy. Two men said:

Our tribe, our culture, doesn't allow people to say "This is what you must do, this is what you will do"...I think that's tacky, one person doesn't do that to another...

...It's...acceptance...They'll grow up to their full capacity if you just allow them to do what they're gonna do, but if you interfere with them you can stunt their growth...Your job is to nurture...that particular animal... flower...tree...individual...If you will nurture them they'll grow to their fullest capacity of what they're meant to be on this earth...It's when you interfere with them that causes the problems...We do that with children...we don't allow them to naturally grow to their own...potential. We're always trying to impose some...of our little twists and bends on them 'cause we want the tree to grow this way so we start bending it and tying it down this way to get something that we want out of it as opposed to just letting them grow the way that they would normally grow if we didn't interfere with them...

A woman who was raised as a young girl by an Indian grandmother and then later went to live with a non-Indian mother described struggles over autonomy, again showing the importance of this value in the Native American perspective:

...I think about being around my grandmother...not having a lot of rules...and yet there were so many nuances to follow...She was pretty autonomous, she didn't have any need to yell and scream...I was a good kid around her...also real creative...you have a Native American style of things...allowing kids to try things, experiment, skin their knees, fall out of a tree, make mistakes, not getting too upset about it...letting people learn the lessons by doing it and being there and being supportive...It's very different than having lots and lots of rules...When I went from living with my grandmother to living with my parents, I could never get...okay with my mother and her "shoulds" and her rules...My mom and I had a lot of battles...lots of times she used to call me "a wild Indian"...I always wanted to reshape my mom and I couldn't do it, and she always wanted to reshape me...

Consensus

Some of the aspects of culture mentioned had to do with group processes, related directly to leadership style, something Oitzinger also found to be stressed in Native American writing. For example, consensus building, listening, direct access to leaders were discussed by quite a few of my respondents. Several woman spoke about this:

...Based on tradition, everything was consensual and it involved the community...everybody...had a voice, or represented a certain area, a sector in the community...

...Can you imagine what would happen, we'd actually have decisions that people could live with if we stopped voting on them; we wouldn't leave people out...I'm really collaborative...that's the way it's done in our tradition...Everyone has a voice...

...If somebody from the community has issues, they can interrupt whether it's the agenda item or not...They can speak as long as they choose to speak...So there's some real democratic practices that are still going on...

...There's no layers in between...leadership...and the grassroots people on the tribal level...I have found throughout the years...[that] putting an executive director in between the people and the Council, or the chair person...the administrators...hasn't worked very successfully. It might work for a year or two but the whole time the grassroots people are fighting [for]...direct access to the leadership...It's real important to tribal communities...The leadership has to be...much more responsive right to the community itself; I think that differs...tremendously...they really are answerable to the grass roots people...

The men agreed:

> ...I'm most comfortable with a team sort of concept and working in trying to reach some form of consensus...It probably goes back to my own traditional tribal...way of doing things...

> ...If you ever get a chance to be at a tribal council meeting, they go by majority but yet traditionally it used to be consensus...In order to get things done everybody had to agree and they weren't time oriented...We'd meet for whatever length of time...to get what we need done and once it's done, it's done...There wasn't a time constraint...

> ...It's going to be based...on...consensus, some sort of cooperative management...not...on the leadership of an authoritarian person...instead, on the leadership of a person or group of persons who are very skillful at organizing and building consensus, people who are able to move a group, or convince a group to be moved...

Hence, these individuals showed a strong preference for consensus decision-making, flowing directly from their beliefs in the essential equality of all persons. And they stressed that the decisions that eventually were made were more effective, in that the entire community had, by that point, bought into them.

Gender Balance in Cultural Context

Balance, in general was also seen as a worthy goal to pursue. As one man put it,..."There [is]...part of a process, you're in balance with the world around you..." Another man said:

> ....Everything has to be in order, everything has to go in harmony -- nature and man, man and man, man and a woman -- everybody has to go together.

Traditional gender systems within these cultural groups were also seen as balanced, important for the over all world view we are exploring in this book. One woman said:

> ...the other thing that's different in our culture...which I see very different from the non-Indian world, is we've always had this understanding...It comes through in the stories...that for men and women there's an equal

balance...a complimentary...understanding that we...couldn't be without each other...

Male and female roles were both deemed essential to the healthy functioning of the group. A man said:

> ...Men...especially the ones who have been more traditionally oriented, are heavily influenced by women...The women will do a lot of things to make sure that the man looks good...He's representing the tribe, the family, the clan; it's real important for him to be doing what he's doing...at the same time, a male needs to...respect the women's roles and always will...

This gender balance was argued to arise from the high respect given to both men and women. Unlike in the dominant U.S. cutlure, women were highly respected. A man said:

> ...I think Indian women that come from the traditional perspective...if they are walking in that position in their own community...are held in usually very high regard...I simply cannot talk back to an Indian woman...The acknowledgement is there, their power to give life men don't have, it's just there, it's innate within them...I respond...that way...

Many respondents also commented on Indian women's decision-making power. Several women said this:

> ...The backbone of our government system down here is really women...Oh men have an office but it's really women...There might be a man in charge of the...program...There's men working in the tribal office, but primarily it's women, especially in the more important programs...

> Women have always been looked on as leaders...regarded as being very special

> ...In the Iroquois way, you probably know, the women select the chiefs and also can impeach them...As I've watched that process, I see people get together and talk about things...

> I keep saying "Wait, Chief is just an empty title" because throughout the ages, it's the women who have told the Chief...men don't do anything unless women tell them to do it, even in today's world, look around

you...It's the women who are the movers and the shakers, the men don't move unless the women tell 'em to...

Men agreed:

...I was taught that the female had all the power...She gave the directions from the home; she was in charge of everything...took care of...everything from outside the door...the livestock...and protect the family...The female's role was to care and nurture the family...The man, if he had a decision to make, it wasn't made without his wife...His decision would be strengthened or changed with his wife's help...the lady of the family had a stronger hand in making decisions...No matter what kind of decision it was, it had to get the stamp of approval from the lady of the house and, if for some reason, she saw that this man was not providing for her the way he should be...she could kick him out...He took nothing else except what was on his back; there was no such a thing as lawsuits...child support, uh-uh, you lost everything if you were a man...Women are powerful in my tribe...I think it's like that in most Native American tribes...If you leave out all this modern-day political stuff and go into a tribe and live with them, a traditional tribe, you'll...observe it...The man can't come home and say "I want this and that for supper," uh-uh, you get what you get, by George...If your wife's gonna make mutton stew, mutton stew and firebread is what you're gonna get...you can't have your t-bone steak tonight...If you don't like it, tough...The lady had the power in the family; she managed all the financial decisions...If you wanted a couple bucks gambling money, oh you hadda do something special to get it from your wife...plus the permission to do it...

Comparing Native Americans to Euro-Americans, one man said:

...The traditional leaders were women, the Council of Female Elders was like the Supreme Court; you did nothing that the Council of the Grandmothers didn't say was all right...You ask any traditionalist, and they'll admit that...How did it get to be the other way around, because the Europeans treated women like furniture...I say to [groups I talk to]..."Pretend I'm Jean Nicolet and this is 1634 and here I am and you are all Menominees and Winnebagos and a few Potawatomis" 'cause that's who was at Red Banks near Green Bay...What he [Nicolet] was asking is he wanted to talk to the king. They didn't have any king...I sometimes embarrass some of [them]...but I'll look out and figure that woman looks like she's probably the oldest woman in here and then I'll say "This is an honor" but I'll point to this woman...and I'll say "These young men kept pointing to you" [as the leader] and [Nicolet] said "No, no, no, no, no, I wanna talk to the chief"...I tell [them]..."Nicolet and those that came after him, never got it through their heads that the real leaders were the women" and this is absolutely true, they were true matriarchies and I know the anthropologists...don't like it when I say this 'cause they say I can't prove it...and I say "What the hell is your proof...all this stuff written down by middle-class, white, Caucasian males mostly,"...

Partly, this high respect for women springs from the regard given elders, particularly grandmothers and aunties, in these cultures. As one woman put it, "I've always learned from my elders." A man said:

When there's a council of elders...all the elders together, they talk in common...spirituality comes in...

...I think females are...very strong in certain ways, as far as Natives are concerned...how....we...survive all these things...My grandmother was a role model...she didn't have any education; we were in poverty but she raised six of us...My dad was not a good role model for me because he was the alcoholic...The women were the ones that were the role models...we kept the family together...

A man talked about his grandmother:

Grandma was a wise lady...People came from all around, for counseling, to her...My grandmother did not have a Ph.D., she wasn't a professor, she was not educated, but she was well respected by the medical...community in my home town, as well as the Christian leaders in the community... Everybody knew Grandma...she knew what kind of herbs and plants...could be used for certain illnesses...people would come to her...sometimes in the middle of the night, and they didn't pay her, she didn't ask for anything in payment, she'd just give them advice...or if she had whatever they needed, that one plant or root...whatever they needed...if she had it on hand she'd give it to them...She was a great teacher...I used to sit through my classes here...I know how people interact, how different races...are, because I experienced it already; Grandma told me about it...Grandfather...my elders, they...taught me all this stuff...it wasn't out of a book though...They had great wisdom, a wisdomologist...

...If I need to learn anything I come back to auntie and mom and say "Well, this is happening or this is going on, can you explain this to us"...that's how we're learning...

Work and Cultural Values

It was obviously very important to these individuals to be able to apply these values to their workplace endeavors. Some talked about the stress of not being able to implement these values. A woman said:

> ...When I left libraries...computers were not [here]...When I came back everything was computerized...you constantly have to learn technology... They have their own requirements...I have to get my second masters degree and then they look at university service...outside service...not necessarily publishing, but...at...how you're doing your job and where I have a hard time...being a human being and being raised a Native...I don't necessarily agree with this...I want something where I'm gonna make an impact, I want something where I'm gonna live for my passion or things that will carry me through...like my education...I can really broaden it...to say "Okay, how can I...in some way benefit Indian people and make a difference in their lives?"...

A man said:

> ...They hired me to run the Indian Studies Program and to teach...The situation got very difficult for political reasons...the anomalous position that I was put into...I was seriously compromised by the institution because, on one hand they were saying "We want to have these classes because...representing the real, or true history....is important; we want...to have our students know Indians, respect them"...I was doing classes on Indian culture, religion, all that sort of stuff, history, education and I don't know a thing about any of these things...I was an Indian and that's what I knew and I had never read anything about being Indian and so I felt fraudulent, I felt compromised, I felt very used...I had a negative standing at the university...I was there to accommodate political correctness ...not...because I deserved to be there so I was tolerated...but I was also rather good and I gained the respect of some of my colleagues, people invited me to talk in class, people asked me about issues...We had a lot of contact with people outside the university who didn't realize that this was all a sham...We did a lot of presentations to schools and sometimes to government agencies, like to the mayor's office staff...By that time I had had enough of the compromise in Indian Studies; I was burned out...I had developed a kind of professional persona and I didn't feel that I should accept the kind of treatment I was getting anymore...

Another man said:

> ...You take the industry or the military concept of leadership...I was certainly active in this in the Department of Public Instruction...to a lesser degree, in the university...Much more micro-management sort of style...to an extreme...to a point where it's oppressive, not healthy for the individual...Very highly...bureaucratic in different kinds of decisions...It's when you know the right thing to do...what should be done for the benefit of...students in this state, Indian and non-Indian...They make the decisions ...ignore that information...because superintendents will get angry if you do...or say that...

As might be gathered from the descriptions above of cultural components, many similarities existed between men and women in these groups, much more so than in my original sample of mostly Euro-American managers. In contrast to my earlier interviews with Euro-Americans, these men were not less likely to list all the many tasks involved in their jobs. Both men *and* women seemed equally engrossed in doing the work, in accomplishing the tasks involved. Both men and women recited long lists of tasks that need to be accomplished *and* the need to focus on people, to work as a team. This stands in contrast to results from my original study, where the men focused more on their image or importance and on giving autonomy (Chapter 3). And it is similar to my findings of African-Americans (Chapter 8).

Community and Service

Tribal traditions, such as that about shared leadership, provided an important basis for how they went about managing or leading in their respective situations. These individuals attempted to implement the essential values they discussed. As with the African-Americans, being of service to others was critically important. In this case, it was equally important to men and women regardless of their work setting. Almost everyone I talked to stressed that leadership was an opportunity to serve, not advance oneself.

> ...it's a...sense of...knowing that...you're doing your best to serve other people...that's the best role...you can hope to play, to serve other people well, not to serve yourself...

Two men said:

> ...We look at things more on the human side...putting yourself in the next person's shoes and experiencing what they are experiencing, their hardships, and then trying to...get help for them or help them do things that they can't do, attending to their needs...It's reaching out and helping people...

> ...I travel 200/300 miles, 400 miles just because someone gives me tobacco to go do something...out of my own expenses...go all the way up there and do the things [traditional ceremonies] that I need to do, because that's my responsibility...I'm expected to do that...People give you blankets and different things and some people give you more...but...you're expected, as a leader, to take on that burden of helping people, so people become the most important part of who you are, the group becomes really important...

As with the African-Americans in the last chapter, community remained important, even in success. A woman said:

> ...My family and I talked about the "I" and the "we", all the pressure there was when I was going to school to be this "I," to climb the old ladder, claw your way up to success...I'm a part of a "we" and I've never lost sight of that...Because of the "we," this community and my family, I can do all of this...

A man said:

> ...I thought what was important was that we do something to help these groups of people out there that have a language that's going to disappear if we don't intervene, and may disappear if we do...That's what I thought was important and that's what I use my training to do...

A woman commented on a job she had recently held:

> ...I didn't wanna pass up the opportunity to try because I'm well aware of the needs and saw the potential...of the organization...to make a difference in the lives of people...so I took the job and worked for a year and a half...

Another woman said:

> ...My parents always said that we were here to help each other and if I
> were in any position where I could help someone, it was expected that
> that's what I was gonna do; that's always exactly what my parents did...

Several men said:

> ...leaders, I think, need to reach out...and look at the people that way
> instead of fame and glory, the way they run after it...It's all wrong; I
> think, that's why...everything's so messed up because of the way they
> thirst for power...The leaders back home...they didn't do that.

> ...That's what I like...when you can do something that's really gonna
> make a major difference and help someone...

A woman summed this up:

> ...knowing that by doing what you're doing, you're doing your best to
> serve other people and that's the best role that you can hope to play, to
> serve other people well, not to serve yourself, that is a key component of
> leadership...

Notions of Leadership

Harking back to the notion of circular structures, rather than
pyramids, these individuals believed that leaders were not privileged
individuals sitting at the apex of a triangle. Rather, they were servants
of the people, following their bidding. For some, the leaders actually
were the people. One woman made this observation:

> ...It's how you respect what you have and how you respect others...being
> conscious and attuned to the needs and the wishes of "the people that you
> lead"...We have a traditional chief...he always has a bunch of people in
> his office and we would always...talk...One person who was non-Indian
> made a comment "Well...just tell 'em to do that, I mean you need
> something done, tell 'em"...Chief says "...I can't do that"..."What do you
> mean, you can't do that; you're the Chief, if you want this done just tell
> the people to do it" and he said "When the Chief starts telling his people
> what to do...then you won't be Chief for very long...I'm here for the
> people; I'm here to do what they want me to do, not what I wanna do,"
> and that's the traditional way, that's a true leader of the people.

A man concurred, discussing his own experience:

> ...I looked around...at my people here who were leaders, they had a lot of
> problems during their tenures...It's...their daily way they treat each other
> and the people they lead...If they go ahead and start doing things...get a
> swelled head...they lose...people's confidence and...votes and they wonder
> what happened...People have problems because they got people mad at
> 'em...they're trying to be a boss...I can tell you, sometimes when they
> want you to...be the boss, they'll let you know...

Several other men also agreed:

> ...Dominant leadership tends to be still a feudal type of mentality
> ...basically you got the kings and the aristocracy on top of the pyramids
> and you've got the masses on the bottom and so most of the resources are
> confined to the people on the top...and then it's...doled out incrementally
> as you go down the line...Most of the people in a feudal type of thinking,
> either they own the land or you work for them and you are the servant of
> these particular people...That's a different type of leadership...

> ...I think what's different for American Indian people is that leadership is
> considered a burden...I mean you're chosen to be a leader but it's also a
> heavy burden on you because you have responsibility for all these
> people...The pyramid gets switched upside down...You're a leader...up at
> the apex of it, the rest of it is all sitting on your shoulders...so leadership
> then becomes a real strong burden...you're expected to do a lot...to give
> up a lot of things to be a leader in the community...You're expected, as
> a leader, to take on that burden of helping people so people become the
> most important part of who you are, the group becomes really
> important...My mother-in-law is from Stone Lake and even with my
> wife...[her father] was always doing things for the community, for the
> people around him, long hours of the day, different times of the night,
> giving things away, that was expected.

Because of this belief that in fact "the people" are the leaders, certain
qualities are prized in those filling leadership roles. The ability to
empower others is very high on this list. Several women made similar
observations:

> If you believe in yourself...that you can lead the people, but in a way they
> lead...that's the key...If you're gonna do anything or help anybody...That's
> where our leadership forgets sometimes; they get so caught up in keeping

with the outside world...Being in a leadership role is to...empower people to come in and express their own views...I say "Why don't you come in...and tell us how you feel...We need to hear from you and by me just saying these things isn't enough, but your voice is louder than mine"...

...It's real easy to get seduced into power and...illusions of status or having power over people...What I'd like to see in terms of community relationships...that people...were respectful...that's cultural, but to a large extent it transcends any culture...What I see being the most pivotal but unrecognized and unsung kind of leadership is the leadership it takes for individuals to work toward empowerment...To give you an example: my mom came back to the community when she was...50 maybe, and was the health administrative planner for the tribe and wrote the grants that funded the Chippewa Health Center and had to fight that through the system, and people would give her a hard time...At the time they don't seem like large contributions and to my mom it wasn't a status thing, it was simply the thing that she could do in her job that would improve things for people...

Since "the people" were so important, a willingness to listen to others was stressed as an essential component of leadership. Several women said:

...It's something that I try to do...even just working with Indian students...I need to listen to them and that they each have something to give, that we can learn from each other...and so...as far as management...I worked within the university bureaucracy, but I also have realized that to work with Indian people we need...to work differently...If you're working with Natives or indigenous people and they're on this level and the university is on this level...if the university wants to serve Indian people...they need to go to the level where the...indigenous people are...

She also believed that:

Every day...this growing person needs to be just doused with love in any way possible...what do we do, how do we show respect, how do we listen...

Several other women said:

...One of the first things I learned when I became chairman was you have to listen...Somebody came in and reported that their child was put in jail and that the jailer broke his arm and I was so upset and I went down there and I raised cain and everything else and then I found out that it wasn't true...it wasn't even broken...So I told myself right then "You hafta listen, you hafta hear both sides of the story" and I've always done that...If somebody tells me something I always say "...I have to hear the other side of the story before I make up my mind if I'm gonna do something or not"...

...I'm the type to listen to other people's ideas...let them talk and let them feel that it's theirs too...I'm constantly giving them positive affirmations and nurturing them and that's what it takes...a lot of patience...to bring people up to that point...I think through the tribal system they don't hear enough of that..."You're doing a good job"...Every Monday morning we have staffings...and we use the talking circle because...it helps us if there's any problems with each other...You can do surface things...but when you're in a talking circle...you can't lie, you can't hide anything because when you have the feather or the medicine's there you have to tell the truth and sooner or later if you don't you'll get caught...Each person has an opportunity to talk about anything they want to and at that time if they have a feather or if they have the sweet grass or whatever medicine that helps 'em...it gives 'em strength, more power to get that out...

Input and Consensus

Implied in the need to empower and listen is the belief that everyone has a voice, something to contribute. Several women said:

...Sometimes [non-Indian] people pressure me to be a top dog...I'm generally pretty resistant to it...We will make the time and we will sit down and work on it because...it's very important...how you make decisions and that people do it together...I try to do that as much as I can...A school administrator said to me once when we were in big chaos... "The thing I've noticed about your people...it doesn't matter who's talking, everybody listens...the guy might be a total idiot, nobody tells him to sit down and shut up, they let him have his piece and when he's done he sits down and the next person talks...Ours doesn't work that way...why do you put up with that, with letting this idiot talk?" and I said "Everyone has the right to their opinion and we respect that"...It doesn't mean we agree with him or we're not sitting here thinking "I wish he'd sit down" but it's...respect.

...What I guess I've been taught and what I've observed in the Indian community is that when you do something you're doing it for the common good of everybody...When it comes to...leadership...you do it with everybody...holding an equal status...being part of the effort and part of the team...I think it goes back into some of the values...in the Indian community...

...I use a giveaway kind of leadership...a kind of leadership where creativity is really important...It's important for everybody to feel good by having their ideas valued...people feel good about who they are...There needs to be some practicality in getting there, but I think you get there by having vision...If I were to define something that I thought was a sin, and I don't use that word, but it would be to block that creativity...To me that's really not okay; that's a kind of abuse...Leadership doesn't belong to one person; it belongs to all the people who are in the circle, and how they are doing what they are doing is important...To me a good leader is a person who can let people dare to dream their wildest dream and help them to get to their dreams...

For them, building consensus is the leader's most important task. Several men said this:

...You've got to figure a way to get the people who you're leading to believe that what it is you want them to do is their idea...You can't tell them to do it, 'cause then people resist, so you persuade them to have it be their idea...That's the old way of leadership...The leader...leads with...consensus and it's not a commander...See the commander, like when I was in the army these jerks...would say..."Do this and do this" when they just sit back and drink cocktails...Some of my buddies died in Korea for that very reason that they told 'em to "Take another hill and another hill" and then they'd take the hill and then they'd get ordered to pull back and they'd say "Why" and "Well it's battalion headquarters" and the next day "Take the hill" again...That's why they call it Mount Bloody Mary, this one hill in Korea...My philosophy on leadership is that you lead by example...You never ask anybody to do something you won't do...You get 'em going and then you pull back and let another generation continue...

...I guess my style would be one of being very empathetic...The constituents that I've worked with predominantly have been American Indian, although there were other minority people, people of color, involved with that but I'm most comfortable with a team sort of concept and working in trying to reach some form of consensus...It probably goes back to my own traditional tribal...way of doing things...very personable...I have very good interpersonal communication...skills that enable me to...help towards getting...people to develop ownership things into an idea or project...

...A kind of cooperative arrangement...I'm not comfortable telling people what to do, but I'm comfortable talking with the people about what needs to be done and then deciding who's gonna do it...I'm okay with asking people what to do...When I've been in charge of programs that's the way I've run them, I've never had much authority...When I worked with people in tribes in workshop situations or consulting, I first decide what it is they want to do, what it is they're willing to do and then I tell them how they can move toward what they want...I believe in power-sharing, I guess it would be called co-operative management...I don't like hierarchies, I don't trust them...I don't like ambition either; I'm very suspicious of...people acting for themselves...Those are cultural traits...It worked well in the classroom...with the people that I had to work with...support staff...the community people...the tribal people that I did program development with...They had a great deal of trouble with anthropologists and linguists, sociologists, some of the people who work with them in a professional capacity because they felt they were being told what their language should be or what their culture should be or who they were, rather than being able to explain or to share who they were, and that "We, the experts, will tell you" approach was something that I was very, very sensitive to because I'd felt it first-hand myself and I knew how not to do it...

Part of reaching consensus involved facility in playing the mediator's role, mentioned by a few of the men:

There was a lot of friction...I could understand the guys on one side of the shop and the...guys from the other side...I could go back and forth...and mediate "You guys can't say that no more"...and all the time I'm getting it...both sides, but it worked out pretty good...We all made out, our contracts at least we thought were okay, we never got enough money from the corporation...but we got the benefits...We fought for it all together...Keep together, the working man's rule...Mainly for the tribe it's mostly like a peacemaker...I find it kind of rewarding 'cause I'm helping...I can pay the tribe back 'cause it's 24 hours a day, there ain't no rest when you're a judge...a lot of complaints I hear about everybody, pro and con, even myself, people complain about me...I try to listen to 'em, give 'em that little dignity of trying to answer 'em...I never overstep...as far as telling people "I'm a judge"...

...I can listen to a lot of people arguing...at the office...I do not get involved anymore...for me those are the type of leadership qualities that a person should have, be able to stop, look and listen, realize...Suppose there was a fight that broke out...you'll have all the whites on one side, all the Indians on the other...I...possibly would...try to become a mediator...I'd probably get killed in the process though...I'm not one that easily falls apart at the seam...if I'm caught in the midst of something, if something happens in the tribe...and there's some big fights going on... and it involves me directly, I will not back down...I'll use all the initiative and imagination that I've had for survival...

Because leaders were seen as servants of the people who build consensus, with "the people" having a strong voice in decision, a strong preference existed for a team work approach. Women talked about this more explicitly:

...I was a strong believer in grass-roots...I think it's up to the people...I coached basketball for six years...Didn't know a thing about basketball...the kids taught me about basketball..."Okay we need a coach" and "I don't know anything about basketball"..."Well we'll teach you"...they're like 11 and 12 years old and now they're all adults...I really enjoyed those years because it was interesting to see them and I never made one compete with the other; I always stressed the team and that everybody out there could do as well as the next person...For a while there it worked, until...we had a problem with crack and I dropped a few of the kids, they weren't clean enough to stay on the team...

...I wanna be a teacher, 'cause that's what my mom did, not just with me but with her staff...Her approach...to teach others 'cause you can't do it all yourself...That's one reason why teams work so well, 'cause you build on each other's strength...

...I didn't realize at the start...how powerless the previous directors had been...they had no say in programming...anything...When I came on board, management style was chain management...There was a lot of privileged kinds of things going on...money set aside...big money, for travel all over the country; it was being spent unwisely so I said "We are going to get equipment"...I'm computer illiterate..."I want the best, you guys better...know"...They really enjoyed that; it was hard for them at first to set aside the time to do team staffing but after a while they really appreciated it, that you give them some say over the program...

...a lot of them have a hard time directing people...everybody has...a team approach...with minority people, than to have levels of administration ...Maybe that's why I...see more of a team effort...

...I see, within cultural diversity programs...a power struggle going on with the non-diversity/diversity staff...Those of us that are diversity staff would like to...sit down and work things out whereas the non-diversity staff, it's like "That's not my job" and "Shouldn't that be the administrator's job?"...They're trying to make sure they separate the levels of who does what, when and how and to whom...I see the diversity staff wanting to "Let's just all get together and work this out as a team"...I see more of a team style management with diversity people...

The way of teaching was also important. Several stressed the importance of leading or teaching by example, through modelling or leading a good life. A woman said this:

...I know I'm really good at empowering young people and other people that I work with...I'd stand up for anybody...it's like if there was an injustice in the world I'd be there...I turned into a crusader...

Several men said:

...The best way to teach it is to role model it...to live it and once you start to live it then people will see...you don't have to teach...You are teaching it in that sense...people will then use it...

...You're willing to work...You never ask anybody to do something you won't do...So you lead by example and then you get these people to believe that it's their idea, and they really will believe it...

Their concern for others did not mean these leaders simply allowed those they managed to do as they wished. Despite their emphasis on individual input and cultural sensitivity, there was still a concern with adequate job performance and a willingness to enforce high levels of excellence. One man said this:

...One thing, when you're working with just a few people like this in a small place...it's kinda hard to then turn around and have to say "Now wait a minute, you're doing all that wrong and this is the way it has to be"...they take it personally but you have to let that go and say "Well, no, this is my job and my job is to see that you do your job well and if you're not doing your job then it's reflecting on me"...Since I've been here I've had to do a number of corrective interviews...what it is they're doing wrong, what they need to do to improve it and how long they have to improve it, or if they don't what's gonna happen...You can do that and you can talk it over, then after you do that then you have to write it all down, document it and settle it, that way they know what they have to do...Then copies go to personnel or the chairman...and if they don't do that well then suspension without pay, then after that termination...But they still have all the things that they can do...For instance, if they don't like what you're saying they can request a meeting with your supervisor and they have to write everything down...It seems to work...first you try and smooth things out...officially taking that step but once you take it...I've had employees mad at me, then after a while..they start improving and things start rolling along...whatever the problem was is improved...

A woman said:

...Once a person's hired I look at...their job descriptions and what they need to do...There are very few people in here...maybe 3 out of...11 or 12 jobs that I evaluate...if people don't make meetings, if they're late, if they don't attend the proper training, all those things to me count as what kind of employee you are...I make that evaluation really reflect how I feel as supervisor and a lot of people don't like it, but it's real clear on there what I want changed...

Imposed vs. Traditional Culture

Discussions about leadership style sometimes led to explicit comments about fundamental differences between traditional and dominant cultures. Several respondents discussed these discrepancies. This was framed most often in terms of conflict between responding to U.S. government requirements and adhering to their own culture. One man said this:

...A lot of Indian people still...go by majority but yet traditionally it used to be consensus...Culturally-wise...your priorities...values, what you think is important...affects the leadership process...You address the creation and all the levels of knowledge and the creator...When you're thinking that way...your world view is different...

Among some of these individuals, a concern was with the lack of values in the dominant society. A man said:

...Within the university institution there's this feeling like "We have to keep watching them" or "We don't know if they're doing what we say that they should do"...There isn't that...inner belief, that says "Okay, they know what they're talking about, let us support them, let's see how it goes"...I hate to use a model but perhaps the military where...you have a bureaucracy, and the generals...

A woman talked more generally:

...I don't believe that white culture really values...even acknowledges human life...White people look at other people of color, or even themselves; they look at the differences more than they do the similarities...

A man talked about moving away from the reservation as a child:

...It was...from coming out of...an area that was...peaceful and loving to a world where...you gotta stand on your own all of a sudden...People don't like to share or help out...There's a different kind of culture...As a young kid that's what I seen...growing up...I didn't like it but I dealt with it, that's why I went back and forth all the time...

A woman discussed the dissonance she felt between cultures:

...There's such a vast difference in being white and being Indian...like when I was a Catholic, for penance they said "Say 15 Hail Marys, three Our Fathers, and maybe about 10 Glory Be's"...That's nuts, why do I have to say 15 Hail Marys, you think that Hail Mary would hear the first one...why do I have to put so many Our Fathers in there...Supreme Being, he could have heard the first Our Father, and the Glory Be...and the litanies that we'd chant...They say Indians are paganist, they chant, well gee whiz, those Catholics are top brass in that area...I'm closer to God sitting in a teepee...worshipping Him all night...I don't have to go to church every Sunday...

A woman working at a university said:

...It's just a way of thinking, I'm in a situation where...the rules and everything takes precedent...If you're on time...even the way I...look at things...I don't plan a half a year ahead of time...I do get my work done that's required...It's a different way of thinking, different way of working...Sometimes I wonder why...we make them jump hoops...what kind of hoops are they, does that make me a better person...I really question tenure...I love it when they say..."What do you want to do?"...and I'm going..."It's my passion getting to meetings on time"...I just have a difficult time...the system is greater than me...There's something in me sometimes that...rebels, I have this streak...there's these things you have to do...Everything has to be defined in a certain way that will be acceptable within the university environment...I think that there are so many things that there could be partnerships in but I think the university is male-dominated, also...majority-culture dominated...The indigenous people...we think differently and we look at things differently.

...I think that with Native groups it's not as rigid...as structured...In non-Indian groups...it's very structured and you end up with people in leadership positions that have no business being in leadership positions...you get that authority ego stuff that gets in the way...It does happen but I don't see it happening as much in Indian groups, except for tribal councils but that's another story.

...Since I had experience with both cultures, it was real clear to me that...my dad's family was real cold and unkind and the community in which I lived was real status oriented and real competitive...Then I'd come to the reservation and people were warm and accepting and funny and you felt like you were part of the extended family and welcomed, so it was real easy to choose which one of those I'd rather be...

In...the non-Indian world or in business or in education, power seems to be more important and how one is perceived as having power, and the one with the most power is the leader and the one that even has the most coercive power is the leader...along with that power goes money...in the dominant society...In the traditional way, it's not what you have...

...I always found that I...liked talking about...how the earth is connected to us...They [Euro-Americans] lack that, the spiritual part of that, even the emotional part of it and so if you take that with some leadership...that's what you get...those that maybe are self-serving...

Does this Difference Actually Exist?

Some of our respondents wondered if there really *were* such clear-cut differences between the two cultures. Two men said this:

You got a very assimilated, culturated people and you've got a vast majority in the middle, between a bi-cultural perspective...you've got the two oppositional ones...very traditional people on one side who are very skeptical of people who are very assimilated...

...The principals of leadership differ from society to society and they will differ within societies...The[y]...can be in several modes...Let's take...a good sized tribe...we're going to have at least three different modes of leadership...The first mode of leadership will be the traditional mode...based on tribal tradition; it's one that is going to be a direct lineal descendent of the pre-contact mode...It's going to be based probably on a consensus, some sort of cooperative management; it will not be based on the leadership of an authoritarian person; it will be based, instead, on the leadership of a person or group of persons who are very skillful at organizing and building consensus...Some tribes don't have that kind of leadership...The second mode is political...based on the overlay of federal and state policy...It is a system which depends on the leadership of elected officials whose principle of leadership is law, on one hand, and expedience on the other...Their interests are not consensually determined; in fact, quite often they're the opposite...They are often in a position of forcing the people to do things...the federal government, the state government, local governments...They're often at cross purposes with traditional...values...Some tribes have formalized arrangements so that they can have a level of political governance and a level of traditional governance...Other tribes haven't and sometimes it leads to serious conflict...The Wounded Knee incident...came out of that kind of conflict 20 years ago...Economic leadership is...entrepreneurial; it tends to be driven by outsiders who are looking for gain on their own part but not always...I would say that two of those modes are western, the political and the economic...There are many different styles of leadership in the west, non-Indian...Some of them are consensual and cooperative, some of them are political, some, as I've described it...economic...I don't think that the modes of leadership are really any different or the styles of leadership are any different but I think the propensity...to choose one mode over another is different...There are some Indian groups that are very authoritarian and some modes of leadership that are very authoritarian but they are in the minority...I think that Indian groups tend toward cooperative systems. I think that western groups tend toward authoritarian, hierarchical systems that produces a lot of conflict...I don't think that there's such a thing as a white way to lead and an Indian way to lead; I think that there are leadership strategies which have been developed by humans everywhere; different groups favor different strategies for lots of different reasons...There are many different strategies for leadership, and different cultures...optimize different...strategies...I think that Indian cultures tend to optimize cooperative modes, or non-authoritarian modes of leadership but...Indians can be very good at authoritarian modes of leadership...the Aztecs -- the pre-contact Aztecs -- or Maya, or even the Natchez, heaven help them, were very authoritarian, high regimented, strongly stratified communities and they totally placed a high value on...inherent authority...They were atypical, I think, but the fact remains that they were just as Indian as anybody else, but they were very "western" in their approach to leadership...So assuming that styles of leadership are different for Indians than for non-Indians has to be handled carefully because it can be a red herring...That's what Sitting Bull said..."Go and learn from them and bring back what's useful...we have much to teach each other"...I think that the Indians are just as... incomplete, as anybody else...Being Indian doesn't guarantee anything...there is no ultimate truth, even inside a brown skin, that people in white skin don't inherently have access to...That's been the basis of the relations and the base of interest in Indian culture, I think, in the popular line and I think it's very unhealthy...I don't think that that's true but I do believe that there are things that Indians do that are different from things that...non-Indians do and sometimes the comparison is instructive, and it works both ways...I think that there are things that Indian people learn from non-Indians too...The book on being human is not fully written yet...

One woman talked about tendencies she had observed among Indians:

...I think that's human nature, I don't even think that's necessarily a native perspective...I can't lump all Indians...I don't think you have to go to ceremonies to live in a traditional way...I think if you have respect for life, respect for the environment...for all things, and you just strive to live in a "good way"...that's the traditional way...

Another woman agreed:

I think that there are different styles...and...kinds of leadership and that some people are real uncomfortable with one kind of leadership or another...What I am comfortable with might be very uncomfortable for some people who like a lot of structure and one I'm uncomfortable with...I don't think that that is about being Native American or about being non-Indian, I think that's about a style...of being what you choose...I'd like to say that "Yes, there's a real difference" but, frankly, my experience in _____ tells me that that isn't so, that some times in some parts of...Native American places...things get real rigid, and I think that's more about dysfunctional systems and a need for control than it is about being Indian or non-Indian...For Indian people a lot of times dysfunction is...about contact in some way or another...

Afterthoughts

Despite these last few disclaimers, it seemed obvious to me that these Indian people espouse some fairly consistent notions of how society should work, including ideas of equality, respect, and participation. That is not to say there were not problems, as there were with the African-Americans discussed in the last chapter. Some of these Native Americans discussed this explicitly. A few men lamented departures from their traditional culture:

> ...The tribal communities have adopted the white leadership way, and have rejected the American Indian leadership way, and that's where a lot of the problems have occurred...even a lot of those Tribal Councils...it's not Indian way...

> ...Sometimes individuals who have moved away from traditional perspectives...have moved into main dominant society's view of how government should be run and leadership is run...basically is that it's a man's job to be leaders and woman has nothing to do with it at all...So they've taken...some of the dominant values...

Despite such problems, efforts were great to live in a "good," "Indian" way. These findings show how drastically cultural setting can alter notions of management or leadership --- and related ideas regarding gender differences. Here, men and women, much more consistently than the African-American managers, ascribe to and use the "new" models that we have been describing, even more explictly than the other groups we have considered. Joan Tronto (1987) has illustrated a convergence of feminist notions of how society ought to be restructured with the thoughts of various marginalized class and racial groups. Again, given our tendency to look at these bodies of inquiry independently, we may not be aware of the convergence involved. It is only by taking a more holistic perspective that we become so aware.

Chapter 10

THE NEW WORKPLACE

> Feminist discourse and practice entail a struggle for individual autonomy that is with others and for community, that embraces diversity - that is, for an integration of the individual and the collective in an ongoing process of authentic individuation and genuine connectedness.
> Kathy Fergenson *The Feminist Case Against Bureaucracy*. 1994.

All of the voices we've heard -- African-Americans, Native Americans, workers, women -- suggest some pretty fundamental changes in the workplace. What are they? As these voices continue to rise in prominence, how might the "new" workplace look? What is the common message coming from all of these groups? They all have emphasized equality, participation, and co-operation; showing concern for facilitating others' development; exercising power *with* rather than power *over* others. They have also talked about an integrated approach, in such ways as connecting work with family issues, understanding the personal is the political or the public, and emphasizing a deeper cultural belief that, in fact, all in life is inter-connected.

What is the new order, as seen in its totality? Several writers have speculated about this. For example, Gene Marshall (1988) in *Repair and Replacement* lays out the five qualities of a replacement movement: one that is holistic, honors the individual person, builds human scale structures, emphasizes cultural transformation, and is itself an eco-movement. These features seem to appear in one form or another in the various perspectives we have considered.

As I said in Chapter 1, we like to believe our current ideas are really new, but in reality, they are circulating through complex feedback loops, growing and extending through time. Some of these ideas about integration have been around for a long time, advanced by those who early on understood that there is a connection between such issues as gender, race, and class. Such ideas have existed in indigeneous cultures for a long time, as seen in the perspectives presented in the last chapter. Certain members of the feminist movement have also perceived these inter-connections. For example, Mary Parker Follett, who lived from 1868 to 1933, was an educated woman who turned her extensive knowledge to matters of business. She deplored domination and devised a win-win method of conflict resolution, articulating a law of the situation (circumstances constantly change and evolve) and terms such as inter-departmental cross-functioning (communicating across hierarchical boundaries) and collective responsibility (the ability to see the impact of one's work on the total organization). She espoused positive labor-management relations, favoring approaches that allowed for integrating all differences and meeting all needs. In fact, she stressed the need for integration throughout life, for a holistic perspective. She urged employers to consider the perspective and needs of workers, and called her approach "the art of getting things done through people." In her emphasis on the importance of people and their interactions, she can rightfully be considered an often ignored founder of the human resource management school (Karsten, 1989). Some of these same principles were articulated by African-Americans and Native Americans in Chapters 8 and 9, where working with people was stressed, as was incorporating their various needs and perspectives.

As we search for new structures that would solve problems we seem to be facing, what is the new contract being sought by workers? We could adopt the changes being urged in the management and worker participation literatures (Chapter 6) which entail autonomy, dignity, and participation. We could develop apparently new managerial styles, like "the relational manager" type suggested by Leavitt and Lipman-Blumen (1980). They have noted the apparently cyclical rediscovery that "people really do need people" (p. 27) in the workplace. Many societal trends are pushing us in the direction of relational management, and Leavitt and Lipman-Blumen discuss the importance of shifts among young people away from careers as a central life focus and more upon "general lifestyles." No longer is the worker content to just go along with the dictatorial, controlling company. One often cited example of this trend is the increasing tendency of male executives to refuse transfers because of their wives' and children's needs.

Yankelovich (1981) laid out very clearly the terms of the new contract workers of all ages seem to be seeking, one that would be endorsed by the marginal voices we see rising throughout these chapters. He notes an increased emphasis on values as guides to one's behavior at work, also, the desire to make a valued contribution *through* work. He argues we increasingly expect to find intrinsic satisfaction in the *doing* of the job, to find meaning and purpose there, a sense of accomplishment. Hence, the trend is away from authoritarian management styles toward more people-sensitive ones. We are seeking, in Yankelovich's terms, to "elevate...the 'sacred/expressive' aspects of [our] lives, and...to downgrade the impersonal, manipulative aspects." (p. 7) In his view, self-denial will no longer be accepted by the newer labor force. Rather, he argues an "ethic of commitment" is being constructed, in which our rebellion against the old rules has now passed from the "reject everything" phase into a consolidating phase where connection is the crux of our lives. As Leavitt and Lipman-Blumen note, "The hunger for warm, affectionate relationships appears to be growing in the United States." (p. 30) Yankelovich believes our new social order will be structured around a need for closer and deeper personal relationships and a switch from instrumental values to more expressive/sacred ones, critical parts of the new paradigm discussed by the voices presented in previous chapters. He supports this with survey and interview evidence showing many Americans feel socially isolated and are searching for community. Ultimately, he believes our new ethic will recognize "the interdependence of all forms of life." (p. 256) Pointing to the decay running through our system, he argues this new ethic will revitalize our society and meet our challenges, especially in the workplace. In sum, workers are calling for more authentic work lives, where one feels a sense of having made a positive contribution. Managers are encouraged to operate from an implementing, problem-solving, path-finding mode (Leavitt, 1986). If this is true, a restructuring of the workplace is inevitable.

This notion of widespread transformation is erupting on many different fronts. Mark Satin, editor of the newsletter *New Options*, has made observations similar to those made by Yankelovich. In a re-evaluation of the 1980's, he is optimistic a new approach is currently being constructed. "I think the 80's were a lot better than the commentators realized," he says, noting many described the 80's as "The me decade...The wannabe decade...The decade of glitz and greed...A decade of death" (1990: 1). He argues the 80's in fact "laid the groundwork for realizing the longings that were first brought to mass consciousness in the 60's." He discusses several trends of the 80's that point to the crystallization of a new paradigm, a new approach to life. These trends include the emergence of the "caring individual" archetype (replacing that of the "rugged individual"), growing concern for the environment, the changes in Eastern Europe and the Soviet Union, a renewed concern with "love" (contained in the title of three best seller books), and the emergence of post modern (less structured) forms in everything from architectural designs to social theory. He ends by showing how these themes were reflected in popular culture, particularly rock music, throughout the decade. Again, this new direction involves a concern with expressive/sacred values and an ability to form deep, sustaining relationships. The ability for individuals to develop their own unique strengths, within the context of community, is essential for meeting the needs being articulated.

In fact, we can see the beginnings of this model, which includes a concern for ethical soundness and morality in the workplace all around us. It is seen in a recent study of first-level managers in a Fortune 500 company (Derry, 1988) who experienced a fairly high number of ethical dilemmas. Their moral conflicts tended to revolve around instructions from their superiors that contradicted their own and/or the company's policies or moral standards. Examples included being told to down-play a known health hazard of a product, subvert the import laws of another country, or fire a person for non-work-related reasons. When asked about the basis for moral decisions, in addition to citing standard sources such as the Ten Commandments and Golden Rule, they said:

> Giving people their dignity...Helping others...Loving others...Contributing to society...Striving to be professional...Not benefitting at another's expense...Integrity to one's own values...A balance that allows us to survive as a species. (p. 9)

I was reminded of the values the Native Americans stressed in Chapter 9 as guiding principles for them. These Fortune 500 managers, half of whom were Caucasian men, show a concern for caring, connection, dignity. Several of them expressed dismay at what their supervisors had asked them to do, although a significant number found when they perservered, their bosses finally came to agree with their stand. Here, we see workers striving to construct the new ethic discussed by Yankelovich, experiencing conflict with those using the old paradigm.

In the last chapter, we found Wisconsin Indian people emphasizing the importance of living by certain values -- to be of service to others and not seeking personal glory in leadership positions. This also seems to be true of women, as a group. For example, Martin, et al. (1988) found women strongly agreed, across class and racial lines, about the types of personnel policies corporations ought to adopt. They strongly supported the work ethic, showing more commitment and willingness for self-sacrifice than men.

Joline Godfrey in her book about women entrepreneurs called *Our Wildest Dreams* (1992) also argues women tend to operate by what she calls "new" or "human" rules, which involve conceiving work groups as webs (with no main controller), seeking meaning *and* money and a balance with the rest of one's life, letting things grow naturally, doing no harm in a sustainable way. These rules, she says, stand in stark contrast to the "old" rules which involve conceiving work groups as pyramids (with a definite individual in charge); work, work, work; seeking money alone; letting the buyer beware; doing whatever damage can be gotten away with for the sake of profit ("use it or lose it"). In her view, women entrepreneurs are motivated largely by the opportunity to make some valuable contribution to society.

Barbara Shipka exemplifies the concern with "making a contribution" in her consulting work, discussed in *When the Canary Stops Singing* (1993). And Astin and Leland (1991) discover it in the women public officials they interviewed. In a chapter subtitled, "A passion for justice and social change," they report one women saying, "I really measure my life by the extent to which I can help effect change." They argue that these women adopted priorities from the modern women's movement, including vision, personal commitment, empowerment, and risk. As more workers seem anxious for sacred, intrinsically meaningful values to be incorporated into their work lives, perhaps women and people of color, in many ways left out of setting the tone and underlying values in our workplace, can lead us in the needed direction.

The exact nature of some of these values was discussed in my interviews with Wisconsin university administrators (Statham and

Swoboda, 1990). Several of the women I talked with asserted they
were guided by "values" -- "right and wrong" -- rather than by
practicalities or political expendency. One woman put it bluntly:

> I'm not really one to compromise a thing -- if it's right it's right
> -- and that's the way it is. Maybe with men...they have to look at
> things more...pragmatically.

Earlier, she had stated when it came to administration, "My principles
are my philosophy...[They] tend to be very student- oriented."
    Another woman described interactions with a sister who wanted her
to leave higher education and go into "the business community and
[make] three times my salary." She said:

> ...I would still look at it as selling out. I have to believe in what I am
> working with and I can't believe in chemical companies...I can't work for
> corporations. I like to think it's a principle.

Another higher level woman said:

> I have never really thought about a career change. Although I've known
> folks...that say these skills...are generic and transferable...there is some
> truth to that, but I also think you have to have some sense that what you
> are doing means something...Public education is who I am, what I
> am...So, it is my way of giving something back. That's probably the
> most significant reason why I couldn't think about changing into the
> corporate sector. I don't think the values are there that I would find
> useful.

This woman related another value that guides her in her work.

> My first boss...taught me...that if you enjoy saying, "No," and if you
> enjoy inflicting pain, then get out of this business...

Another woman said her job gave her the "opportunity to promote those
values...cultural pluralism...which I worked on since I was a teenager."
In stark contrast, only one of the male administrators I interviewed
discussed values as guiding his work, and his comments were somewhat
negative, with him being "intrigued" by a former (male) boss who had
attempted to do this and had failed at his job. For him, being guided
by personal values, rather than practicality, was an unwise thing to do.

The value of cultural pluralism was mentioned by several of the women, particularly when they talked about how they would change higher education. Five of the eleven women mentioned "increasing tolerance for difference," increasing the numbers of nontraditional, minority, and women students. This they saw as valuable in itself. One man mentioned this, but it was couched more in terms of responding to market factors than as a goal valuable in and of itself. Other women mentioned the value of becoming more student centered.

In sum, then, these women administrators showed a tendency to make decisions based upon their own morality or sense of ethics, their desire to do the right thing, make a contribution. This echoes the tendency toward expressive/sacred values Yankelovich claims to be characteristic of the new workforce and reminiscent of the framework laid out by the Wisconsin Indian people discussed in the last chapter. The African-Americans also stressed the importance of being of service in Chapter 8. These women also expressed a desire for and comfort with a more diverse workforce, something demographers tell us will soon be a reality. Perhaps these women managers, as well as others like the African-Americans and Native Americans I interviewed, can take the lead in fashioning the new contract between workers and employers Yankelovich spoke about so eloquently, if provided the opportunity.

In a sense, these women also show a more integrated or holistic approach to work. Unlike the men, they do not consider their values or sense of morality to be separate from work. Rather, they try very hard to integrate their values into their job situations. These values become part of the ends they attempt to achieve. The values themselves also show strong respect for the dignity of the individual. All of these factors are characteristic of many marginal groups' views of work and management or leadership outlined in previous chapters.

The rising of these marginal voices combined with the need for diversity more generally may be a very powerful force for change. A *MS* report called "Jobs for women in the nineties" by Julie Bailey (1988) suggests women, for example, may have a special contribution to make, noting that "nurturing diversity makes good business sense." Quoting Lennie Copeland, a San Francisco consultant who produced a series called "Valuing Diversity" for thirty *Fortune 500* corporations, Bailey notes:

> Management teams consisting exclusively of white, male clones won't be
> able to come up with the most creative ways of reaching the ethnically
> diverse U.S. marketplace of today and the future (p. 75).

Women of color, in particular are often pointed to as especially
powerful forces for change. For example, Johnetta Cole, president of
Spelman College, is described as using "a new style of leadership...non-
narrow, non-chauvinistic and intentionally humane" (Edwards, 1989),
echoing approaches of women and African-Americans we have already
seen. Barbara Holmes (1989), in studying black women administrators,
asserts that:

> Consensus, communication, and co-operation are at the heart of the
> feminine style of management; competitiveness, hierarchical structure,
> with the aim being to win, are at the heart of the masculine style (p. 9).

Perhaps the Euro-American, white, male style, not simply "masculine",
would be a more apt description here. Of course, not all white men use
this style. Remember the discussion in Chapter 2, where the distinction
was made between cultural or societal emphasis on what is considered
masculine or feminine, as opposed to seeing these characteristics as only
pertaining to individuals.

New Contributions

Much literature exists about the potential contributions women might
make to the workplace, based upon the specific changes being called
for. Given the shape of workplace restructuring, women as leaders
seem to be a logical outcome. I use this literature as an illustration of
how a marginalized group can make critical contributions, transforming
the institution in the process. As we see other marginalized groups also
possess these -- and broader insights -- the potential for transformation
is even greater.

This idea that new approaches contributed by these excluded groups
can prove enormously helpful has been appearing in various guises. In
1989, Sherry Seib Cohen published *Tender Power*, in which she urged
women to "use our own strengths," which she says involve combining
"firm direction with the genuine empowerment of others." In this
"feminine context," workers are motivated to produce because they feel
good about themselves and the place they work. This is certainly the

crux of the new ethic Yankelovich sees emerging in our society, the new paradigm being heralded by others such as Capra. It is also a type intrinsically tied to cooperative approaches. Cohen argues women know best how to deal with the change that will constantly be demanded of our corporations, and goes on to say that women have so far not worked as authentic persons, but as "split personalities," trying to mask their "female traits," by instead using the male model. The American Indians I interviewed reported being quite up front about their alternative strategies. If these various groups were aware of their similar impetuses, it could have a greater cumulative transformative impact as they come to more frequently hold leadership positions in the workplace.

Community and Connections

Several features, aside from the emphasis on values as guides for behavior, have arisen with some frequency. They are the emphasis on building community or connections between the people in the workplace, flattened hierarchies and teamwork, and integration of the personal with work. I begin with the first, the emphasis on connections between those at work.

We saw that the African-Americans and Native Americans discussed in Chapters 8 and 9 emphasized community and connection. This seems to be important to workers, more generally. It seems this is also true of women's approach. After a considerable amount of research, Leavitt and Lipman-Blumen (1980) have concluded women use a more relational approach that is much needed in contemporary affairs. They found even young high school girls to be more motivated by "relational" aspects of management (i.e., using teamwork, contributing to another's success), an approach deemed "more appropriate for the future" (p. 37) compared to boys' more competitive and power-oriented style better suited to the traditional, segmentalist organization. Leavitt and Lipman-Blumen argue that even in early studies, the best managers were actually those who were both task and people oriented, a fact often overlooked in these studies.

Many other writers also point to women's greater facility in working with people. For example, Kagan (1983), reporting on results from a national survey, found human relations concerns to be high on women's lists, things such as valuing the people women work with, feeling like a part of a team, treating co-workers with care and respect. Hersh-Cochran et al. (1987) discuss women's flexibility and perceptiveness of people (noting also their lack of contacts, poor knowledge about career move timing, and late career starts).

In the past several years, this idea has literally exploded onto the scene, with many books appearing that emphasize women managers' abilities to work effectively with others. Patricia Aburdene and John Naisbitt (1992) greatly expanded this perspective on the basis of hundreds of interviews done for their book *Megatrends for Women*. They believe the inclusion of women into formerly male-only domains will enhance the spread of a partnership approach to all endeavors, quickening the spread of worker participation. Nicholson and West (1988) found women managers report showing feelings more often than men and being more sociable, fulfilled, intellectual, and optimistic. The authors believe that women have different motives toward their careers, have higher growth needs, and are more self-directed. Sally Helgeson, in her book *The Female Advantage* (1990) did an in-depth study of four women, showing how women might transform society by bringing the "feminine principles" of caring, communication, and collaboration to their leadership roles. She found their styles to be inclusive, open, flexible, caring, and available to employees. Patricia Lunneborg in *Women Changing Work* (1990) reports results from 200 women in 10 non-traditional careers which showed women adopt a nurturant approach to co-workers and a service orientation to clients, again evoking this "ethic of caring," a concern for the individuals involved. She argues women tend to use power differently than many men -- not power "over," but as the ability to share resources, a point also made by Hunsaker and Hunsaker (1991). And Patricia Yancy Martin (1993), looking at feminist practice in organizations, argues it emphasizes connectiveness, co-operation, mutuality over competition and individual success. It seems this is the world women might well try to create, if given the opportunity to do so. Of course, some observers are less than enthusiastic about women's increasing dominance in certain fields. Philipson (1993), for example, worries the decline of the male perspective -- and male presence -- in the area of psychotherapy will in the end lead to less creative contributions being made to the field, partly because women are not being trained to make creative changes.

I found an emphasis on connecting, communicating, relating in my own data. Several women from my original interview study reported themselves to have good people skills, to interact well with their subordinates:

> I guess I'm not a scientific manager...I'm not the paternal type manager...but I would try to help them [subordinates] learn...

> I'm probably not the most businesslike supervisor...I know I'm not terribly efficient; I don't care to have that type of attitude...you know, crack the whip. I feel more family- oriented to the whole lot of them.

Their secretaries agreed, saying their women managers were very people oriented. "I don't think I've had a man boss that was quite as good as her in that respect," one of them said. A similar point was made by a school administrator in a study done by Susan Chase (1990):

> I'm convinced...that strong female leadership is the kind...of leadership needed in urban school districts today...there is a mothering element that I'm not ashamed to admit...that becomes very, very important when we have to face crises that are hitting school campuses today...and men, by their very nature, the way we groom them to be macho, are not comfortable getting in their cars, going to the hospital to see about a kid...

These women were not, however, *only* people oriented. The old order stresses hierarchical relations and asserts we must be either person *or* task oriented, that it is impossible to be both. However, the newer theories of management are now arguing managers who are people-oriented and sensitive, along with being concerned about accomplishing the task, will be more successful in the coming era. And, as reported in previous chapters, the women I interviewed were *very* concerned with doing the work, accomplishing the task at hand, as were the men of color I interviewed.

Teamwork and Flattened Hierarchies

The second characteristic, teamwork, is related to the first, connections to those at work. Again, we have seen much evidence that the marginal voices considered here emphasize its importance. A great deal of evidence suggests this is a critical aspect of many women's approaches, hence their potential contributions to the workplace. Marilyn Loden (1985) argues that more women and people of color in the corporate ranks will cause companies to change the way they are run. She believes most women's preference for the team approach and a consensus style will put them in good stead with the American companies of the 1990's and beyond, as do Rizzo and Mendez (1990) in their book *The Integration of Women in Management*, meant to be a practical guide for integrating women. The same might be said for other marginalized groups.

Sargent (1981) similarly argued that many traditional female qualities women might bring to management would be welcome and productive in the workplace. She envisioned an androgynous style, incorporating elements from both traditionally male and female approaches that would move us from the segmentalist, hierarchical, authoritarian workplace criticized by Kanter where the emphasis is on short range, tactical goals, and seniority to a participatory workplace where long range excellence and self-management are emphasized.   This, according to many observers, would enhance our position world-wide. In her view, women would play a crucial role in this transformation, a prophecy reiterated by Blanchard and Sargent (1984) and Naisbitt and Aburdene (1985). Considering the possible additional impact of other marginalized groups, the potential for transformation seems even greater.

Julie Bailey, in her *MS* report on jobs for women, concluded women are team builders with an enhanced ability "to connect with people." (1988)   She further cites Marilyn Loden's belief that women demonstrate less vested interest in proving they are right, but show more interest in finding an outcome satisfying to all. As early as 1976, Jackie St. John defined "women's ways of leading" as "organic...shifting" and asserted this approach, for the first time, admitted the possibility of a relationship among equals in what had before always been hierarchical relationships.   A New Society Publisher's pamphlet using this approach asserts:

> Shared leadership in a feminist vision, then, values the morale functions highly and sees that the power of the group in the long run is as dependent upon the nurturance of its members as on its efficiency in particular tasks. Moreover, all group members develop skills and caring in morale-building, with men, as much as women, fulfilling that function (Koopeli and Lakey, 1990, 20).

It seems groups other than feminists also espouse this vein.

For teams to work effectively, hieracharcies must be flattened. In one example of this, Carolyn Wall, vice president of the flagship station for Murdock's Fox Broadcasting Company, is reported to "roam the halls" visiting people "a lot, to stay in touch" (Rosch, 1989, 109). According to this report, she is anything but the aloof, elitist superior. To work as a team player, she must give up her elitist position in the "old order."

Looking first at women's supposed propensity toward equality, participation, and cooperation, I found specific terms were being coined to describe women's unique approach. For example, in writing about a "Female Ethos," Judy Rogers (1988) noted the goals of connection between others and individual dignity are furthered by using *heterarchy* as opposed to a *hierarchy*. Heterarchy permits leaders to work more effectively toward empowering others by "valuing the contribution of each person and the unique perspective he or she brings to the organized enterprise." (p. 6) This echoes what several Native Americans said in the last chapter about empowering others. Specific practices entailed in this type of "transformative leadership" would include an emphasis on "relationships, process, groups, networking, intuition, feelings, and perceptions, and above all, on collaboration" (p. 6). This description is reminiscent of changes called for by writers such as Kanter -- and by the relationships established between women managers and their secretaries in my original study of men and women managers, where women focused more than men on their relationships with their secretaries, treating them as individuals with career paths of their own.

Again, this notion of women using more team approaches appears in many places. Marilyn Loden had previously asserted that "feminine leadership" is less hierarchical and more team oriented, with the leaders viewing themselves more "at the center" of the team rather than "at the top" of the hierarchy (p. 119), reminiscent of the "work" model used by Native Americans in the last chapter. Rogers believes the co-operation, intuition, and collaboration at the heart of the feminine leadership model is already being espoused by most respected scholars on leadership and, if adopted, will ultimately be "in the best interest of both male and female worlds" (p. 8). In philosophy, Nel Noddings (1984) has noted the "female approach" as one concerned with caring and relatedness and the uniqueness of individuals (again, echoing the Native Americans principles discussed in Chapter 9). A report of her work appeared in a 1987 issue of a magazine called *Business Ethics*, which featured the theme "Toward a feminine ethics: How does it differ from masculine ethics?" (*Business Ethics*, 1987).

Judi Marshall (1985) in her book about women managers used the term "communion" as distinct from "agency" to connote women's sense of power and efficacy obtained through connections, "our sense of being at one with other organisms" (p. 65). Agency, a more popular term in the literature on individual power and control, is actually more relevant for Euro-American men, who are socialized to obtain their sense of power and well-being from independence, assertion, self-expansion. This difference, she argues, affects how men and women manage.

Here we find some glimpse of a workplace transformed by women's input, where communion and heterarchy are valued above agency, image-building, and hierarchy. Marshall's vision is one clearly formed by feminist influence. In her book, she documents her journey to free herself from notions of equality as promised by the patriarchal world. Cathy Ferguson (1984), in her classic book *The Feminist Case Against Bureaucracy* (quoted at the beginning of this chapter), states the feminist transformation of the workplace values and facilitates connectedness, integration, and dignity for the individual.

Others suggest women's rejection of bureaucratic approaches. Rodriguez (1988) reported how a counter-bureaucratic structure worked in a shelter for battered women. Paying all employees the same amount, she argued, helped maintain a flat hierarchical structure. Women in other situations are found to reject key components of bureaucracy. Ice (1987) reports that clergywomen reject the "built-in rigidity of parish life" and other aspects of church bureaucracy. One woman minister asserted, "I emphasize collegiality and mutuality rather than difference and reverence," and another said, "I'm personally and spiritually more nurturing...more concerned with wholeness," and still another woman said, "I'm infuriated when I see bureaucratic efficiency used to squash people..." (Ice, 1987, 108). This reminds me of the problems with bureaucracy recounted by Native Americans in the last chapter.

These same tendencies were noted by Kathleen Torpy (1990) among women administrators in higher education. She laments the "paternalism" inherent in many quality of working life experiments, which, she argues, doom them to failure. Paternalism to her is "a policy or practice of treating or governing people in a fatherly manner, especially by providing for their needs without giving them responsibility" (p. 8). This is certainly the nature of bureaucratic structures. Torpy instead argues for "maternalism...the practice of treating people in a motherly/humanistic manner...[including] a concept of connected knowing, capacity for empathy...shared experiences... interact[ing] so that others may achieve their potential" (p. 9).

This rejection of bureaucracy is voiced by other women. Author Deborah Tannen, in an interview with *Working Women* magazine (Lusardi, 1990) states that:

> Women are much less comfortable with the idea of hierarchy. They use language to achieve rapport; they want to get their way, but they prefer to get their way by having everyone agree. They don't like to pull rank (p. 92).

Faith Popcorn (1991) talks about building her company, Brain Reserve, along similar lines:

> I began by filling up the ranks...with my sister and her friends and my friends...My former colleagues were horrified. "If you want to be a marketing consultant, *act* like one...Give your staff important-sounding titles...Develop a scientific approach...Don't share information...Hire some MBA's"...I never wanted a traditional corporation, with each employee sitting robotically in his or her office. I tried to create a community for thinking...What inspires productivity the most is freedom...and freedom begets creativity (p.11).

And Paula Forman, an executive management director with an advertising firm said to Mary Billard (1992) in a *Working Women* interview:

> I don't think command-and-control management is ever effective in this business. It's about creativity, and I can't command creativity.

Several of the African-American women in Chapter 8 made similar statements.

Some argue women and other marginalized groups may alter the way power and other resources are distributed in the workplace. Kanter (1983) stressed power is accumulated by relationships we form and by completing our tasks. Jobs that empower, she argues, provide discretion, visibility, and relevance to the key functions of the group. The vision of the new paradigm would spread these resources around, give all workers discretion and a job with relevance, and re-do the job segmentation described by Braverman that increasingly dissects jobs into meaningless tasks.

Major et. al. (1989) found women more likely than men to favor distributing workplace resources on the basis of need, again considering the individual's situation. As Naomi Scheman (1989) said in her opening remarks for a National Women's Studies Association conference, in women's hands:

> Leadership can be empowering of the many rather than engrandizing of the few

Some of these same aspects of women's approach were reported by women administrators in the study I did with Wisconsin university administrators. First, these women emphasized teamwork more than the men. While there were many similarities in the reports men and women gave about doing their jobs, teamwork was an important emphasis, discussed more often by women. While some overlap existed between both sexes, a trend existed in what I call perceived locus of influence. The men more often saw what they had accomplished as individual achievements, while the women more often discussed their work as group or team efforts. I was reminded of Marshall's point about women exercising power *with* more than *over* others, and also of the points several Native Americans made in Chapter 9. For example, one of these men said:

> It's nice to have a budget with some discretion about how it's spent...I [can] say "Oh well, we can print up the brochures through our office"...That's a good feeling.

He went on to say that:

> It's like, "Isn't this great, I've touched all of these people..." I feel I'm largely responsible for all of this activity. If it weren't for me, these things wouldn't be happening.

Another man said he liked to:

> ...build something, put some things together, put a structure together, give it some direction...Some people say "You like control." It's not that, or it may be part of it...I have...a lot of experience and I feel, "Hey maybe

I can contribute something here."

Several other men stated "the ability to influence people is power," and one went on to say:

As an administrator, I have all the power I need...only the power to persuade people.

He distinguished between being faculty and being an administrator as:

...the difference between playing in an orchestra and being the conductor. There is a desire to see everyone doing their job and having this thing work in some kind of harmonious way.

He explained his return to administration after several years on the faculty:

...There were several things I started, and I was interested in seeing those things continue...it seemed like the opportunity to have some input on the school or college.

The women were more likely to describe themselves as part of a process, not as the main causal agent. In somewhat similar fashion to the Native Americans described in the last chapter, they were likely to have a view of a total process. Their concern for the dignity of others is seen partly in their concern of facilitating others' success. One woman asserted her job entailed:

...making it easier for those who want to teach to teach. Someone has to do the paperwork, and take care of the housekeeping details and I think the _____ position is really doing that, for the people that want to teach.

This is reminiscent of Native American's views that leading is, in reality, serving others. Another woman said:

I never demand anything...Very seldom would I say, "You will have this by such and such a date"...it's just my style to ask more in a form of a question, "Would you please do this...Would you...have the time to get it done by then?"

In return, her secretary, whom she had recently gotten promoted:

> ...has really been the most supportive person to me...she is always
> encouraging; she covers for me...I'm sure if she was not on the job, my
> job would be much more difficult...She makes my day run very
> smoothly...And if my day is not going well, she is always the one who
> says, "What can I do to help?" She is always there for me.

This woman expressed a strong preference to "work co-operatively," as
did many of these women -- along with other groups discussed in
previous chapters. One of these women said:

> I find it gratifying to put people together who are able to
> work...collectively, collegially as a team...Giving them, enabling
> them...the responsibility and leeway to carry out that responsibility...that's
> exciting to watch people take hold of their operation and make something
> happen to it.

Another woman, who teaches management courses at another institution, reported instituting quality circles among the grounds crew.

> ...At first they thought it was a bitch session. They were surprised that
> they actually had some input...They had never been asked their opinions
> before.

And another woman reported trying to institute that kind of team-work.

> Once I get the [her subordinates] together as a real team that can think
> about the good of the institution as a whole and then exert some
> leadership in their [units]...I will feel that we're in better shape...

Many of these women saw team work as the only effective way to get
the job done.

> ...I think that if people have ownership, they are more enthusiastic about
> doing it [job].

> ...The only way we can be successful is if everybody participates.

One woman reported how her department had effected a great deal of
change by:

...work[ing] at this as a community, as a staff, with the cooperation and knowledge of other student services people as well as faculty.

And another woman said:

I think part of making a difference...if you are an administrator is measured by the success of the people who are in your organization...What you can accomplish for the people that you are here to serve -- the students.

While these differences tended to exist among men and women, there were several exceptions, especially among the men. It is probably the tendency for many of these men to have a more people-centered, team-work approach than Euro-American men in other settings, such as private sector companies. Several of them, even the men quoted above, expressed a great liking for working with people, whether it be students or faculty. They have, after all, chosen a field where a major purpose is to help others develop. This might make them very different from the male managers discussed in Chapter 3. One man said it best:

I love working with people...to delegate authority and allow people to exercise it...I've committed my life to teaching, especially helping people develop. As an administrator, I'm doing the same thing.

While many of the men expressed this sentiment, they were simply not as consistent, nor did this emphasis come through as clearly as in the women's comments. There were also a few women who expressed the more male-typed sense of control.

I like the freedom...the ability to establish time and move...I allow and like participation...but I also recognize that I have a high need for control.

I believe in working cooperatively...[but]...when push comes to shove, it shall be done.

Interestingly, these two women were also somewhat more traditional in their views of gender roles than the other women and had for many years been marginally attached to the labor force, not really committed to advancing in a career.

In general, however, the approach women seem to be using in managerial positions follows quite directly from women's more general life sensibilities. Marshall (1992) also connects these tendencies directly with the paradigm shift Capra claims to have observed, arguing women managers tend to follow the new paradigm, whether consciously or not. Similarly, Roberts and Thorsheim (1988) found women leaders to be more comfortable with a "holistic interconnection" style of leadership that emphasizes relating to others as total persons and concentrating on interconnections, while men more often used an "interdependent freedom" style that emphasizes autonomy.

These attempts at transformation are coming amid other attempts and calls for organizational change. For example, a special issue of *Conscience* (1988) examines the position of women in Catholicism in this country. It ends by calling for widespread change within the church bureaucracy, from recruitment/affirmative action to educating women and paying them a just wage. If these recommendations were truly followed, the Catholic Church would surely be transformed, less male-dominated, making it more representative of the total population's religious experience and needs. Women and other marginalized groups are having problems in other fields. A 1989 article in *The Wall Street Journal* (Trost, 1989), lamenting the "long pipeline" women wait in to get a break in media, says bluntly "women's advancement often requires direct intervention from top corporate officials" (p. B3). The author reported on a study done by the New Directions for News think tank. And a previous *Wall Street Journal* story (Hymowitz, 1989) described the extra efforts a company like Corning had to make to *keep* blacks and women once they had been recruited. Efforts to improve women's standing occur elsewhere. Our federal government has ordered all departments and agencies to take initiatives to improve women's standing in their work forces (U.S. Department of Labor, 1985). Some observers view all of these efforts as fruitless, believing the only solution to be a complete deconstruction of the bureaucracy, a total redesign of our system (Rowbotham, 1987). Part of this re-structuring will undoubtedly come from the combined impact of women and other marginal groups, as they gain greater voice in the workplace.

The Integration of Work and Family

Integration and holism is another essential ingredient of the new approach. From the perspective of feminists -- and others fashioning this new view -- it is important old schisms are rejected. For instance, being concerned with the individual does not mean the work will not get done. It is *not* a matter of one or the other. Both can happen at once. Another implication is the notion that personal and professional lives need or ought not be totally separate from one another. One's personal life *ought* to be considered in making work arrangements -- without the penalties implied in recent discussions of the "mommy track" (Schwartz, 1989).

A propensity toward integration is also seen in women's views of professional accomplishments, how feelings about them are often colored by successes or failures in one's personal life (divorce, marriage, etc.). Men, psychologist Harriet Braiker reports, are more likely to separate their feelings about personal and professional successes and failures, while women tend to view all aspects of life as connected. Her discussions (Solomon, 1989) look at the two sexes' views of accomplishments, showing men can more easily separate personal and professional successes and failures, but women are more likely to see them as a gestalt.

Another issue that has received much attention is that of conflict between the demands of work and family. The new workplace must be flexible enough to allow workers to attend to both. As Ellen Bravo (1995) puts it in her new book that offers many practical suggestions about this issue:

Facing the job/family challenge will never be simple, but it can be livable and fulfilling. Anyone who wants to should be able to have a family *and* a job -- and to feel good about both of them. Getting to that point will require change in how businesses do business, how society values family, and how families share the work at home. (p. 7)

Again, these ideas have been around a long time, in many ways are now being re-articulated. Riva Poor was an early advocate for a four-day, forty-hour work week. Jane Mouton has passionately (and effectively) argued for a managerial strategy that simultaneously maximizes production *and* people-orientation. Christal Kammerer is a West German consultant who successfully introduced the concept of "gliding time" to many firms in her country, helping to solve a difficult problem with absenteeism (Stead, 1985).

A very concrete example of women negotiating this dilemma is seen in Betty Beach's (1989) book, *Integrating Work and Family Life*. She interviewed men and women who arranged to do their work in the home. For most of them, childbearing pressures motivated them to seek this alternative. One of her respondents (a man) talked about women's approach:

> Women have always had that tradition...they've been brought up having a thousand and one little jobs to do around the house every day...The time is very fluid for a woman. It's like the tide going in and out, whereas for man, it's like a drawbridge coming down and going up. (p. 19)

Both the men and women in this situation talk about how fluid their lives have become, how children and chores flow in and out of and intermingle with the work that they do. And how much they *enjoy* this, how they cherish their time with their children.

These families are in the throes of "redressing the work-family imbalance," (p. 3), according to Beach, a major responsibility of late twentieth century American families. As another of the men put it:

> I feel that your life should come first...your work should come second...it's so easy for work to become your entire life. (p. 91)

While this particular man was, admittedly, hierarchically ordering the various realms of his life (work and family) to some extent, the overall gist of his and others' remarks exemplified the *integration* they had achieved in their lives. For them, this often meant no longer giving work the clear priority often expected of those pursuing careers in the usual way. Homework had allowed them to step aside from that dictate, at least temporarily, and get back in touch with their own priorities. Many of them talked at length about their relief to be freed from workplace pressures.

> I can't stand to have somebody stand over my back and give me orders all the time...I can't hack that (p. 95).

> ...the atmosphere was terrible...It's certainly not pleasant punching a time clock. I've never worked in a clean mill. I've worked in plastics where you get the fumes. I actually would break out in hives (p. 95-96).

And the deadlines too -- [now] there is no late work or trying to get away early in the traffic. Also, I don't have to get all dressed up every day, which is something I don't like to do (p. 96).

Much of this former "hassle" time, they now devoted to their families.

Another example of women bringing more integration, a more holistic outlook to the workplace is seen in the only academic discipline ever created solely by women, that of Women's Studies. As Pearson, Shavlik, and Touchton (1989) show, the Women's Studies discipline is based upon a critiques of 1) knowledge fragmentation into discrete disciplines, 2) compartmentalizing lives into the professional and the personal, 3) separating ways of learning into cognitive and affective, and 4) juxtaposing a conflict between scholarship and politics. The way the discipline is structured -- and proceeds -- acts to integrate these traditionally separate pursuits. Again, holism and integration was seen in other voices appearing in earlier chapters, especially among the Native Americans.

A New Look by the Original Respondents

I also saw some of these same trends in the summer of 1990, when I briefly re-interviewed my original sample of managers in three workplace settings. (See Appendix I for more details.) When I asked them about problems facing the workplace, many similarities existed between men and women. The most common problem mentioned by both genders was the need for a well-trained workforce. They also stressed the need for technical and analytical training and bemoaned the lack of both traits in the younger workers currently joining their companies. One man expressed astonishment that these workers expected to become "instant yuppies." One woman noted that companies are often slow to provide the necessary training, and one man predicted companies will soon begin to do so.

Other problems mentioned by both sexes with some frequency were the increasingly fast pace of change, accompanying information explosion and the need to deliver quality. However, beyond these similarities, men and women responded very differently. Men mentioned problems arising within the workplace, such as the drive to provide quality service, the need to balance human needs with automation, the move to flatten management hierarchies, the need for customized training, the changing technological culture (from mainframes to PC's), the lack of company-worker loyalty in our increasingly mobile society.   One man talked about the need for daycare, saying "last year, in my department, I had nine ladies pregnant; seven came back, but we lost hours and days because of it." He felt flex-time and on-site daycare would help solve these problems, adding "too many quality workers with years of training are forced out of the work force" because of these problems.   Women mentioned some similar issues, such as the need for flexibility to accommodate family demands,   career   goals,   automation,   the   growing   trend   toward consolidation, efficiency, and accountability. However, they more often mentioned trends arising outside of the workplace that will have a tremendous impact nonetheless, such as environmental issues, the globalization of the economy, demographic shifts that will result in fewer young workers and new retirees, and the increasing number of minorities and women who will enter all levels of the workplace and change the culture radically. Only one man mentioned two of these issues.

With   these   respondents,   as   with   the   administrators   in   higher education, women seemed to be wrestling with broader ethical or moral issues. They were more immediately conscious of the fact corporations would   soon   have   to   take   some   responsibility   for   solving   our environmental problems.   Indeed, they seemed to feel corporations *ought* to do so.   They were thinking a great deal about both the desirability and the fact of a more diversified workforce and believed companies would have to move quickly to meet the needs of these new types of workers.   They were concerned about demographic shifts, particularly the growing number of retirees and shrinking numbers of new workers, and worried about the growing loss of talent and experience of the older workers. Again, women managers undoubtedly have a great deal to offer in seeking solutions to these problems. They may be much further along than these men, as a group, in pondering both the issues and the solutions.

Interestingly enough, women who were considering these broader issues were more likely to have been promoted. (Having been promoted did not predict these attitudes for men, since they never mentioned these broader issues.) This gives some support to my argument that women moving into higher managerial ranks will bring a new, more female-identified perspective with them. The women who received promotions were also more likely to have expressed a desire to move up in their first interview. (This made no difference for the men, since almost all of them expressed this desire.)

Men and women also differed in their assessment of how women would fit into the new workplace. Most respondents, both male and female, felt no real gains had been made; women, they felt, were still very disadvantaged. The men with this view were somewhat more likely to blame the women for their lack of progress saying "women downgrade each other." While two women did express concerns about women being "their own worst enemies" or "perpetuating the myth," and another stated that women cannot take time off for children and still expect to move through the hierarchy at the same rate men do, that was not the majority view.

The men more often talked about how well the women were doing in their companies (as proof of progress), while women more often talked about the contributions women could make. They stated women were "less vested" in the status quo, so were "more willing to dig in and make the necessary changes." One woman stated women were more entrepreneurial, "more...analysts...can see how to avoid [previous mistakes]...can see better the cause and effect of organizational process." Another woman claimed women were better able to cope with the frustrations of solving today's problems, and another felt women would bring more nurturing into the workplace. One woman talked about how much she liked the "peaceful...wonderful...feminist workspace" she had found. One man talked about women's strengths for management, saying he thought women had "more stamina to handle today's problems." We see in all of these data sets, studies, and theories a belief that women, as a group, do have much to contribute to the workplace by means of transforming it. By offering a more holistic, co-operative, participative approach, women possess many of the qualities companies are now spending millions to instill in their (mostly male) managers.

Of course, I am not implying all women are exactly like the more generalized description I have been constructing throughout this book -- or that no men possess any of these qualities. I do believe, however, these tendencies exist between men and women and that excluded groups have much to offer by means of improving and/or radically changing all of our institutions.

I also do not mean to imply women have no problems to overcome, that all they do is altruistic, moral, and virtuous. Of course, such is not the case. There are several much discussed problems, among them women's supposed tendency to sabotage one another (Madden, 1987; Briles, 1987). Despite arguments of authors like Madden and Briles that women are their own worst enemies, evidence mounts that in fact women are quite willing to support each other, helping to boost careers whenever possible. Such evidence appears in recent articles about women in business and nursing (Ball, 1989; Watts, 1989), in broadcast television (Conant, 1990), in academia (Pheterson, 1988), and in managerial jobs (Statham, 1987b), hence bolstering the claim women prefer a more co-operative, person-centered style that fosters integration and allows for individual initiative. The next chapter will trace something of the process whereby these changes may become more widespread in the workplace. In the meantime, there are some negative misunderstandings to counter.

Further Evidence of Difference

In the last chapter, we saw the importance of placing approaches to management or leadership in the context of the cultural imperatives operating for those interviewed. This is also important for women, to see their approaches at work in the context of their more overall life experiences. I have admittedly taken a particular view in my analysis. I recognize the importance of both capitalism and patriarchy in shaping our current social life (at least in the Western or Euro-centric world), although at times I may emphasize the importance of patriarchy more. Afterall, the patriarchal system has survived, maybe even helped to shape, a succession of economic and social orders, ranging from nomadic life through domestication, feudalism, industrialization and capitalism, and into our post-industrial world.

I am anxious to see the woman's agency; she is not merely a passive pawn of social forces. As Hunt (1984) puts it, the woman is an active participant in the process of social construction of gender. A major component of the approach women seem to be taking is that of concern with the relationship, a tendency noted previously in a multitude of literatures that discuss woman's commitment to "the other." Simone de Beauvoir (1952) presented one of the earliest articulations of this concept, and Jean Baker Miller (1976) has used it to note -- from her clinical practice -- that men tend to "center around themselves, women around 'the other'" (p. 69). Women's identity has traditionally come largely from relations to others. Small wonder, then, women are so concerned with nurturing their relationships, as Gilligan indicated in her ground-breaking research on moral development published in her book *In A Different Voice* (1992). She found men tend to perceive moral dilemmas in terms of abstract moral principles and use moral calculus to derive rational solutions. In contrast, women use a more inclusive, integrated approach, employing a very different set of criteria, one that emphasizes care and connection as the highest order of functioning rather than autonomy and abstract principles, emphasizing the overriding importance of the relationship. In this sense, women might be less likely to separate their personal relations from autonomous principles; rather, they see each as the context for the other. Simply put, Gilligan argues women employ a "logic of care."

It should come as no surprise, then, that women have developed finely tuned interpersonal skills. In fact, these traits appear quite early; even as infants, females are much more aware of others' cues (Brothers, 1982) and are more responsive to these cues than males (Chodorow, 1978). While Gilligan's thesis -- there is a particularly female approach to moral development -- has generated a great deal of controversy, many other writers have since expanded upon her ideas, applying them to other areas, broadening her ideas to include connection or integration more generally. A notable example of this is a book by Belenky, Clinchy, Goldberger, and Tarule, (1986) called *Women's Ways of Knowing*, a study of the development of intellectual functioning. Here, again, the authors find women most comfortable in learning situations that allow them to integrate past experiences with the present, thus taking a more holistic view of their total life situation. They point to many ways our current system of higher education discourages this, putting women at a disadvantage. For example, in science -- and in many social sciences -- we are explicitly told to discount our past experiences, that error will be introduced into the learning process if personal experiences are considered. As in Gilligan's work, an alternative developmental sequence for intellectual development is discovered by these authors. Before their study, sequences derived from studies of men had been assumed to apply to both sexes. Previously, it was thought that higher orders of learning involved the ability toward abstraction, taking things out of context. This was not the highest level of intellectual functioning for the women; context remained quite important.

Lillian Rubin, (1983) in her studies of couples in intimate relationships, also found women emphasized connection and men autonomy. These couples found it difficult to be intimate, since they had such different perspectives of the relationship and expectations of each other. Gardner (1981) has observed differences among modern music composers, where women tend to compose music using a cyclical, as opposed to linear, form. She argues that the [masculine] linear form is more point-centered and tends to move onward, never returning, while the [feminine] cyclical form is more integrated (returning) and expansive. Cheatham and Powell (1986) report that women community organizers take a more personal approach, integrating their work with their personal lives in both the flow of their work and in the spaces where they do their work. They also report that women architects design more integrated, less isolated space. Loden (1985) and Shakeshaft (1987) report that women managers and administrators use a more holistic approach, where personal and professional lives are less segregated and workers are seen more in the context of their total life situation. As a result, women administrators deal with workers and subordinates more holistically.

We see such trends in other areas as well. Soviet fashion designers argue for the woman's newly found [in their country] "right to be different," to exemplify the "woman's approach" in their lives (Kunitsina, 1988). Anscombe (1985) reports women artists have contributed a unique perspective, more often integrating their work with family activities. A very important woman painter of the sixteenth century, Sofnisba Anguissola, newly "discovered", is said to have painted portraits in more intimate ways than her contemporaries and teachers (Campi, Michelangelo, Gatti), making less of a distinction between everyday life and art (Perlingieri, 1988). Contemporary artist, Helen Frankenthaler, is said to have marvelously integrated her personal and professional life (Wallach, 1989).

Contemporary women novelists are said to produce novels along similar lines. Two notable recent examples are *And Ladies of the Club*...by Helen Santmyer Hoover (1982), an historical novel of epic proportion, where real life experiences are skillfully blended with known occurrences to give one the flavor of how life was actually lived during the post-Civil War period (the author intimates that she *intended* to write an epic novel from a woman's perspective) and Marge Piercy's *Gone to Soldiers* (1987), about which the *New York Times Book Review* has said:

> In many male war novels character development is sacrificed; the "woman's touch" here is excellent. The battle front is not all blood and guts. There is also the grief of separation from family and the mitigating solace of friendship.

Again, the integration of the personal with the historical is evident. *MS Magazine* said the book is "...refreshing in its transformation of a genre associated mostly with men into a form that treats men and women equally." And *The Village Voice* said the novel "...moves as easily from battlefield to home front as it does from female to male perspective." All in all, women are said to take a more complete and integrated view of a situation, to see many sides, particularly those having to do with relationships.

Women historians' work is sometimes described along similar lines. Bonnie Anderson and Jane Zinsser (1988) have recently published a book called *A History of Their Own* that, according to *Ms Magazine* (Wartik, 1988), "makes familiar landmarks and heroes...mere footnotes to a new vision of history -- one told from a woman's-eye view." The telling focuses on "place and function" rather than "dates and events," showing us life as it was actually lived by women throughout the ages. Considering woman's approach in general, a quote by May Sarton in *A Woman's Notebook* perhaps says it best, "Women's work always tends toward wholeness."

Feminist legal scholars argue for legal criteria that emphasize fairness and caring. In this system, courts would focus on the intent, not the letter of contracts, and reward those who tried to be fair. "Caring" judgements would require individuals to provide care to their victims (*Business Ethics*, 1992). And Penrose (1987) reports that women humanized the social environment in The Netherlands after the government ordered all ministries to integrate women's concerns about family, discrimination, and so on into their missions. In political polling, it has been clear that women, as a group, often share certain political views having to do with concern and caring for others. This phenomenon is sometimes referred to as "the gender gap" by the news media. (See one example, Thom in *MS*, 1988).

Some argue women, as outsiders, bring to our social life different conceptions of power relationships and, so, have enormous potential to transform our system. Helen Hughes in a *Chicago Tribune* article (1988) talked about women's ability to integrate right and left brain functioning. As she put it:

> ...one day one of my students stood and said: "Oh, I know why that is --
> because women always have to hold the baby with one hand while they
> stir the pot with the other hand" -- meaning you've got to use everything.
> You've got to use both sides [of the brain] all the time. I liked that.

She has made these same arguments in *The Creative Woman*, a magazine she publishes.

Anne Wilson Schaef, in her 1981 book *Women's Reality*, expands upon these notions. She too argues women have a unique perspective on the world, particularly after breaking free of the reactive system of behavior many women adopt to deal with a hostile world. As she has observed through years of therapy with both sexes, the emerging Female System involves synthesizing, constantly growing and changing, delights in paradox, seeing differences as providing growth opportunities, whereas the White Male System involves analyzing, defining, breaking the whole into parts, seeing difference as a threat, fearing paradox, favoring dualism and hierarchy. As Lillian Rubin noted among couples, these very different stances make it difficult for men and women to interact successfully.

Erica Jong (1988) has argued in today's world, women bring the "true counterculture," the "new paradigm" into existence, in our valuing of relationships more than things. She believes the experience of childbirth is "radicalizing," and has given us this "counter culture".

Dallas Cullen (1992) has argued how women's potential has been severely undermined by society's pervasive attempts to insist that women behave like men when they cross over into "the male universe." She looks particularly at the self-actualization literature, focusing on the research done by Maslow. She argues that his approach -- asking women in that historical period the types of questions he asked about sexuality, for example -- was degrading to the women involved. That Betty Friedan uncritically accepted Malsow's resulting "discovery" that men and women had similar self-actualization needs, she further argues, has led to an ideology of valuing only those women who act like men.

Examples of women actively attempting to modify aspects of society, to build an alternative reality abound, not only in the works I have already discussed, but other places as well. A recent copy of Co-op America's quarterly publication *Building Economic Alternatives* includes a directory of all member organizations. *Many* of these organizations are women-owned. One in particular caught my eye; an organization called "Womanswork" which produces "quality women's work gloves, work clothes, and accessories" and dedicates itself to "strong women building a gentle world."

Some of these same tendencies are seen in the field of science as well. Arditti (1985) has suggested that science in a feminist society would be life-affirming, not destructive, as many argue our science/technology system has tended to be. Dill (1985) also argues that feminist theory stands for a society in which individuals do not have to limit others' options to achieve their own. Christie Farmham Pope (1988) also forecasts that the feminist future will include -- celebrate -- diversity of all kinds. Pyum (1969) and Oakley (1976) have urged us to re-evaluate such feminine contributions as the value of housework and childcare.

Another idea relevant here is the notion women would, if left to our own devices, create a more humane, less warlike society and world, an idea being debated, fiercely. The notion that women might, if given a voice in society, put an end to war was taken up by Virginia Woolf (1938) in *Three Guineas*. She quotes men of her time who thought:

> ...women might win the vote which...would enable them to make war a thing of the past. The vote is won...but war is very far from being a thing of the past (p. 42).

However, Woolf saw women standing as "outsiders" to professions, indeed to all of society, committed to:

> ...obtain full knowledge of professional practices, and to reveal any instance of tyranny or abuse in their professions. And they would bind themselves not to continue to make money in any profession, but to cease all competition and to practice their profession experimentally, in the interest of research and for love of the work itself, when they had earned enough to live upon (p. 112).

She also called upon these "outsiders" to refrain from supporting any activity that contributed to war. In this sense, she saw (hoped) women would, as they became more prominent in the work world, bring about major social transformation.

Anderson and Zinsser (1988) note the long history women have had in contributing to socialist and collective endeavors and to nonviolent philosophy. They see Woolf as critical in this regard, particularly *Three Guineas*. They also quote Helena Swanwick, who published *The Roots of War* the same year Woolf published *Three Guineas*. Swanwick said:

> Women do, I believe, hate war more fervently than men and this is not because they are better than men, or wiser, but because war hits them much harder and has very little to offer in return (p. 405).

Here again, women's outsider status is thought to impart a particular, group perspective.

Others have made explicit ties between feminism and nonviolence. A pamphlet published by the War Resisters' League (Feminism and Nonviolence Study Group, 1983) asserts that "sexual divisions in society operate to support and perpetuate wars" (p. 9). In their view, women have become part of the "war machine," raising sons to participate. And in this sense, women have a special role to play in undoing this process because of our role in nurturing and childrearing. The War Resisters' League believes nonviolence will come to our society only after drastic re-socialization. They do not view women as "true guardians of life on earth," but as individuals damaged by the current system (along with men) and capable of organizing to make a difference.

Others believe women do have a special vision to offer. Again, the mothering angle is crucial. For example, Sara Ruddick (1989) believes mothers raise children to be nonviolent, but that something else happens to young boys along the way. Mothers, she argues, focus on how to solve problems in peaceful ways. She further argues that mothers plus feminists plus women in resistance present "an imaginative collective" that can transform our world.

Some women have begun the work of waging peace. Ruth Sivard publishes a masterful book every year, *Worldwide Military and Social Expenditures*, exposing the domestic to military spending ratios of nations across the world, in the words of author Deborah Baldwin (1990), "how nations sacrifice human health and welfare in order to arm themselves for war" (p. 34). She works from her own home, using background and contacts made from long years of working for the U.S. State Department in Washington, D.C. Rebecca Christman (1988), a bright, newly trained defense contractor engineer, opted instead for a career in medical research, saying:

> I see conventional nuclear defense projects as making nuclear war inevitable. Consequently, I feel I should not contribute my time and skills to the effort. My opposition to nuclear proliferation is intuitive, not rational (p. 152).

In making her decision, she presented a dilemma to others, such as those with the federal government and private industry who sought to hire her, possibly raising their consciousness, as well.

Jacqueline Haessly (1988) founded Milwaukee Peace Education Resource Center and Peacemaking Associates. Of her programs aimed at children she says:

> We can assist [peace education] by...address[ing] not only the dilemma of the nuclear threat but also enable students to develop as responsible men and women, able to appreciate and affirm the rich diversity of peoples and cultures who share space with us on Planet Earth...Thus the creative imaginations of our children...could be redirected toward solving problems that...include access to adequate food, shelter, education, health care, arts, recreation...(p. 4).

Daniella Gioseffi (1988) has put together an anthology that gives an international voice to women's outcry against war. And Cheatham and Powell (1986), in their 30,000 mile trip through Canada and the United States, found countless women acting for peace, teaching peace, waging peace, and imaging peace. Consider the open ended fast begun by eleven German, Spanish, French, Japanese, and United States women on August 6, 1983. They fasted for forty days, some of them to dangerous physical conditions. Said one of them:

> We have to take peace as seriously as they make war...We've got to put our lives on the line, take some risks...We can't have business as usual...The arms race is the most dangerous symptom of a racist country. The arms race is the most evil manifestation of the patriarchy (p. 209).

Many studies have shown that women prefer to solve problems using a participatory rather than a hierarchical model (Meeker and Weitzel-O'Neill, 1977). This follows directly from women's tendency toward personalizing work relationships (Kanter, 1977; Nickeles and Ashcraft, 1980) and inclusion of others (Gilligan, 1982; Spretnak, 1982). Also motivations have different weight. Women do work for money but are less enthusiastic about the motive of power (even women in positions of power -- Nickeles and Ashcraft, 1980; Hennig and Jardim, 1977), more often saying they are motivated by the opportunity for self-actualization or by the intrinsically rewarding nature of their jobs (Nickles and Ashcraft, 1980; Kanter, 1977; Hennig and Jardim, 1977).

Assuming holistic approaches are a positive aspect to bring to the workplace, some previously negative conclusions drawn about women as a group can be turned around. For example, in psychological and problem solving tests, men have been found to more easily "break set," to derive novel solutions not dependent upon the context in which the original information is presented. This finding, the consistency of which has been called into question by Maccoby and Jacklin (1979), has been used in a negative way against women, used to support beliefs that women are less creative, more dependent, and afraid to take risks. Seen from the viewpoint of integration, however, it has more positive connotations. Perhaps women see more clearly how elements in a situation *are* related, appreciating the strengths of these connections. If so, women may be better at capitalizing upon existing strengths in given situations. Also, it is possible the questions asked in the testing situations were gender-biased. Assuming the ability to "pull a situation apart" is the highest order of functioning may have resulted in male-biased tests.

Take also the greater permeability of the boundaries between work and family that women often experience. In general, their work activity is more easily interrupted by their family involvements on both a day-to-day *and* more long-term basis than men's work activity (Pleck, 1977). Some researchers have bemoaned this tendency and encouraged women to be "more like men" in the labor force (Sandell and Shapiro, 1978; Polackek, 1979), to work more continuously and restrict their family's interference in their work lives. Others have urged instead that work patterns become more flexible so that both men and women may nurture their family relationships (Barrett, 1979). Women are more likely to experience this conflict partly because they view their lives more holistically, without neat compartments that barely touch one another. They are not as willing as men to keep one sphere out of mind while concentrating on another. And their approach is placing pressure on our work institutions to change, to become more flexible, in many of the same ways urged by those advocating change in worker/manager relations. Career theory (cf. Sekaran and Hall, 1989) suggests solutions to the "asynchronisms" in career and organizational progressions experienced by working women -- *and* their husbands -- that create systematic pressures on organizations to change. So, rather than seeking ways to allow women to divest themselves from family involvements, perhaps we need to rebuild our public (formerly men's) sphere so this holistic approach can be perpetuated by women and taken up by men. This is certainly the hope of those who are beginning to ask, as women move further from their traditional roles, "If women don't do the nurturing, who will?"

Concluding Comments

The last several pages present ideas and evidence that many in our society find discomforting. Even ardent feminists are nervous about the "essentialism" potentially inherent in any formulation of women's "difference," as a group. I believe the widespread resistance to this notion has prevented us from moving forward as quickly as we might with needed transformations. Seeing these views as also prevalent among other marginal groups shows a way around the essentialism bind in that it is not only women who have these views. They seem typical among different types of marginal groups. (Although, again, not *all* members of these groups have these views.) Perhaps looking across all of these groups also points the way to fruitful avenues of coalition-building between the groups involved.

Chapter 11

How Change Happens

In the last chapter, we explored the content of the new paradigm that may be dawning, the exact perspective the marginal voices we have heard are putting forth. In this chapter, we consider *how* such change may occur. Recall the notion I began with in Chapter 1, that change occurs in part through cycles of feedback loops, constantly reintegrating elements from the old reality. In the social realm, I believe paradigms shift through a series of sudden spurts, interspersed with periods of rethinking the old in terms of the new, and vice versa. Because of this process, new ideas may ultimately have a revolutionary impact on our social processes, despite apparent short-term setbacks. The force of the new ideas may simply be too great for resisting forces to contain. If ideas truly are important forces for change, then a first indicator of change may well be the massive appearance of a new set of ideas.

Certainly, aspects of the new paradigm that seem to be growing -- notions of greater equality, connection, and participation -- can be seen in many different areas. Consider a few of the many different, sometimes surprising, places they appear. For example, Shirley Maclaine in one of her books, *Dancing in the Light* (1985), claims to have been highly influenced by the new developments in physics, though she does not specifically mention Capra. She is especially interested in the idea all living matter has consciousness, binding all creatures and matter tightly together. Greenpeace literature abounds with references to the new paradigm, to the coming together of many different social movements based upon the shift from a mechanistic to a holistic world view. The Realistic Living Press has published several pieces detailing the basic principles of this new world view, illustrated in a 1988 essay by Gene Marshall called *Repair or Replacement? An Essay on Ecological Politics*. Here, many of the ideas about ecological preservation espoused by organizations like Greenpeace are reiterated. Judi Marshall in a 1984 book *Women Managers: Travellers in a Male World* published by John Wiley credits Capra with helping to develop a new world view favorable to women. This, she argues, is inherent in the points he makes about domination and control, his strong argument for greater equality and participation. Elizabeth Dodson Gray in a 1982 book called *Patriarchy as a Conceptual Trap* makes similar points, discussing Capra specifically.   Charlene Spretnak (1986), speaking from a cultural and eco-feminist perspective at a conference organized by Capra for the Elmwood Institute he established, talks of the need to see more clearly our connection with nature.   If we continue to believe we control nature, rather than coming to see ourselves as *part* of nature, she says that we will ultimately destroy ourselves.

From this perspective, re-education, modifying consciousness, is essential for bringing about the needed changes. Modern society has many tactics to prevent us from acquiring this new vision. Television and advertising entice us to strive for "the good life," as defined by the old order, with no concern for the implications of our desires -- their impact on scarce resources or the economically poorer segments of our society or the world. Government and big business have attempted to control the media to put forth a certain view of reality, making us fearful of radical change and almost resigned to the specter of chemical, nuclear, or another environmental catastrophy. In the writings discussed above, by contrast, a sense of hope is seen, a belief in the ability of the individual to reassert control over his or her life, a sense of dormant agency. And specific suggestions are emerging for how we might re-educate ourselves (Rizzo and Mendez, 1990).

Thus, part of the paradigm shift argued to be occurring involves an economic and social order that will ultimately differ radically from that currently existing. Both capitalism and patriarchy, as predominant trends in our economic and social institutions, respectively, are very likely to be transformed, since both systems tend toward exploitation.

Increasingly, social observers see these two systems as linked, both acting to give the few privileged their place and both needing to be addressed for true social change to occur. I am arguing in a quasi-Marxian fashion, that these systems may actually contain the seeds of their own destruction, perhaps more gradual and from different means than Marx had envisioned.

The old order that shows signs of impending demise has posed many problems for individuals attempting to lead full and satisfying lives. As we have seen, workers without voice in what happens in their work setting experience frustration, hardship, and eventually, alienation. The results of this are not only unhappy workers but also poor work performances. These structures must be changed, then, for the good of all of us, not just for the sake of workers.

The new paradigm I see dawning involves greater participation, equality, and dignity for all. Marjorie Kelly writes often about "the turning point between the old ethic and the new." For her, the crux of this change is:

> ...that democratic capitalism is spreading...When the world lived in...a monarchy...[the old ethic]...made perfect sense...What is dawning now in our society is a realization...that financial prosperity and well-being...must be rights...open to all. (1993b, 7)

She talked about an *INC.* cover story proclaiming "the old Us/Them style of management no longer works" and a *Business Week's* report about the coming paradigm shift from autocratic to inspirational leadership styles that value teamwork over individualism (Kelly, 1992b).

In the same magazine, *Business Ethics*, Anita Roddick, founder of The Body Shop, says:

> There's a change of mind taking place in the modern world. It's reflected in many social movements that have to do with alternative values, equality of relationship, cooperation, caring and nurturing, social justice, human ecology, and personal values. The only area that has missed out are two institutions -- the political...the business institution...This is where capitalism is moving. It's got to be kinder and gentler, it's got to take ownership, it's got to be protective of the planet...it has to allow people to have more input into the process of running their job...We need more equitable distribution of wealth; people need to have ownership of their companies...I also think the Third World will demand a different economic structure...I go around the world...I meet people who are

thinking exactly the same thing...We're never connected...it's instinctive knowledge. We all have [the] sense, this is the right way of doing it. (1992, 28)

What Roddick is espousing here is the new paradigm approach many others have written about. Dispersing wealth and ownership so widely is really not capitalism as we know it. Yet, notice how she still refers to something so drastically different from what we have had these last several centuries as "capitalism." Naming the new seems almost as difficult as conceptualizing it. Even those working for change cannot simply drop all attachments to the current order. It at least provides a frame of reference.

When very new developments seem to suddenly burst upon the scene, as in the recent demise of the Soviet Union and the Eastern European block, we do not always grasp the full implications. Politically, this change has been heralded as a sign that the West has won the Cold War, that capitalism has triumphed. Some writers, however, are cautioning that it may, in fact, be a signal that a much deeper transformation is in process. Drucker, in his book *Post-Capitalist Society* (1993) notes that the collapse of the communist states has signaled the beginning of a new era, but that the same forces are also making capitalism obsolete -- the entire order will be transformed. Lane Kirkland, president of the AFL-CIO, agrees:

> It is a myth that the collapse of communism is the victory of capitalism...Both...have something elemental in common. Both can atomize society...Both can be lethal to the institutions of civil society...Free markets...have their own severe limitations. They do not, unless compelled, discern the difference between employment and exploitation. (1992, 21)

Burawoy and Lukacs (1992) demonstrate convincingly both systems suffer from similar defects of industrialism, particularly increasing exploitation of workers.

As we move toward widespread change or paradigm shift, we do not grasp all of the pieces simultaneously, and we only grasp individual pieces gradually. This is, in fact, a very complex process involving many aspects of our society -- gender relations, relations at work, race relations, family forms, etc. We tend to see these issues as segmented and to work on them in isolation from the others, not seeing the total picture. Sometimes, we do not see the complete picture even within separate issues.

Appreciating and incorporating any of these new approaches and perspectives is resisted strongly by certain segments of society. Judi Marshall (1992) describes reactions to William Torbert's *The Power of Balance: Transforming Self, Society, and Scientific Inquiry* (1991) in which he takes up the feminist challenge to incorporate the personal/private into the professional/public. He has written a book about transforming leadership that makes heavy use of his own personal experiences. Marshall admits to feeling "embarrassed...yet intrigued" (p. 364) by his openness and emphasizes that Donald Schon, in the forward to the book, says he finds the confessional quality of the book disconcerting. He is uneasy Torbert does not accept the conventional boundaries between the personal and professional.

Here again, even those supportive of "the new order" find themselves resisting or uncomfortable with certain aspects of it, when actually confronted. Incorporating the sensibilities of the excluded groups (such as women) will not immediately gain wide acceptance -- sometimes even among certain segments of those groups themselves who have strongly internalized the prevailing ("old") paradigm. This is seen in looking at how companies incorporate what might be a unique approach among women. It is increasingly true gender role ideology is coming to support women's efforts in managerial positions, and management philosophy accepts major elements of their style. However, as these paradigms shift, they do not necessarily do so uniformly throughout society. Some industries change more quickly, while others lag; some individuals adopt new attitudes and outlooks more readily than others. Just as new technology is not instantly embraced by all, neither are new ideas. While the merging of these trends has been accompanied by marked increases of women managers in general (U.S. Bureau of the Census, 1985), in high tech, food, and metal industries (Simpson, 1984), in factory management (Baron, Bielby and Davis-Blake, 1986), and in small business ownership (WEAL Report, 1984), much controversy exists about this different approach to management.

In spite of this resistance, ideas supporting the worker participation model are spreading rapidly. Eugene Carlson in *The Wall Street Journal* discusses a book by Jay Hall (1980) which argues problems in the workplace are caused by bosses who believe "people don't want to work anymore" and "it's hard to get good help these days." Hall is reported to conclude that 95% of all companies hold these [*Theory X*] attitudes toward their workers. This information is summarized under the bold headline "Workers Aren't the Problem, Theorist Asserts; Bosses Are." Indeed, Hall does stress the need for worker participation and outlines certain conditions that will promote it, including factors that encourage the expression of creativity and commitment to work and the organization.

INC. featured an interview with Jack Stack, who negotiated a leveraged buyout from International Harvester in 1985. The company's progress, seen as a great "turnaround" by others in the business, was accredited largely to his management style. His employees own most of the stock and participate in what he calls "The Great Game of Business." He involves them in the process of helping the company be profitable, giving them all of the information he has and the responsibility for taking action (*INC.*, 1989). This is certainly a company run with the new paradigm approach -- empowerment of workers, flattened hierarchy, individual responsibility. These new ideas seem to be spreading.

The growing prevalance of these ideas is also evident in popular sources aimed specifically at women. For example, in *Working Woman* magazine, women managers are counseled to remember subordinates' feelings will always enter in and so must be considered (Quick, 1982), to develop mutual commitment with workers when delegating (Swindall, 1985), to stay in touch but not reduce subordinates' authority (Sheppard, 1985), to build teams of subordinates who are jointly responsible (Bradford and Cohen, 1984), and to show consideration for their secretaries (Winston, 1986). In *The Executive Female*, a workshop at the sponsoring organization's annual meetings on traditional vs. nontraditional leaders reflects Kanter's segmentalist vs. integrative classification for organizations almost exactly. (Traditional leaders resist, seek status, resent, push, direct, defend, are static, inconsistent, rigid, while nontraditional leaders confront, reassure, lead, expect, offer, talk quality, express concern, seek integrity, are accountable -- Young, 1984). Also in this magazine, women are encouraged to delegate decision-making (Lindo, 1986) and listen, explain, clarify when giving criticism (Port, 1986).

A newsletter for administrators in higher education called *The Administrator* contains many of the same exhortations. The adaptive organization is said to facilitate the replacement of "authority-wielding [work] crews --[Now] employees work through parallel communication links instead of burdensome chains of command." Work commitment is enhanced if 1) everyone has a sense of ownership, 2) teamwork is the norm, 3) rewards are shared, 4) information is two-way, 5) challenges to the status quo are seen as the norm, 6) learning is emphasized (December 29, 1986). Managers are encouraged to adopt a coaching style, with no implied threats or invasion of privacy (November 9, 1987), recognize subordinates' personal needs (October 12, 1987), learn to communicate with them "the way they want to be communicated with" (June 22, 1986). Managers encounter problems when they show callousness toward others, fail to keep their promises (November 9, 1987), try to instill threats in subordinates through abrasive behaviors (June 22, 1986), or fail to trust the staff and view themselves as irreplaceable (January 8, 1990). Managers are encouraged to 1) identify tasks, 2) hire or appoint the right people, 3) make sure they have authority, 4) set mutually agreed deadlines, 5) establish a monitoring process, 6) communicate confidence, 7) allow people to accomplish tasks as they see fit and make mistakes, 8) reward completed work effectively (March 28, 1988). Subordinates report they are more satisfied when their managers exercise personal authority instead of some pre-determined kind (November 11, 1989). Using Kuhn's notion of paradigm shift, the newsletter argues that linear thinking which has resulted in highly specialized and fragmented tasks and analytical managers who measured their worth by power over staff and outcomes, is now succumbing to a new view that the world is dynamic, complex, diverse, and constantly in flux (July 9, 1990).

Even in academia, where new, popular ideas are often slower to emerge in research reports, several studies in major sociology journals flow from this new perspective on management. Carroll and Huo (1986) report that the task environment of the organization directly affects work performance, something Fiedlar had proposed years before. Ridgeway and Johnson found the existence of a status hierarchy reduced the negative emotions expressed in a work group, at the expense of lower status workers. "The hierarchy makes [them] the target of the bulk of task behaviors that elicit negative emotions ...[and]...also constrains them to turn their frustrations against themselves..."(1990, 1209). Hence, they argue, hierarchy can be counter-productive. Fligstein (1987) reports many of those involved with American business are dissatisfied that too much attention is paid to short-run (i.e., quarterly) profits and not enough is being paid to longer-term manufacturing quality. Product and personal integrity is apparently becoming more important than short-run gains. Hirsch (1986) reports contemporary hostile take-overs are generally conducted to permit a loss with dignity. Interpersonal finessing becomes critical for those wanting longevity in the higher echelons of corporate America. Even in China, where management as we know it is a fairly new endeavor, the emphasis is on long-term planning and managerial competence (So, 1986).

In sum, these popular and academic sources show the spread in acceptance of the new management strategies -- incorporating elements of *Theory Y*, contingency theory, the integrationist perspective -- described in Kanter's *Change Masters* and popularized in Blanchard and Lorber's *One Minute Manager*, among many other sources. As Leavitt and Lipman-Blumen have argued, the new paradigm involves a shift from a *direct* (get-it-done, task oriented, competitive) to a more *relational* (sense of belonging, help others succeed, form intervening relationships with coworkers) style.

Changing Belief Systems

Much of what was true about and is now changing in the old order also concerns the relationship between male and female. As with the process of paradigm change in science, as Kuhn described it, the recognition that something was wrong or amiss with the old order simmered for awhile on our political backburners. Friedan (1963) named this feeling in her book *The Feminine Mystique*. Yet, just as Kuhn describes the process of change, in much of society, these problems were not at first given real credence. Nor were they seen as connected to other developing problems, such as pressures for civil rights or worker rights, when in fact the impetus for such changes was occurring on the global level. As stated in Chapter 2, *The Feminine Mystique*, was seen as the first major recognition in our own era that "something was wrong" for women. Others, such as Malcolm X's autobiography, signaled the urgency of other issues. All of these early formulations were followed by several other very influential books and magazines that made us conscious of our taken-for-granted reality about gender or race. In all of these cases, a greater understanding of discrimination follows, as taken-for-granted, "natural" realities are challenged.

Because of the new interests and awareness, we, as a society, are in the process of remaking our very basic beliefs about the nature of human life, a paradigm shift. Past revolutions within the patriarchal order have targeted race and class oppression. These include the French, American and Russian Revolutions, the Ghandi-led Indian uprising, and the American Revolution and Civil Rights Movements, among many others. They have certainly led to the current revolution involving gender -- in some ways quite directly. For example, many of today's feminists began their social criticism as members of groups opposed to the Vietnam War and/or racial inequality. Later, they came to see the centrality of gender oppression in their lives, as they experienced it even in these supposedly radical groups. This also happened during the anti-slavery movement that led to the Civil War. From that experience grew suffrage sentiments. Taken together, attempts to correct the inequality inherent in the current predominant world view will require a major revision of our philosophy of life.

In all of these areas the struggle exists over integrating our insights into mainstream thought. This is an issue with which Kuhn has not explicitly dealt. How does paradigm shift occur when the impetus, the new reality which does not fit into the old perspective, comes from marginalized groups? When these insights spring from gender, race, and class oppression?

The tendency to see the new perspective as footnotes or unimportant deviations results in attempts to isolate the view-holders or viewpoint. This has certainly been the case in the academy. Major efforts are required to integrate woman-centered, feminist, race, and class analyses into traditional disciplines and curriculum. (See the report of the NEH-funded project attempting to do this by Aiken et. al., 1988.) Token men and women are promoted to positions of power, those who uphold the old paradigm. Some groups resist the change strenuously (cf. D'Souza, 1991).

In time, however, I believe even these strategies will prove insufficient to prevent change from occurring. As Beauvoir was, I remain hopeful, despite the fact that full change has not yet occurred. It seems that things have moved too far from the old order to ever go back to that place again. As T.R. Young (1988) has put it, "History is on the side of workers, women, and the Third World." As we wait here in the in-between phase, with our anxieties and occasional attempts at reversal, it is as if we are suspended, not knowing where the world is heading. I wonder if this is not how social change has always felt -- scary and painful while also challenging and exciting.

The view I am taking here, that fundamental change is occurring, that the old order is declining, is certainly one open to debate. There are sociologists and other social scientists who would argue things are, in fact, not changing very much at all, that marginal groups are simply being prepared to play a different type of subservient role in society. While I recognize (and worry about) this possibility, I essentially take Beauvoir's view, that we are simply too far along the road to not change. If we accept Kuhn's theory of change, we cannot expect to see all of the ramifications immediately. There will be a great deal of lagging behind and resistance and attempting to force the new reality into the old among various aspects of society with only very few instances of obvious, fundamental change, for much of the time. Yet, it is my belief the future is being created now, from the interaction of those men and women working under new conditions. And if we look closely enough at their lives, we may see glimpses of the future. As a result, a total reorganization may occur as, for example, a history curriculum built on critical events in the lives of African-Americans world-wide, not primarily on wars organized and pursued by the dominant group, or workplace processes truly based on the concepts of individual competence, dignity, and autonomy. Clemens (1993) argues such change will occur when material is presented to potentially sympathetic actors in terms roughly familiar to them.

Moving Beyond Hostility

Some of my data about interactions between men and women may suggest some general patterns about how we move beyond the intergroup tensions involved in our current phase. This may occur in stages, since women's approaches may generate a great deal of hostility among men in the early stages of the process. Such seemed to be the case among the managers I spoke with. In my original interviews, a woman manager was one of the strongest proponents of the person-invested approach used by most of the women. She said:

> I'm more people-oriented...I delegate and make them [subordinates] very accountable for what they're doing, but I guess the people side of me says

make sure you see them once in a while, know what they're doing...I
meet weekly with them to be sure...their objectives are being met...I go
and visit the different departments; I talk to people individually...their
perception of the staff and people is important. If they perceive us as
being on the top floor and no one caring, I don't want that. On the other
hand, you could visit daily and create problems.

A male manager who had previously worked for her (she was still a
level above him in the hierarchy) said about her:

She doesn't delegate enough...she stays too much involved in the nitty
gritty of the work. She doesn't have confidence in the people working
for her.

He felt she was "looking over his shoulder," as he *expected* complete
autonomy from his supervisor (*his* management model) and so,
interpreted her style as lack of confidence in him. This man was one
the clearest examples of the image-engrossed style discussed in Chapter
3, using many self-aggrandizing images in his description of his job.

What is the future of male/female interactions in the workplace?
Are we deadlocked in a situation where those using the old model
continue to resist the insights of those using the new? Or will women's
style in particular come to be incorporated into how we normally
proceed? Some of my data hinted at a mechanism that might facilitate
this: mentoring.

Mentoring and Change

Mentoring is one way men can show explicit support for the women
attempting to break into the managerial ranks. And it was true some
men supported women managers in this way, even if they did not
totally endorse their style. A few of the men, whether consciously or
not, seemed to actually change their own style when they were
interacting with female subordinates, to incorporate more of the people
orientation women utilized. The men who did this in the original
interview study were cited as mentors by the women managers who
worked for them.

In that study, both men and women discussed mentors. Since
mentors frequently are direct supervisors, the general quality of
supervisor/subordinate relationships are important in this regard. To

the extent sex differences complicate relationships with supervisors, they also affect the mentoring process.

While surprisingly few of the individuals I talked with claimed to have had a mentor (fewer than half of the women and one-third of the men), women were more likely to have mentors than men, especially at the higher supervisory levels. (See Appendix I for more specifics.) This patterns was surprising, given the literature which suggests that women typically have fewer mentors available to them (cf. Bowen, 1985 and Cook, 1979,) or perceive more barriers to obtaining mentors (Ragins and Cotton, 1991). However, it was also true of the Wisconsin administrators I interviewed. Here, too, women were more likely than men to say they had purposely set out to become administrators, and that, in the process they had had important mentors. Two of the highest level women administrators had worked for or been associated with high level women administrators as undergraduates:

...as a student in college I worked for the president's office a good bit. So I really went to meetings with her [president]. I chauffeured her around...I really learned quite a bit. The president was not a person or an office that was far removed or unknown to me.

...I am so big on role models...I remember, I was...sitting in the freshman convocation at ____ which had a lot of women in the administration...All I was thinking about seeing all those folks up there was that someday I was going to do that, too. I think the fact that there was a woman dean -- at that time a woman acting president...really said to me -- not only do I want to do it, but I certainly think I *can* do it.

Several women also mentioned husbands, even former husbands, as mentors. These women also more often had degrees or training in management or administration.

The men said they did not have mentors; as one high level man said, "Mentors no, encouragement yes." The majority of these individuals, both men and women, said they more or less drifted into administration -- or were drafted by others. Some of them had actively resisted. It seemed to "just happen" to them. One man said:

...I was just walking down the street one day (talk about coincidences, being in the right place at the right time), I ran into ____, who was at that time part of ____...somehow he remembered me...he said, "____ what are you doing?" I said, "I am finishing my degree..." He said,

"Have you got a job?" I said, "No." He said, "Why don't you come and
see me. How would you like to go to _____?"

He started at a brand new campus and later was offered a job at
another campus by this same individual. It amazed me that he did not
call this man who helped him so much a mentor; he said he had no
mentors. This sort of thing had happened to several other men as well;
it had happened to none of the women.

In the years since the mentor literature began to appear, we have
developed a considerably more complex view of this phenomenon.
Kanter, as early as 1983, worried we expected too much of these
individuals in formal terms, that workers were more in need of
"sponsors" who would provide periodic assistance, rather than mentors
who work with a person closely, grooming them continuously for a
period of years. It has also been pointed out immediate supervisors are
most likely to serve as mentors and, in fact, this protege-type
relationship is part of supervisory work (Roche, 1979). Specific types
of mentors are now discussed in the popular parlance: sponsors,
information sources, feedback sources, etc. Also, peers and co-workers
as well as supervisors can assist with some of these functions. Given
the complexity of the situation, I suppose it is not too surprising that
the majority of the individuals I interviewed claimed to not have
mentors. The formality and extensive commitment implied by the
mentoring term may belie the numerous sources of help from those
they work or have worked with.

Regardless of the exact nature and form of the mentoring
relationship, it seems when it does exist for women, it *can* function as
a major mechanism for communication between the sexes about
management. In this sense, it is even more instructive to see who the
mentors were and what functions they performed for these women. In
the first study, that of managers in three settings, ten mentoring
instances were reported by women. (See Appendix I for more details.)
Seven of these ten instances involved male mentors, supervisors these
women had or were working with. Often, the same man was
mentioned as mentor by several women in these organizations. The
seven instances of male mentoring involved only three men, one man
in each of the three settings. It was generally recognized that these
men were concerned, caring, non-sexist men with the patience and
aptitude to be "natural educator(s)." These were qualities mentioned by
all of the women when talking about their mentors -- supportive,

caring, protective, instructive -- generally "bringing me along."
Mentors also "pushed" and "challenged" these women to set their sights
higher than they might otherwise have:

> He forced me to re-think my career goals...challenged me to set broader
> goals...to where I could honestly say I wanted to be a junior college
> president.

> Because of him, I am doing things much beyond my actual experience.
> He has given me so much responsibility.

The emotional support, the "pats on the back," were seen as being
equally important. They felt their mentors also helped them by giving
them responsibility, in some cases out of necessity:

> He had heart trouble and was sick for awhile so he kept giving me more
> and more of it until eventually I just took over.

Sometimes mentors gave more responsibility because of a need to have
someone to "rely on, to trust." These women often felt their mentors
gave them autonomy or "positive control" but appreciated that it was
coupled with a willingness to "train me, discuss different issues...He
always had the time." Mentors were also useful as models; many of
these women discussed adopting their mentor's styles or practices,
particularly in the way they dealt with subordinates:

> I watch him. He knows how to stroke you on the head...I've
> learned...from how he handles his staff.

The three men cited as mentors by several women in each institution
seemed to use different strategies with male and female subordinates.
I interviewed one of these managers. He described himself as
autonomy-invested, and his male subordinates enjoyed this approach.
"He lets me make my own decisions," one man said. Another
described him as "fairly meek," adding, "He leaves me alone." And he
was very critical of a female peer's approach. His women
subordinates, however, tended to see him differently. They described
him as a "wonderful natural teacher," someone they saw as investing
in them and helping them to develop.

In another of these settings, a similar situation existed, in which the same man was cited as a supportive mentor-type supervisor by quite a few of the high-level women managers, yet the men who worked for him saw him as autonomy-invested, someone they even bypassed when seeking resources or dealing with important issues. A surordinate to one of these men said he had the habit of "going directly to the Director"...and that his supervisor "understood and agreed" with being bypassed.

In contrast to the women, the men who did have mentors saw them as fulfilling more limited functions than those the women mentioned. Several men were taught specific things by mentors.

He taught me about people, observing them. He used to be in law enforcement.

He encouraged me to do things so I was successful.

He was in charge of indoctrinating me when I first came to the company.

However, for the most part, these men saw mentors as someone they might "check with before making decisions," someone who might supplement their own considerable skills and expertise. They did not, however, describe relationships that were as complex or affectively charged as those described by the women. They also did not report the same level of teaching, but more often giving advice about specific problems when asked. And there was not the same pattern of one male acting as mentor for several men in the organization.

This pattern I discovered led me to wonder about these men who were seen as mentors by so many aspiring women managers in their organizations. It was my impression these men were well-respected in their organizations, people who *could* successfully help these women advance. Is this a usual pattern across organizations? Are there usually key people who can eventually help to move women into higher positions, removing some of the barriers women currently face? Is this part of the way change occurs?

The fact these male mentors seemed to adopt a more female-typed, person-invested style when dealing with women indicates that, at some level, they recognized the existence of different management models and sanctioned women's approaches, at least when interacting with women subordinates. The management literature has for some time stressed the importance of flexibility, of being able to use different approaches in different situations. Perhaps, through time, the most effective managers will be those who are aware of many differences and are able to alter their own style when supervising a diversity of individuals. Several questions remain to be answered. What influence do these men have on the workplace and attitudes about management? And are they able to function as change agents, helping to make the environment more accepting of women and their styles? Certainly they help the women to feel more at ease, more comfortable in finding their own approach in this new world. But many barriers remain.

Change Shown Through the Mail

In looking at how change occurs, I offer yet more data, here as an indication of just how gradual this process can be, how much society struggles to re-interpret the new in terms of the old. This evidence consists of a collection of ads or fliers for management training seminars I began receiving shortly after completing data collection for my original studies and began my own experience as an administrator. These fliers were collected over the last nine years.

Trends here illustrate the point that change does not occur suddenly. What appears as abrupt change has actually been building for quite some time, as we successively attempt to incorporate the new into a more familiar framework, through various feedback loops devising a more complete and integrated perspective. In this case, the change might ultimately be profound, as more excluded groups gain access to positions of power. Exchange theorists have long maintained (cf. Scanzoni, 1976) and more general feminist theorists have recently affirmed (Chafetz, 1990) that women's access to "resource-generating work roles" is a major factor driving the transformation in gender roles we are currently experiencing in our society. As these groups gain access to higher levels of the work world, that transformation ought to become more powerful. Thus, for example, we ought to see more complete modifications in perceptions of women managers, leading to changing notions of what management *is*, as women managers become more numerous. This does seem to be occurring as more individuals gain experience with women managers (see Chapter 4).

The fliers show the gradualness with which we come to incorporate new approaches (in keeping with Kuhn's notion of how paradigm shifts occur). Shortly after I began my research on women managers, I became a manager myself. For all of these reasons, I became part of new networks and began receiving many brochures for management training seminars. I am not certain whether all women administrators in my geographical area received the same type and/or volume of advertisements. I am also not certain how exhaustive my collection is, although I suspect by the number of repetitions *and* the appearance of new companies that it is a fairly representative collection. Over the nine-year period, I received ads from approximately 40 different companies. (A few of these companies were divisions of other companies already represented.)

These brochures reflected an interesting process in developing awareness about women's approaches to management. From the beginning, several trends were immediately apparent about the seminars these brochures were advertising. On a mundane level, the workshops became more widespread over the time period, a factor that apparently lowered the cost over the five year period. What cost $150 or more in 1984 and 1985 began to cost around $50. Typically, a few firms entered with fairly high prices, then other companies entered the market, driving the price down. In fact, one of the original companies lowered their price a year or two later by more than one-half. These trends reflected the fact that more women were entering management and taking these seminars. In addition to these lower-cost seminars, several companies began to offer very expensive specialized seminars that involved training in specific areas, e.g., training to be a consultant ($495 a day) or to be a trainer ($295 a day). This trend reflected women's move into specialized management positions. Also, by the end of the time period, several companies were offering very expensive all-purpose developmental programs that lasted several days and cost as much as $7,000.

Second, the seminars, as a group, had come to cover a more diverse set of topics, yet the content of individual seminars became more specific over time. For example, in 1984-85 companies were offering seminars on topics like writing or time management. The following year topics included team-building, presentation skills, risk-taking, getting results, working with difficult people, negotiating, and The One-Minute Manager. The next year added to the list were listening powerfully, leadership training, setting priorities, and designing sales literature. By 1988, topics such as problem solving, leadership from diverse places, communication skills for supervisors, and profit planning appeared, followed in 1989 by specialty workshops dealing with being a consultant or trainer.

One thing that struck me about many of these topics was the amount of resources increasingly devoted to teaching supervisors to use or develop interpersonal skills. This trend has intensified to the present time. In 1989, fliers appeared for workshops dealing with constructive conflict resolution, abusive relationships, and working successfully with people. Emotional issues were referenced: "How to stay charged without blowing a fuse" one brochure offered. In the 1990's brochures began appearing for workshops that included pictures of over-sized, angry, or otherwise emotional people. It was apparently seen as more acceptable to use emotional approaches, not *only* the rational, controlled ones used almost exclusively to that time. Other issues, such as family violence, dealing with difficult issues, clowning were the subjects of some workshops.

However, this is *not* to say that the tone of rationality was disappearing in general. At the same time, there was an explosion of offerings dealing with personal and general communication strategies, marketing, finance, fundraising, etc. By 1993, we had perhaps come full-circle. The large pictures had disappeared, and I received a business-like flier for a workshop titled, "How to manage conflict and maintain emotional control." Yet, by 1995, some of these angry pictures had once again appeared.

Most interesting for my purposes were the trends in the content of the seminars aimed specifically at women. The earliest seminars were concerned with image projection or general professional development. The concerns quickly progressed to more specific issues -- power communication, leadership, management, executive skills, stress management, managing for excellence, getting published, developing entrepreneurial skills, and assertiveness training. Also, local groups (hospitals, women's centers, women's organizations) began getting into the market, and national companies began offering other avenues of learning, such as cassette, video, and reading programs. In addition, there were perceptual developments concerning women managers in some of these brochures. In general, there was a progression from seeing women managers as needing help in learning to manage, to asking questions about any "real difference" that might exist between men and women, and finally, to wondering if women had unique contributions to make in this area.

This latter insight took quite some time to develop and, in fact, there is some ambiguity in these fliers -- sometimes within a single seminar or across offerings by a given company -- about whether women need help or whether they can offer it. Some companies began by announcing seminars using fliers that presumed women's naivete and inexperience when it came to management. One of the first fliers I received in 1984 was for a seminar called "Image and Self-Projection for Professional Women." On the inside, a long list of benefits of the seminar included the identification of:

- 5 "female" mannerisms that say you're a lightweight
- 4 unconscious fears that hold women back
- 5 power-robbing appearance mistakes even sophisticated women make
- ways of working effectively with men

The flier goes on to say women are not taught to project an image of power and, as a result, others (even other women) refuse to accept them as power figures. Here, the onus was clearly on the woman to change her behaviors, to learn to manage her self-presentation so she would be taken seriously. This message is even more clear in a flier I received from this company the following year (1985) for another seminar called "Power Communication Skills for Women." Here, part of the copy reads:

Let's be blunt. Most women do not know how to exercise power as effectively as men.

The flier goes on to list "what women need," things mentioned in the first flier. The presumption seems to be women are totally unprepared for management, though no one explicitly *says* this is a new undertaking for women. The dramatic increase in the proportion of supervisory positions held by women is not mentioned explicitly in any flier I received until 1987, when it is tied to the idea of androgynous management styles and discovering the "real differences" between men and women.

In the earlier fliers, we get the idea to be "feminine" is to be ineffectual, to be a poor manager. The thrust seems to be toward training women to fit the male model. This company repeated these same two seminars (plus several others) for five years. In 1989, they advertised a new seminar called "Management and Supervisory Skills for Women," where no disparaging comments were made about women in the flier; rather, basic managerial issues such as making decisions and using resources were stressed, as was "determining your own style." This evolution of a single company illustrated how the fliers as a group changed over time -- from presumptions of women's ineffectiveness to explorations of the possibility women may have unique strengths to build upon and contribute.

Another company early in the period was offering seminars and conferences for women managers that purported to show women:

- low power feminine behaviors to avoid
- [to] take charge, not advantage
- proper use of authority

Here, the presumption was not just women were powerless but they would misuse power if they had it (they would "take advantage)", suggesting a stereotypical fear of the powerful woman. A conference sponsored by this company during this same period included a workshop with a flier that asked if women managers *could* maintain a sense of feminine values, although it seemed most concerned about whether or not men and women could stop competing with one another and start working together.

In the second half of this time period, voices were already exploring the possibility of different styles: for example, offering workshops that encouraged women to determine and develop their own unique strengths and styles. Seminars with this focus were usually sponsored by professional associations or larger, more established companies, such as the American Management Institute, or by organizations specifically geared toward women, such as the Business Woman's Training Institute. A flier for one of these seminars, called "Moving Up! A Seminar for Today's New Woman in Business, Industry, Government, and the Professions," promised participants would learn to:

- Exercise authority without sacrificing femininity
- Use "woman's strengths" for the benefit of yourself and your company
- Gain a better understanding of the different needs of female/male relationships in your organization.

Another seminar, called "Leadership Skills for Women," promised women would learn to:

- Win the women's way...A 5-point plan that will get immediate results.
- Discover your natural leadership skills...and use them to get the job done.
- Use your leadership style to get the most from your employees -- willingly.

In addition to asserting women *did* have something valuable to bring to the managing enterprise, these seminars also touched upon the subject of sex discrimination or sex-role stereotyping. The fliers implied the source of women's problems lay more with the system in which she worked and less with the woman herself.

One workshop dealt partly with the idea that "women [were]... shaping the meaning of leadership," and another with the idea that women would be effective leaders in a multi-cultural environment. Others acknowledged women were affecting various institutions, such as women and the law. However, this change has not necessarily been on a straight linear trajectory. A few years ago, some of the companies offering workshops exploring "women's style" began to back off of that stance a bit. One of these companies developed a workshop called "High impact skills for women" that re-asserted women's need to fit into the existing process:

- Identify and eliminate words, gestures, and speech patterns which rob you of power
- Use communication techniques that result in predictable, positive responses from people
- Get people to like, respect, and support you
- Perform confidently in tough situations

The implication here is that women are having problems doing well in managerial positions. Another company moved from helping women identify their own strengths to, in part:

-Mix masculine and feminine traits in a formula for success and learn the "balanced image"
- steps to the sexless formula for success

Seminars by many other companies also seemed ambivalent on the point of women's strengths vs. women's problems; they projected both views. For example, one flier for a seminar called "Self-Presentation for Profession Women" warned about the hazards of using "female-speak," but at the same time argued each individual ought to build upon her own strengths, allowing for the possibility of the use of a different approach by women. Another flier for a seminar called "Today's Woman Supervisor" warned about the "Cinderella Syndrome" and promised employers to teach female managers to stop doing others' work, to delegate, so they would "stop burning the midnight oil," a tone that seemed to presume incompetence. However, this flier also noted while management tasks were the same for both sexes, each used a different approach and women often faced barriers such as the "good old boy network." Still another flier for a seminar called "Image and Communication Skills for Women" stressed the importance of teaching women to let go of fear of success, fear of competition, self-sabotaging tendencies (concepts that have not been well-supported empirically), while at the same time stressing the importance of discovering the "real differences" between men and women (particularly in how they think) and encouraging women to build upon their strengths. While I am not certain how this conflicting message was handled in the workshop itself, the message of the flier was that women ought to (simul-taneously) change their style and keep their style.

In the throes of trying to master a new managerial position myself, I found these messages confusing. The few workshops I attended also had this effect, or I found myself resenting the suggestion we ought to, without question, adopt men's approaches. I honestly felt I had more to contribute, that I might know some better ways. Early in 1986, a flier arrived that caught my eye. It was for a seminar called "Managing for Excellence: For Women Managers." The flier asserted women managers were changing how things were done along the lines, of *The One-Minute Manager*, *In Search of Excellence*, and *Megatrends*. The workshop would explicitly deal with how to encourage worker participation, consider the whole individual, improve information flow, develop interpersonal skills even more completely, and discuss such things as employee rights, informal networks, and performance standards. The focus sounded very futuristic and seemed to argue women are having and would continue to have a very positive effect on the quality of our workplace. It was interesting to me that this flier arrived just as I was coming to a similar conclusion, that this newly emerging managerial style was a better way to approach administration. Everything was beginning to point in the same direction. For years, we feminists had argued a new approach, the decline of patriarchy and other oppressions, would be very good for society as a whole. It would help us see our way clear of many of our major problems. Now, I was beginning to see specific evidence that it may be happening.

Over time, the volume of brochures I received aimed especially at women significantly declined. However, in 1993, I received an explosion of them again, this time from an array of perspectives. Several companies or organizations continued to offer similar workshops offered in the past, although the company that had advocated for a "sexless approach" a year or two before had dropped all reference to this and offered, instead, to explore:

- How your personality influences the way you lead
- What works for others -- 10 characteristics of successful women

The idea women have something valuable to contribute seemed to be growing, as there were offerings from new companies with a new perspective on women's managerial strengths. One workshop was titled "Learning from Women." Another, dealing with "taking the next step," included Sally Helgeson, author of *The Female Advantage: Women's Ways of Leadership* as a panelist. Another workshop proposed to explore:

- 8 positive trends for women in the 90's
- The "female universe" and the "male universe" and how they differ
- Negative labeling of women who move into the male universe and what to do about it
- Gender differences in approaches to communicating, reprimanding, management, and nurturing

Another dealt with women in a wide array of positions and promised to reveal "the secret advantages women have in business."

Since 1993, the content of the brochures I've continued to receive (primarily from the same companies) has become evenly divided between seminars obviously aimed at women and the problems they encounter as managers and apparently gender-neutral seminars. The latter are of two types, one dealing with technical skills such as writing, grammar, presentations, designing promotional materials. The second type is aimed at promoting supervisory skills -- interpersonal skills, manager as coach, self-directed work teams, or simply "how to supervise people." Interestingly, the majority of these seminars are being offered by a single company, one that experimented with special offerings for women but is now treating the development of "people skills" as a standard need for all managers.

A second company is responsible for most of the fliers I have received aimed specifically at women managers and their supposed difficulties in the workplace. I received a flier for the same workshop repeated at least three times titled "Conflict Mangement Skills for Women." This flier featured a cartoon woman saying:

Be Honest: Do you ever:
- back down on an important issue instead of sticking to your guns?
- overreact and make a difficult situation even worse?
- allow unresolved anger and resentment to hurt an important relationship?
- become angry or frustrated when dealing with difficult people?
- let people take advantage of you?
- feel trapped in seemingly unresolvable conflict?

This shows many of stereotypical problems some of these companies (and others) were assuming women managers experience. The same company repeated another offering "The Essentials of Credibility, Composure and Confidence" showing a color photograph of a very professional-looking woman on the cover and a sub-title "A One-Day Seminar for Working Women." The inside text dealt extensively with the need for women to maintain confidence and composure in the face of difficult pressures, an implication women may find it difficult to do so. This company also offered a seminar, "Assertive Communication Skills for Women," as well as others (repeated) on "Managing Negativity in the Workplace" and "How to Work with Just About Anybody!" While these were not aimed specifically at women, they use some of the same codewords, such as "how to innoculate *yourself* against the negative influence of others." A few other companies had offerings on these topics -- managing conflict, maintaining emotional control, self-esteem, peak performance. Half were aimed specifically at women, one "Dealing with Conflict and Confrontation: For Working Women" promising to show "How to keep your cool, stand your ground, and reach a positive solution."

A growing number of fliers continue to be aimed at women in secretarial positions, offering specific skill development (Word Perfect, telephone, receptionist skills), professional enhancement, and in one case, making the transition to the managerial ranks. A limited but more diverse array of offerings dealt with such issues as stress management, health, personal happiness. I received one flier for training to be a trainer (much less expensive than before) and two for conferences that dealt broadly with "Women in Management" and "Managing in a Multi-cultural Environment: Strategies for Women in Leadership Roles."

These fliers suggest a process whereby change may be occurring in the population at large. New ideas are received cautiously, subject to denial. At first, women managers were seen as needing instruction in the prevailing model. In essence, attempts are made to fit the "new" into existing models. It seems the ideas are being continuously processed through feedback loops, in this case, feedback from actual or potential workshop participants -- what sells and what doesn't sell, what people have to say. Eventually, workshops appeared that acknowledged "woman's approach." This eventually progressed to the idea that women might actually have something to contribute ("What We Can Learn from Women"). While a new perspective may seem to suddenly come upon the scene to those not directly involved, the new perspective is usually articulating the viewpoint that, in retrospect, we had been stumbling to all along. The ideas are, in fact, subject to constant refining through this feedback process.

Concluding Observations

The data reported in this chapter suggest some of the mechanisms in the process of paradigm shift. I am arguing that inclusion of marginalized groups will push us more firmly in the direction of expanding equality, with greater emphasis at work (and in other institutions) on freedom, dignity, social justice, and respect. The fliers show us the way we hear the "new way" deepens and transforms itself through time, although they also show how we tend to see issues in isolation from each other. No issues other than gender were discussed in any of those fliers. The response of male mentors suggests that certain key individuals may serve as "bridge people," living and enacting both realities or paradigms during the transition phase. The overwhelming amount of places these ideas are appearing show how new approaches may build below the surface of general societal awareness, seeming to suddenly burst forth from many sources.

The problems with our current order have, after all, been discussed very early in the industrial revolution by such writers as Karl Marx. And still later, at the beginning of our current phase of technological revolution, Elton Mayo (1945) noted:

> ...The industrialized world is facing now...industrial, mechanical, physicochemical advance so rapid that it has been destructive of all...historical and personal relationships (p. 8).

He argued, even then, that midlevel managers "of extraordinary skill in the direction of securing cooperative effort" (p. 118) would be essential in leading us out of our impasse. However, so far:

> ...technical competence earns recognition and promotion whereas skill in handling human relations does not...[W]ere it not for these men...the unleashed forces of modern technology would spin themselves out to doom and destruction...[Yet] these men go unnoticed and unrewarded... (p. 118).

If the approach put forward by women and other marginal groups is adopted, what exactly is the future for the workplace? A transformation toward greater worker participation, for example, even though currently presented as tinkering with the present system, would, in fact, result in a fundamental change. Management specialists advocating such changes, by and large seem to assume we will continue to have capitalism. However, following a Marxist logic, it is possible our system is sowing the seeds of its own destruction, that the exploitation inherent in capitalism has become so counterproductive it will force a transition into a new type of economy and social order. Certainly, a drastic increase in worker participation -- a greater sensitivity to worker needs -- contradicts the basic mechanism of capitalism, the essence of which is profits. Incorporating perspectives of many different groups -- women, people of color, working class people -- will significantly modify our system.

When certain individuals have the opportunity to reap the rewards of their own efforts monetarily, they will find a way to do so. As long as those individuals do not directly pay the cost of any environmental or personal damage done in the course of work and production, exploitation that increases profits would likely continue. If steps were taken to stop these practices, we no longer have capitalism, at least not as we currently know it. If corporations were made to pay for the environmental damage they caused, no matter how far reaching or indirect, they would proceed differently. If worker complaints about job de-skilling were listened to and acted upon, things would change. If the most vulnerable, such as migrant farm workers, are no longer exploited, we would have a different system.

If we do away with such practices, profits will shrink, perhaps, in the short run. Is this really capitalism? Who will make and enforce such regulations? Would the market, then, be the ultimate regulator? Pressures are mounting in the wake of such incidences as the Exxon oil spill and the Bopal tragedy. As Bellah and his colleagues (1991) put it:

> The corporations and the world economic system in which they are enmeshed grew up "over the heads"...of the people and even of their leaders. Misunderstanding...them...Americans...even more than the other citizens of most nations, allowed them to produce whatever unintended consequences they would, some of which were serious indeed (p. 72).

We seem to be at an impasse about how to go about making these changes, though increasing numbers of observers and workers agree they need to be made. Many of us are disillusioned with big government. It did not work to have someone else take the responsibility for making all the changes for us. Somehow, we have all got to take back our own power and insist on accountability by those institutions that supposedly serve us, a point Ralph Nader and his organizations have long been making and Jerry Brown based his presidential campaign upon. This sounds simple but it is a tall order. We are all being programmed, by many institutions (mass media, schools etc.) to become more and more docile and passive, submissive, to experience life vicariously through what we see on television.

The importance of human relations has long been recognized, yet steadily ignored. And now management experts are urging its use. Will this provide a window of opportunity for marginalized groups? Will they be able to execute their preferences, use their talents and expertise to transform our workplace? Will a true paradigm shift occur?

Chapter 12

IMPLICATIONS FOR SOCIETY

I believe it is clear, from all the evidence I have been able to amass, that women and other marginalized groups, given trends that seem to exist among these groups, have the capacity to bring remarkable changes to the workplace. The perspectives of these individuals, who have experienced first-hand the problems and inequities of the current system, have the potential to bring significant change to any situation. And, of course, the eternal message of feminism and other movements for equality is that such changes will be "for the good of all."

Many in industry and elsewhere are fond of saying these days, "We need everybody's input" or "We can't afford to waste any human potential." Our problems are, indeed, pressing, our challenges great. Some of the Native Americans I talked with framed this yet another way. They pointed to the importance of four governing principles, a repeating pattern in our world. There are four directions, four elements, four races, all forming integral systems. Several said explicitly to me that each race has a particular contribution to make to humanity as a whole. By denying any one race input, we construct social systems that are "out of balance" in some way. They, too, much as the feminists discussed in Chapter 2, decried our society's emphasis on logic, rationality, profit, and material comfort and neglect of needs such as nurturance, sacred expression, concern for the earth.

As with views about "women's strengths," we tend to shrink from such claims as "essentialist." Not all Native Americans operate in just this way. There are many individual variations. But we are talking here about group tendencies, how certain social groups have evolved through time, in response to their particular situation. Standpoint perspectives (Clough and others) argue that lived experiences (materialist groundings) produce certain views of things, propensities to react in certain ways. The data presented in these chapters provide striking evidence for the existence of these alternative perspectives. At the same time, not all group members conform. Some Euro-American males use the new perspective. Some women and people of color do not.

I believe that sorting through this thorny issue is a critical aspect of the way we change our awareness -- how paradigm shifts may occur in the social realm. Partly, our resistance to this idea that a radically new perspective is emerging represents our attempts to hang onto the comfort of the old view, no matter how dysfunctional it may be. However, our resistance also signals a concern that "it cannot be this easy," that more is needed than simply putting women and people of color into positions of power. This will not automatically solve all of our problems. There is a great deal to cycle through the lens of a new perspective, much to rethink and realign. This takes time, something I argue we have been doing in a cycle nature repeatedly over much of our history, coming closer to our ideal of equality, input, dignity for all.

The Benefits of Change

In many ways, making these changes will ultimately prove beneficial for our society as a whole. For one thing, several constituencies stand to gain directly by the inclusion of these groups and their perspectives. Obviously, the groups themselves will benefit, as they gain access to greater shares of societal resources than are currently available to them. They might also fashion organizations more in keeping with their world views and more flexible to the full demands of their lives. However, such changes stand to benefit co-workers, as well, since most show signs of alienation, withdrawal, and/or anger toward an increasingly frustrating and meaningless workplace. For example, women's work activity has increased pressures on men to participate more fully in family activities. Hence rigid career boundaries and expectations that ignore family involvements have become stressful for both sexes. In addition, the changes likely to come to the workplace would address many sources of worker alienation, by redesigning workplace structures and processes to give more dignity, input, and incentive to individual workers. Members of these excluded groups also seem more likely to address moral issues in the workplace and to be concerned about adequately responding to the needs of more diverse work groups.

High level managers and companies themselves would also benefit from their inclusion because these workers may more readily handle contemporary issues companies are facing -- changes in consumer expectations and diversity, the fast pace of change, the need for flexibility, flatter hierarchies, people involvement, to name a few. Despite a great deal of trepidation on the part of many feminists about this fact, women -- and these groups --*do* seem to approach leadership positions, even work in general, with a different perspective than many of those currently in the dominant positions. As Chapters 9 and 10 showed, these marginalized groups more consciously attempt to move institutions in certain valued (or moral, in their terms) directions, while the dominant group often uses a more pragmatic approach. In fact, this latter group may see the invoking of moral principles, as opposed to political expediency, as something that *hampers* one's job performance.

Other characteristics of these marginal groups' approaches to management and work are unique. Much of the literature and research cited in this book point to a more integrated, people centered, team work approach that sees even the leader as a part of the overall flow of what happens. In this respect, the perspective is less hierarchical and bureaucratic. Women, Native Americans, and African-Americans seem to less often believe such control structures are necessary, and in fact, may believe that they actually hinder task accomplishment. Executing this style requires a great deal of interactional skills, as cooperation is of the essence. The manager of the future must be able to sense and fine tune to individual worker needs and motivations.

These differences do *not* mean these groups are focused solely on relationships, or are unconcerned about or unable to focus on task accomplishment, a common stereotype that exists about women managers. Rather, they strive to use their considerable interpersonal skills to accomplish the task at hand. The individuals I talked with were very focused on that objective -- and seemed to be very successful at accomplishing it.   For them, instrumental and socio-emotional leadership seem to work together, not in opposition, creating a model of the "all around leader" more and more being advocated in management circles.

From the moment this new model began to emerge in my data, I have been very excited about the idea that women -- and others --have a different approach to contribute to the notion of management and leadership.   I believe this represents an opportunity for women and other groups, in our attempts to both break out of our former position in society and to transform our society.   Both go hand in hand. Perhaps we can offer what is needed now, in many of our institutions, to solve some very serious problems.   Thus, we can demonstrate -- clearly -- society's need for us, and the folly of continuing to exclude us and our viewpoint.   But *we* must articulate our strengths and contributions clearly.   We cannot expect others will simply see this on their own.   For too long, we have provided the unseen glue that has held things together, our contributions appropriated, distorted, unrewarded.   We simply cannot permit this to continue.   And we cannot fool ourselves into believing that we need simply tinker with our social order, shore it up here, prop it up there.   The order itself is the problem.   A trend is afoot to move from a dominator to a cooperator society.   That is the direction our workplace revolution is taking -- and where our "special strengths" can lead.   However, finding the precise language to articulate such a new approach is often problematic.

Directing Women's Studies

I would like to leave you with one last bit of data, about myself working with the cooperative approach, an experience I found to be hopeful beyond words.   It also offers a few more specifics about how change occurs.   After my disastrous time being Chair of my department, I had a much more positive experience as Director of the Women's Studies Program on my campus.   This occurred in a climate in which two new chief academic officers were committed to increasing the Women's Studies' resource base so our program could grow.   Alas, the social forces of the institution made it a difficult thing to do.   In a faculty governance situation, the historically powerful faculty decision-makers (males) did not support a strong Women's Studies Program.

However, I committed to continue using the co-operative model (which had gotten me into so much trouble before). Our Steering Committee met with our Dean to discuss the program's future. When he suggested that we "go after resources" as did certain notorious men on our campus, we all retorted, in unison, "But we're trying to use a feminist model."

The problems of functioning as a cooperative unit within a competitive one are illustrated by my situation in this position. Our program both consciously and unconsciously adopted a co-operative approach. We had a very active Steering Committee that made decisions by consensus. We never consciously decided to do this; we just did. Each person had a great deal of power, discretion, and *credit* in pursuing projects of interest to her. I did more of the work because I had release time (from teaching) to do it, but I was not the final authority. One of our Steering Committee members said this in a written communication to me:

> One of [my] joys here...at _____...has been working with...the Steering
> Committee...[Y]ou lead by example. You base all that you do on a model
> of equality and cooperation -- not hierarchy and power.

I believe her comments reflected upon the total operation of the program, not just upon my own behavior.

As part of the institution, however, we were forced into competitor-type interactions. Sometimes, this affected my own functioning and that of our Steering Committee. For example, we underwent an institutional reorganization, one that moved us from a relatively loose hierarchical system (as an institution) to a tighter hierarchical one. Before, there was a lot of maneuvering for resources in a relatively flat hierarchy, with much direct communication with the two highest academic officers. There was a great deal of upward *and* downward communication between administrators and faculty -- except for periods of change in administrations. After the reorganization, there was relatively little upward communication, but a predominance of downward influence through a tight hierarchical network.

The implications of the reorganization for the program were very clear. When I reported directly to the Vice Chancellor, both he and the Chancellor were promising more resource support for the Women's Studies Program. However, the Dean told us we probably ought to think about raising new funds from outside sources. (We had a supply and expense budget of $1500, while another comparable (male-dominated) interdisciplinary program had one of $4000.)

We were given space and clerical support to share with another department, something originally much more than other programs were given. The campus power brokers were furious Women's Studies should do so well. (As far as I could tell, little was said about the other department sharing these resources, which actually had a larger share of the resources.) As a result of this alarm, part of our space was given to another school for whatever use that program wished, with no consultation with us. Since that other program set up a computer work station and issued their faculty keys, they had access to our supplies, phone lines, files, and projects after normal working hours. Had this happened to different interests, other departments would simply have refused to go along with such an arrangement. However, we were told we would have absolutely nothing to say about how the space was used or if the space was given to this other unit. Since one of the chief administrative officers read a draft of this account, Women's Studies has received a larger supply and expense budget and all of the space under question, for a related project.

Our Steering Committee members were clear about how we wanted to run our program, but we were not at all certain about how to deal with this competitive structure to which we reported. Each one of us had a different personal reaction ranging from, "We'll just have to make do; it'll never change," to anger or despair. We went in and out of consciousness that we did not want to simply accept the system as given but hoped to create an alternative, one that is transformative in nature. But at certain key junctures (like the meeting with the Dean), we were as a group quite conscious of this desire. This is one, slow way the transformation happens, beginning with certain groups such as ours. There was also a practical imperative operating; our institution needed to attract and retain more students, women chiefly among them. Programs like ours were invaluable in making the institution more comfortable and familiar to women students, through our course content and other communications with students and through our ability to understand and articulate problems of female students, actual or potential.

Hence, resistance began to wane as implications for other parts of the organization were realized and integrated into those other considerations. Also other leaders on campus noticed the "success" of our program and investigated contributing factors. A related department became much more co-operative, taking pains to treat all members equally rather than competitively in terms of salary increases. Representatives from our program began to be included in many campus committees deemed highly important.

It seems that new approaches may become more acceptable -- generate less resistance -- as it becomes clearer to those involved how their critical goals can be furthered by adopting the newer stance. Thus, the conscious framing of issues by groups espousing those stances is very important. However, some valued goals from the "old paradigm" are called into question, a more fundamental issue especially likely to generate resistance.

Other Organizations

These ideas have spread in other types of organizations, also. The process involved here gives additional insight into how change occurs. For example, in my follow-up of managers from my original study, I found that those women who had been promoted (since our first interview) were likely to be one of two types: either they used somewhat more male-identified strategies (little participation, pushing work onto others, less common strategy for women) *or* they used extremely female-identified strategies (working with and consulting others, showing appreciation and concern, etc.). One common characteristic was their intense drive to accomplish the task at hand -- by whatever means they used -- and their amazing ability to juggle many different tasks simultaneously for their companies. The men did not seem to have to keep so many different irons in the fire to attract attention and obtain a promotion. Important for the spread of these ideas is that half of the women moved laterally into bigger companies, and these were women who made fairly consistent use of the new style being described here. Hence, the influence of this approach will spread as the result of women making such moves, since many more workers are potentially affected (in the larger companies), as well as by women receiving promotions.

These ideas are also spread through such media as the arts. Hoy et al. (1990) -- discussing a wide range of women writers including Joan Didion, Annie Dillard, Maxine Hong Kingston, Joyce Carol Oates, Alice Walker, and Virginia Woolf -- find women commonly writing about such themes as diversity, racism, sexism, classism, tributes to women, personal experiences such as parenting, loving, and truth. However, some note that women's communities depicted by women in literature often include the horrific as well as the idyllic, as they explore the various possibilities arising from the human condition. Thus, some wonder what sort of alternative women would create to our current order (Auerback, 1978; Albinske, 1988). This speaks to the concern voiced by those arguing against essentialism, that women are not innately morally superior and would possibly, on their own, give rise to other kinds of problems than those seen in the current social order.

Even so, there are those who firmly believe women and other groups have the potential to lead our society in new directions. This is seen in a variety of claims, ranging from physical endurance to social propensities. Take Dan Buetlner's assertation women may actually have an edge over men in certain physical endurance situations, contrary to common stereotypes. He came to this conclusion after a 10 month bicycle trip with a woman (Mills, 1989). Or Bennholdt-Thomsen's (1989) view that women in Mexico used money to bring the community together rather than using it to make divisions between people:

> Money is used as a means to obtain social interaction...It is this predominance of the social aspect, a female attitude toward money, so to speak which is why women continue to have social strength and to [lead] (p. 4).

I wonder if their practices could be used in the fully developed, capitalistic countries as well, and how such practices will fare in the face of the global economy. Brwyn (1991) argues that we must look "beyond the ideologies of capitalism and communism"...to establish "a new competitive economy with manifest social foundations" (p. 8). In this process, he urges that we begin to emphasize (and measure) cooperation as well as competition.

Of course, the road ahead is rocky. All of this change will not come easily. Those in power will resist; they will continue to misunderstand our approaches and mistrust our person-oriented techniques. Those benefitting from capitalism will try to maintain the system. Such change trajectories do not proceed smoothly. Chafetz (1990) shows the waxing and waning through history in our movement toward equality for women. Kuhn has shown how paradigm shifts always start with fits and starts, only later bursting upon the scene in full maturity. And Adrian McLean and Judi Marshall (n.d.) have produced an entire workshop series showing corporations how to change their cultures to incorporate more diversity, suggesting that this is, indeed, serious and long work.

Re-assessing Our Own Behavior

Some previous reviewers of this book have felt I was attacking white men, implying that everything they have done has been harmful. Or, alternatively, that everything women or people of color might do would be beneficial. Of course, the situation is not so simple. Recalling several sociological principles might help clarify what I really mean to say.

The principle of institutionalized racism or sexism is useful here. According to this principle, patterns of oppression and/or discrimination become encoded in our social processes, in ways such that *individuals* do not feel any sense of responsibility for what is happening. *They* have done nothing "bad," it is simply how "the system" works. This is the level of my analysis, so I am not blaming individuals for the state we are in. I tried to set that framework in Chapter 2 by pointing to imbalances on the societal level between what we consider to be feminine and masculine principles. I have also pointed out along the way that variation exists among individuals in these various groups, and have tried, instead, to focus on general patterns of differences between groups.

On the other hand, the Symbolic Interaction approach I am using argues that individuals do collectively have impact on our social structures, that self and social structure are mutually reinforcing. Granted, we have not all had equal weight in determining the structure and processes that affect us. But, we all play some part in this. Thus, it behooves as all to take stock in our own behavior. How do we each contribute to the problems we hope to solve? How might we further the change process, the acceptance of the new paradigm that seems to be emerging? If we are not able to *name* our problems, we cannot hope to solve them. All of us have a role to play in this process.

Issues and Coalitions

I have one final observation about a factor blocking our process and conversely, a way to advance our progress. One major hurdle is to devise ways of working effectively in coalition, across the issues of race, class, and gender. I gained insight about this need while doing a study of environmental issues in southeast Florida (Statham, 1995), interviewing members of different groups -- feminist, environmental, social justice organizaitons. Members of each type of group showed a preoccupation with their special interest, often denigrating other interests. For example, social justice and feminist group members believed environmentalists cared too much about injured whales and not enough about needy people. Environmentalists thought these groups failed to see the "big picture," that if the biological world were destroyed, there would be no society to care about. Those working on racial issues thought feminists focused too much on the abortion issue. Many such comments were made. However, there was a point about which they all agreed: that the source of all of these problems was greed. One of the early settlers to the area, active in none of these movements, alluded to this issue:

> I guess people got greedy...these developers...pay fabulous sums for this land, and it just got out of hand...

Several women environmentalists also alluded to this factor:

> As people start having children they suddenly are becoming concerned with the future of their children...and they're not thinking in such a self-centered way now.

> People go through their lives and they never notice anything and if they would open their eyes and see what's out there then they would do things differently...We all live day to day, let's have fun today!

Other women echoed the early settler's contention that greed, specifically, was the underlying problem:

> Too many people, too many selfish people, too many money-hungry, or ignorant [people]...the greedy...the space shuttle's busy punching holes, dumping chlorine and the story...is one of the 10 most squashed stories in '91 because of all the vested interest...

A Seminole women said:

> That's right in the middle of Florida...If they're gonna live, the Seminoles...the center of Florida should be preserved...for the wildlife and the water situation...There's just greediness driving everybody...

Two individuals working with a social justice group also stressed greed as our underlying problem:

> What the world needs now is love. If people would just treat people like they would want to be treated, but unfortunately that's not what's happening. It's a money thing. It's greed. It's other things motivating people, and I think inequality is just a symptom of an illness, of a much greater illness...It's all about money...It's all about green...They're gonna get whatever they can...that's a vicious cycle...It stems around power and money...

> Goes back to a theological question. Greed. Stop and think...A pastor ...that I know...did some research. If the wealth of this world were equally distributed, every man, woman, and child on the face of this planet would have two and a half million dollars in their pocket...It's the love of money, not money but the love of money is the root of every evil on the face of the earth...Give you an example of greed keeping people from getting what they need. I went to the food bank to pick up my supply of food, and I said, "Where's all the cheese?" "There won't be no more cheese." "Why not?"..."The Cheese Producers of American said...the distribution of all the cheese...was lowering their prices"...It was the greed of the American producer...You've got people sleeping in drain tiles, but..."you can't put those people in there because" -- greed --" who's going to pay me to let him sleep in there?"...God put the earth in the hands of man...we're raping it, not taking care of it -- greed...The common denominator is greed...

One of the civic/business men I talked with pointed to greed as a major contributing factor to the problems we had been discussing:

> I know the greed in people to make money, and people make money in different ways...I think there should be a Holiday Isle...for young people...I just don't know if we are really ready to develop every square inch...which seems to be the way we're going.

Working around this common perception of greed as a cause may prove an effective way to bring these various groups together for effective coalitions. A recent publication by World Watch posits "the emancipation and empowerment of people" as the most significant movement of the last fifty years, a movement that can be closely tied with pressures toward greater economic equality (less tolerance of greed -- Renner, 1995).

Hopefully, the questions raised in this book about the full contributions women and other excluded groups can and have made to our society will hasten the process of change. Lack of clarity may be one of the major factors that prevents new paradigms from being adopted. My intention has been to help us see more clearly. Fuller inclusion of women and these other groups stands to help us solve critical problems, and some observers would tell us the time is short. As Aburdene and Naisbitt (1992) challenge, "It is time to move from liberation to leadership" (p. xi). Certainly, we face many critical problems in need of a fresh approach. Hopefully, as we more fully articulate our visions, desires, and propensities, we can more consciously create the type of social structures we truly want, that will be more beneficial to all.

APPENDIX

METHODOLOGY, CHRONOLOGY, SUPPLEMENTAL FINDINGS FROM STUDIES

This appendix gives more complete technical information about the studies I have done for this project, for those interested. Some of the data are presented or mentioned in Part I or later chapters, supporting my own points and also those of others.

Original Study of Managers and Secretaries

As I stated in Chapter 1, I began my research in 1983, with a focused interview study of 40 men and women managers and their secretaries (70 interviews in all) in three work settings -- a multinational manufacturing firm, a bank, and a technical institute. Because I was open to the possibility women managers have styles not previously delineated in the literature, I hesitated to rely on popular management typologies, since they have been derived chiefly from observations of men, and so may fail to tap or may distort any distinct style women might use. One major difficulty had to do with the dichotomies in these typologies. The most popular ones involve (implicitly or explicitly) a people/task distinction.

Fiedler's model (1978) categorizes managers as task or relationship oriented, Lewin's (White and Lippitt, 1968) as autocratic or democratic, Ohio State's model (Stogdill, 1974) as structure initiating or consideration oriented. Previously, McGregor's (1960) theory X/theory Y distinction had categorized managers as focusing on either structural task incentives *or* more humanistic concerns, a distinction elaborated upon in Likert's (1967) System 1, 2, 3, 4, distinction. The task/person orientations are often treated as distinct in many of the topologies that currently exist. As applied to women managers, the assumption has been that women use more expressive management strategies, focusing more on relationships and consideration and are also more democratic. Even though the corroborating evidence for this dichotomy was produced in experimental settings where leaders have simply emerged from the interaction (not in situations with actual managers and subordinates), the expressive/instrumental sex differentiation is very widely held in sociological circles. It may not hold up when applied to managers on the job.

Managers may, in fact, perform both functions, something these topologies often do not allow for. If these topologies, based as they are on male behaviors, fail to adequately represent women's management approaches, their use may result in women being inaccurately judged as less effective when they are simply using alternative, though unrecognized, approaches. Such was the case with the female respondents in Kohlberg's studies of moral development as critiqued by Gilligan (1983).

To allow for these possibilities, I used a focused interview approach to gather information about the management styles of men and women managers. I asked them ten very general questions in 60 to 90 minute tape recorded sessions at their place of work. I also talked with each of their secretaries. By allowing them to tell me about their work, I avoided an imposition of pre-conceived categories that may be unlikely to tap the full range of their behaviors. All respondents (including the secretaries) were asked the same questions, though the order varied somewhat if a respondent began talking about a topic on his or her own. Other procedures (including sample selection) further insured the systematic nature of the information I collected.

Sample

I talked with 22 women and 18 men managers in the 3 settings. The institutions chosen were expected to reflect a range in the extent to which women were accepted and integrated into managerial positions. Financial institutions have historically been more open to women, having more women in higher supervisory positions, but especially plentiful at the level of vice president (Korn and Ferry, 1982).

Because she is not uncommon, a woman manager in a financial institution may find fewer problems in role performance than women managers in other kinds of institutions. The manufacturing firm, by contrast, may provide the fewest opportunities and least support, especially the particular type of manufacturing firm chosen here, one which produces heavy durable equipment. A woman manager in this situation will find herself numerically less common and in a less favorable emotional climate. The technical institute was expected to offer a middle range along this continuum: teaching, a traditional women's activity, increases the likelihood that women will be accepted. Management is a different matter, however, especially in the voc./tech. system, which emphasizes training in traditional male occupations (trade and industry).

I interviewed as many women as possible in the highest supervisory positions and did interview all of the women in the very highest levels. Once the women were chosen, I then attempted to locate men at comparable levels and interview equal numbers of them. I thus have a sample of men and women managers at similar managerial levels, in contrast to many past studies, where men frequently are in higher positions in the hierarchy than the women who are interviewed. After completing each interview with the managers, I asked permission to interview their secretaries. None of the managers refused me permission to contact their secretaries and only one secretary (a "temporary-help" employee) refused to be interviewed.

Figure 1A and Table 1A show the position of managers in the organizational hierarchy. Though each organization had its own set of internal and external contingencies, all were similarly structured. Several senior vice presidents (or their equivalents) reported directly to a chief operating officer, who in turn reported to a managing or controlling board and a chief executive officer. The senior vice presidents, relatively few in number, had several vice presidents reporting to them. The structure for each organization is outlined in Figure 1A, along with the actual titles associated with these positions.

In the technical institute, the chief operating officer was called the director, the senior vice presidents were called directors, the vice presidents were called supervisors, and those reporting to supervisors/vice presidents were called coordinators. In the financial institution, titles for the first four levels followed standard practice, and those reporting to vice presidents were often called assistant vice presidents. In the manufacturing firm, there were more managerial levels, chiefly because of size. (The manufacturing firm employed 20,000 individuals, while the financial institution employed 500). There was a chief executive officer, a chief operating officer, senior vice presidents and vice presidents. Those reporting to vice presidents were called general managers or directors, the next level was titled managers, and those reporting to managers were called supervisors.

In general, women occupied lower positions than men in these organizations, although the extent to which this was true varied greatly by company. Women were more often in higher positions at the financial institution and less often in these positions at the manufacturing firm (see Table 1A). Differences in position cannot be entirely accounted for by differences in age, education, years with company, hours worked per week. The men and women managers in this sample are remarkably similar in all but salary. The women, in fact, are even more available for work involvement, given their lowered tendency to be married or to have children. (See Table 2A)

These interviews, lasting approximately one hour, were fully transcribed and content analyzed using Glaser and Strauss' (1967) method of constant comparison. (See Statham 1987a and 1987b for further details about this original study.)

Additional Data

I also have information about the existence of mentors. Surprisingly few of the individuals I talked with claimed to have had a mentor. (See Table 3A). Fewer than half of the women and one-third of the men could unequivocally say they had had one. Several others mentioned people that "might have" been mentors for them. In all cases, mentors in the workplace were past or current supervisors. (Several respondents also mentioned a family member as a second mentor.) I was surprised that women were more likely to have mentors than men, especially at the higher supervisory levels (See Table 4A), given the literature which suggests that women typically have fewer mentors available to them. (See, for example, Bowen, 1985 and Cook, 1979.)

Follow-up

I also did a brief phone follow-up in the summer of 1990 with these same individuals I had interviewed some five or six years earlier. I was able to reach all but four of them. One of men from the financial institution had died suddenly at a very young age. I was simply not able to connect with one of the men and one of the women in the manufacturing firm for various reasons; one of the women from the financial institution had lost her job in a corporate take-over and left no forwarding address. In these later interviews, I reminded them of what they were doing when I first talked with them and asked if they still had the same job. Only four of them did, and one of those with the same job (a man) now worked in Paris rather than Wisconsin. However, at least 50% of both men and women said they had a higher level job. Fifty percent of the men clearly did, but only 31.6% of the women were in jobs that were at a higher level in the organizational hierarchy. Another 31.6% of the women had improved their situation by making a lateral move to a larger company. These moves, they felt, were a step up for them even though they were technically at the same level. Their responsibilities were greater and their chances for further advancement improved. Only one of the women had started her own company. Two women had left the work force (one to raise children), and another had retired (though she was still doing consulting). One woman had experienced downward mobility, though she enjoyed the challenge of her new field a great deal. Another had made a lateral move within the same company. I was unable to obtain any information about two of the original female respondents.

Two of the men had retired (one still consulting), and one was deceased. This man was one of the male mentors for women mentioned in Chapter 11. Another had made a lateral move to a smaller company and another had experienced downward mobility. Both of these moves had been voluntary, and both men expressed relief at being rid of the pressures of their former jobs. I was unable to obtain any information about two of the original male respondents.

Two of the three work sites I had used for my original study had since been involved in mergers. In the first case, one company had been purchased by another. In the second situation, the parent company had purchased a second company and merged the two. Because of this, many of the stories about work experiences involved "living through the merger," being transferred to "headquarters," commuting for periods of time, and/or managing significant reorganizations. Few of those in the manufacturing firm had lost their jobs directly because of the merger. Several had been moved, but most of those who had changed employers had decided on their own to move on. Many of those with the financial institution had been offered jobs at the new company headquarters (in a different town). Several had made the move, and a few had commuted for periods of time, but most had found new jobs.

The women were, overall, more enthusiastic about their new jobs. All of them discussed important aspects of their new situations that they liked a great deal. One woman expressed ambiguous feelings, saying she liked her job "some days," and another expressed disappointment that her "more engineering driven" company was "light years away" from her former company in its treatment of women. And a third woman felt computerization had taken much of the joy out of her work (she was still in the same job). However, the other women seemed very happy with their jobs. Five of them hoped to move up in a few years, often the same women who had already been promoted, while three looked forward to retirement, and the rest were satisfied to stay where they were for awhile. One woman hoped eventually to move "back into teaching." Two women who hoped to move up were also contemplating the possibility of starting their own companies.

The men were, as a group, somewhat less satisfied with their current situation. More of them expressed dissatisfaction directly. Complaints ranged from not liking "the pressure to make money" to not being "100% thrilled with the location." A slightly higher proportion than among the women hoped to move up, and one man was actually in the process of doing so. One man hoped to change areas of responsibility, and another was looking forward to retirement.

Survey of Secretaries

Since that time, I have done additional studies. First, I designed and administered a survey to secretaries in the same geographical area where the original interviews were done, distributing them through secretarial organizations (unions, professional, and advocacy groups) with their regular newsletters and in person to certain departments in manufacturing firms (under-represented in the original survey sample.) This was done in 1986.

While some of the information obtained was relevant for my purposes here, the focus of this study was actually on problems with the introduction of new technology that unexpectedly arose in the original interview study. (See Statham and Bravo, 1980, for more information.) We developed and distributed a survey to secretaries who were primarily members of professional secretarial organizations, secretarial unions (a unified school district and a technical institute), and an organization designed to improve the situation of office workers (a local "9to5" chapter). When contacted through newsletters distributed to the members, the return rate was approximately 50%. When all secretaries in given (non-unionized) organizations or departments were approached and asked to complete the surveys, return rates were approximately 85%.

The types of organizations where the secretaries worked in the second survey reflect this sampling scheme. (See Tables 5A and 6A.) The large number (59.6%) in educational settings are primarily respondents from the local unified school district and technical institute. Those in the manufacturing setting were primarily respondents approached on a department by department basis. Respondents in other settings, as well as some of those in educational and manufacturing settings, were the "9to5" respondents. Demographic characteristic are given in Table 7A, job type in Table 8A.

These secretaries, from many different types of organizations, reported their women supervisors to be more concerned with helping them improve their own career position, to be less hierarchical, and to more often show appreciation and give credit for their work. (See Table 9A.) These women did not, however, perceive their women supervisors to work more often as team players. Both men and women were perceived to do this in equal proportions. The secretaries *did,* however, believe that *they* themselves were more often included in decisions -- treated as team players -- by their women supervisors.

Local Community Survey

Also in 1986, I contributed questions about women managers to a general community survey done at the college where I was teaching. This was a randomly selected sample of 1,000 individuals, using random digit dialing techniques, conducted by the Center for Survey and Marketing Research at the University of Wisconsin-Parkside.

This survey illustrates aspects of how men and women supervisors are viewed, discussed in Chapters 3 and 4.   Notice how men's perceptions compare to women's.   First, Table 11A shows no real differences in perceptions of men and women supervisors when both sexes are mixed together.   However, looking at Table 12A, we can see marked gender differences in these perceptions.   In fact perceived gender differences are often reversed for the two sexes, with women workers believing that women supervisors were more considerate, more likely to give credit, etc. and men workers believing the opposite (Table 12A).

Midwestern University Graduates As Managers

In 1987, I did a follow-up study of a group of highly educated women I had studied previously.   (See Statham, Houseknecht, and Vaughan, 1987; Househnecht, Vaughan, and Statham, 1984 for further details.)   Originally, women who received high level degrees from a major midwestern university between 1964 and 1974 were sent a mail survey dealing with family and work events, including managerial experiences.   Names were supplied by the Alumni Foundation of that institution.   For the most part, only women who received degrees beyond the Masters level were included in the sample.   However, because I was interested in managerial experiences, women who had received MBA's during that time period were also included in the follow-up.   Despite these efforts, the sample is predominantly composed of women with doctorates (72.5%), followed by women with medical (10.6%) and law (6.6%) degrees.   The majority of PhD's were in the areas of Education, Home Economics, Physical Education, Psychology, Foreign Language, and English.   Only 2.1% of the respondents had an MBA. (See Tables 13A and 14A.) Thus, these data can give us information mainly about the managerial experiences of women doctorates, and to some extent, those with medical and law degrees. For the most, these women were born during the 1930's and 1940's and received their degrees after 1972 (Table 13A). The four-hundred seventy-four women who responded to the survey represent a 47.3% response rate, obtained after two follow-up contacts. A surprising number (8.5%) of these women were retired by the time of the follow-up survey. They were excluded from the analyses concerning work, as were the 3.9% who were unemployed for other reasons.

In this study, I was interested in women managers' perceptions of their environment, their own managerial styles, and perceptions of women managers in general. The survey provided measures of several general characteristics, including supervisory status (yes/no), sex of own supervisor, assessment of supervisor (a five-point scale ranging from excellent to poor), specific occupation, and type of subordinants supervised. I was also interested in the implications of being a manager for such factors as job satisfaction and life satisfaction (both global 5-point items) and income, as well as the extent to which managers and non-managers differ with respect to type of PhD, year of degree, and age. All respondents were also given the opportunity to list three factors that contributed to their overall life satisfaction and three factors that contributed to their dissatisfaction. These responses were coded into categories under the general headings of family, work, and personal/self.

The women who were managers were also asked to rate their own behaviors on a scale of 1 (always) to 5 (never) in such areas as delegating, using teamwork, showing appreciation for subordinates, and other ways of dealing with subordinates. They were also asked to list three factors that hindered their success as managers and three factors that contributed to their success. These answers were coded into categories under the general headings of structural factors, interpersonal relationships, and personal characteristics. Respondents were also asked how many individuals they were currently supervising, if they had any say over the pay of their subordinates, and the sex of their own supervisor.

An eight-item scale was included that I had developed from my interview data which asked respondents to rate differences between men and women managers in general. These items included stereotypical perceptions of women managers (too emotional, demanding, not willing to delegate, etc.) and actual differences suggested by recent research (more considerate, hard working, thorough, etc.) I also looked at how assessments of the respondents' own supervisor differed by the sex of the supervisor. In addition to the global rating, they were asked to assess their supervisors' behaviors in 13 areas (listening, taking and giving credit, delegating, being too emotional or sensitive, etc.).

Table 15A gives behaviors reported by these women. Notice the large percentages who say they always pay attention to subordinates' needs: giving credit, showing appreciation, listening to problems. However, equally high numbers say they set high standards. The trade-off between people and task orientation, the assumption that a manager is either one or the other, seems to not be true of these women. They are highly focused on both. These women reported themselves to use many of the tendencies found to be true of women in my original study. However, these women may not be aware they have so much in common. Another set of questions in this mail survey asked them to generalize about differences between men and women managers. Many claimed they could not do this, saying it was more a matter of personality than gender. Often, they simply did not answer these questions.

Another way of discovering gender differences is to ask individuals to describe their own supervisors. When these highly educated women did so, significant differences by sex of supervisor did appear, even though many of them had said they believed systematic gender differences did not exist. They described their women managers as more often using the model they themselves were using. These behaviors are depicted in Table 16A. Women supervisors were more often than men described as working hard, encouraging teamwork, listening to problems, and less often being too emotional (they said their men supervisors lost their tempers a lot) or pushing their work onto others.

I also have some information on the sources of life and job satisfaction among these women. Professional women do not seem to be any happier with their lives and jobs if they are managers. (See Table 17A.) These women managers simply reported different determinants of satisfaction than women who did not manage. The managers relied more heavily upon accomplishments at work, including promotions, recognition, and attaining their goals in arriving at their overall level of life satisfaction, than did highly educated women who were not managers. The *dis*satisfaction of women managers was also more influenced by work, specifically when they did *not* successfully pass hurdles or receive rewards, or when they felt they had too much work. These women managers were also more affected by being lonely in their personal lives or, alternatively, feeling they had no time for themselves. Overall, though, the two groups (managers and non-managers) were remarkably similar in terms of general life and job satisfaction. This may be peculiar to women in this type of occupation. If becoming a manager does not make a professional woman happier, it may be because she feels her job is sufficiently challenging and interesting in its own right. In fact, in many professional circles, becoming a manager may be seen as detracting from doing one's "real work," whatever that may be.

University of Wisconsin Administrators

In 1988, I also did a study of women and men administrators in a different large midwestern system, the University of Wisconsin. It is one of the largest systems in the nation, one that includes 26 two-year, four-year, and doctoral campuses. This study involved a mail survey which asked about management approaches, problems and other aspects of jobs, as well as focused interviews with twenty of the respondents.

The sample is composed of respondents to a mail questionnaire sent to all administrators above the level of department chair in the University of Wisconsin campus system. There are two doctoral campuses, eleven four-year institutions, and thirteen two-year "centers" in the system, with a total of 158 administrators. Return envelopes were enclosed with the questionnaires, and several reminders sent at certain intervals after the initial mailing. One-hundred-and-nineteen or nearly 75% of those administrators completed and returned the questionnaire. The centralized nature of the Wisconsin System made it relatively easy to obtain names and addresses of all administrators.

In addition to the mail questionnaire, I interviewed twenty administrators in depth about their administrative experiences and perceptions. Using the system-wide Administrative Directory, eleven women and nine men were matched by general administrative level, job, and institutional type. These face-to-face interviews, lasting approximately one-hour, were tape recorded and analyzed, using the constant comparative method developed by Glaser and Strauss (1967).

Managerial style was measured several ways in the questionnaires. First, a forty-five item, nine dimension Achieving Styles Inventory (available from the Achieving Styles Institute, Leavitt and Lipman-Blumen, 1980) was included, as it was one measure reported in the literature to tap subtle gender differences. It asks respondents on a scale from 1 to 7 to rate the importance to them of such things as having a challenge, winning, being a leader, gaining respect and admiration, helping others succeed, using relationships for self-gain, and using teamwork. The items have been factored into dimensions called 1) intrinsic direct, 2) competitive direct, 3) power direct, 4) personal instrumental, 5) social instrumental, 6) relational instrumental, 7) collaborative relational, 8) contributory relational, and 9) vicarious relational. (See Table 18A). The questionnaire also asked respondents to describe specific problems they encountered in being administrators, where few gender differences appeared. (See Table 19A.) Basic demographic information was also gathered. (See Tables 20A and 21A.)

The focused interviews allowed more careful probing of these same issues, asking respondents to describe their jobs, discuss administrative or managerial issues (including successes and failures), recount their career paths, assess the institution of higher education in general, and, at the end, hazard a guess as to how men and women administrators are different and the impact women administrators might have upon higher education.

The women in this sample were very similar to the highly educated women discussed earlier. In many instances, however, the men were more similar to the women than in my original study. Even so, women were somewhat more likely to stress giving subordinates credit, considering their needs, showing appreciation, encouraging teamwork, and establishing checkpoints. Men were somewhat more likely to stress giving autonomy and letting subordinates set their own pace.

Looking at Table 23A, note that these men *and* women believe that men supervisors are more likely to delegate, to allow subordinates to work on their own, and to show sensitivity, and women supervisors are more likely to establish checkpoints, to take credit for work, to push subordinates to work hard, to work hard themselves, to push work onto subordinates, to show concern about their positions, and to be too emotional. Here, we again see differences around autonomy given to subordinates, with men seen as giving lots of autonomy and women as establishing checkpoints. Also, women are seen as being very task oriented, particularly in their willingness to work hard. There are also some contradictory assessments here; women are seen as both too emotional and more likely to show consideration. This sounds like a double-edged sword. The woman's sensitivity on the job may be appreciated by many, while others may perceive that she is "too emotional."

Tables 24A and 25A, which look at these trends by sex of respondent, show some interesting contradictions. Males and females do not take the same views of their men and women supervisors. The men are the ones who believe their female supervisors are too emotional and push their work onto others. They also believe their women supervisors are insensitive, while *women* believe their *male* supervisors are too emotional and insensitive. Men are also likely to believe their male supervisors show more consideration, while women are somewhat more likely to see their female supervisors as doing so. The men are also the ones who believe their women supervisors take credit for the work of others. Women administrators saw their women supervisors as more concerned about the supervisors' own positions and less likely to allow them to work on their own, trends not nearly as pronounced among the men administrators.

In sum, then, there are several differences between men and women in the management model they espouse, as argued in Chapter 3. Women seem to believe working *with* subordinates is most effective, and they go about doing this through the types of relationships they foster with subordinates; they exhibit more consideration, appreciation, and other types of sensitivity. They also structure the relationship differently, establishing checkpoints for communications about delegated work. All of this activity is directed toward accomplishing the task, something women work at very hard -- harder than men -- according to many reports in my studies and elswhere. Men, on the other hand, seem to approach the management task with the notion that complete autonomy ought to be granted to subordinates, that to fail to do so constitutes unwarranted interference on the part of a supervisor.

It is also interesting to note that women's perceptions of women supervisors in general is different from men's. Table 26A from this same study shows that women make more favorable assessments of women supervisors than men do, believing they are more likely to give credit, be considerate, know what to do, and work hard -- and less likely to push work onto others.

The Wisconsin administrators also seemed to be giving up their stereotyped perceptions and adopting a more reality-based view. This did not mean, however, that the men came to *like* what the women were doing. They simply began to perceive it more accurately. In certain cases, the women's approach seemed to generate a great deal of hostility, particularly if each gender-specific model was strongly held by each individual.

African-American Managers

Together with an African-American former student at my institution, I did depth interviews with twenty African-American managers and administrators, ten men and ten women, about their jobs (Statham and Neinhaus, 1996). These interviews, conducted in 1991 , lasted from one to two hours and were tape-recorded and fully transcribed. Respondents ranged in age from 27 to 59, with the majority being in their forties and fifties. The average age for women was 45.3 and for men 41.4. Half of the respondents were currently married, with slightly more men being in first marriages. Women were more often divorced and men more often never married. All but one respondent had children, two or three children being the most common numbers. Their job tenure ranged from 1 to 17 years, with the majority having been in their jobs five years or less. Three men and three women had been in their jobs ten years or more.

These individuals were chosen to both simulate my original sample of Euro-American managers (Statham 1987a; 1987b) *and* to represent important types of leaders in the African-American community. In the previous study, managers and administrators from business, education, and banking were interviewed. Thus, we included all three types of individuals in our sample. We also interviewed several ministers, as they are important African-American leaders, as well as two military personnel (Non-Commissioned Officers), another source of leadership in that community. For each female we interviewed from a particular type of organization (and level within the organization), we interviewed a comparable male. Thus, our sample is a matched sample of men and women, controlling for place of work and level in the hierarchy.

This study is a qualitative examination of an area where we were uncertain of what we would find, hence exploratory in nature. And as Collins (1990) has put it, traditional social science approaches do not always yield the types of "truths" we are seeking, so we instead "rely on the voices" to show the reality of our respondents' lives. We were looking for evidence that gender may interact with race to produce differences in approaches to management, by comparing these findings with those from my original study of mostly Euro-American respondents.

We analyzed the transcripts for women and men separately within the various topic areas of basic approaches to one's job, decision-making strategies, managerial philosophies, conflict between work and family, racism and sexism at work, and perceived gender differences in approaches to work. In addition to looking at gender differences per se, we considered differences by type of workplace. As stated, we suspected those individuals working mainly with other African-Americans would experience the workplace differently than those working mostly with Euro-Americans. We had included individuals working in African- American (or other people of color) organizations (mostly self-employed or president -- five males and four females) *and* those working in predominately Euro-American settings (four males and four females). A few of these latter individuals worked in units concerned specifically with people of color (one male and two females). While our results looking within these categories are suggestive, given the small N's, they are also provocative and reflect trends I found elsewhere.

Study of Leadership in Native American Context

Beginning in the summer of 1993, a Native American student from my institution and myself began traveling around the state of Wisconsin, interviewing Native Americans about their notions (and experience) of leadership. This was also a depth interview study -- this time of 29 individuals.

It became apparent very quickly in our conversations that we would not be able to simply replicate the studies I had done previously of mostly Euro-American, and then even of African-American managers. These individuals found it very difficult to talk about something like leadership outside of the context of the culture which supported the practices they were reporting.

The state of Wisconsin is home to eleven American Indian groups, most of them centered around reservations in the northern part of the state. We spent much of our time visiting these reservations and interviewing those who would be considered leaders from both a Native American viewpoint (elders, healers, etc.), as well as those with leadership positions recognized by the outside society (directors of university centers and tribal programs, members of tribal councils, etc.). We interviewed a mix of Indian people currently living on reservations and those living in the urban centers of the state, including representatives of seven of the eleven groups in the state (Ho-Chunk, Potawotame, Menomine, Oneida, 3 Ojibwe). We also interviewed representatives of several nations not in the state, including Otl, Navaho, Abanakee, and Seminole (See Table 28A).

As with the other studies reported here, the interviews were tape-recorded and transcribed, then analyzed using the constant comparison method. It was very apparent how important cultural background was in shaping approaches to management or leadership. While there were differences in amount of emersion in the culture and important differences between these cultural groups, in the issues explored in Chapter 9, there was remarkable consistency in outlook across the various groups included.

TABLES

Table 1A

Supervisory Levels of Respondents

		Financial Institution		Manufacturing Firm		Technical Institute	
		women	men	women	men	women	men
Level 2[a]	Chief Operating Officer	0	1	0	0	0	0
Level 3	Senior Vice-President (Directors, Chief Planning Officers)	1	1	0	0	0	1
Level 4	Vice Presidents (Supervisors, Chief Operating Officer)	3	2	0	0	0	3
Level 5	Assistant Vice President (General Managers, Coordinators)	3	1	1	2	5	1
Level 6	Managers	1	0	5	5	1	
Level 7	Supervisors			2	1		
	Total	8	5	8	8	6	5

[a]Figure 1 contains exact titles for individuals at these levels in the 3 settings.

Figure 1A

Levels Firm	General Stucture Technical Institute	Financial Institution	Manufacturing
1 Chief Executive Officer (Board of Directors)	1 Chairman of Board	1 Chairman of Board	1 Board of Directors
2 Chief Operation Officer	2 President	2 President	2 Director
3 Senior Vice Presidents (Planning Officers)	3 Senior Vice Presidents	3 Senior Vice Presidents	3 Director
4 Vice President (Operations Officers)	4 Vice President	4 Vice President	4 Supervisor
5 Assistant Vice Presidents (Operational Involvement)	5 Assistant Vice Presidents	5 General Manager/ Director	5 Coordinator
6 Managers		6 Manager	6 Technician
7 Supervisors		7 Supervisor	

FIGURE 1A. Supervisory structure of three settings.

Table 2A

Demographic Characteristics of Managers

Salary	Women Managers	Men Managers
12,500 - 16,000	1	0
16,500 - 19,000	3	0
19,500 - 24,000	4	1
24,500 - 30,500	6	0
31,500 - 36,000	3	5
36,500 - 50,000	2	6
50,500 - 70,000	1	4
70,500 - 100,000	0	1
Age		
25 - 29	5	0
30 - 34	4	0
35 - 39	3	7
40 - 44	3	4
45 - 49	2	2
50 - 54	3	2
55 - 60	1	2
61 - 65	1	0
Years with Company		
1 - 5	6	3
6 - 10	7	7
11 - 15	5	3
16 - 20	3	2
20 +	1	1
Hours Worked/Week		
40	1	1
40 - 50	6	5
50 - 60	12	11
Education		
Associate Degree	2	0
Some College	5	1
College Degree	5	5
Graduate Degree	9	11
Marital Status		
Married	13	18
Divorced	5	0
Never Married	4	0
Remarried	0	0
Number of Children		
0	11	2
1	3	2
2	3	6
3 - 4	4	2
5 - 6	0	4

Table 3A

Existence of Mentor by Supervisory Level

Existence of Mentor	Supervisory Level[a]											
	C O O		Sr. VP		VP/Operating		Asst. VP		Managers		Supervisors	
	W	M	W	M	W	M	W	M	W	M	W	M
Yes	0	0	1	0	2	0	5	2	2	2	1	1
No	0	1	0	2	0	4	3	2	4	1	1	1
Mixed	0	0	0	0	1	0	1	0	1	1	0	0

[a]See Table 2A, for a full description of levels.

Table 4A

Existence and Type of Mentor by Sex of Manager

	Male Manager	Female Manager
Existence of Mentor		
Yes	5	10
No	11	8
Mixed Response	1	4
Multiple Mentors		
Yes	1	4
Identity of Mentor(s)		
Current Supervisor	0	5
Past Supervisor	6	9
Mother	0	1
Father	2	0
Spouse	0	2

Table 5A

Industry of Secretaries

	Original Managers - Interviews	Original Secretaries - Interviews	Secretaries - Survey
Manufacturing	40.0% (16)	38.7% (12)	13.7% (22)
Finance/Insurance	32.5% (13)	29.0% (9)	4.3% (7)
Medical/Legal			6.2% (10)
Government			3.7% (6)
Education	27.5% (11)	32.2% (10)	59.6% (86)
Communications			1.9% (3)
Transportation			1.9% (3)
Business Services			4.3% (7)
Computers			0.6% (1)
Retail Trade			0.6% (1)
Wholesale Trade			1.9% (3)
Totals	40	30*	161

*Several of the managers interviewed shared a single secretary. Only one secretary refused to be interviewed.

Table 6A

Supervisory Levels of Secretaries' Supervisors*

Supervisor's Level:

Original

Interviews	Survey	
1. Chief Executive Officer	0.0% (0)	6.4% (9)
2. Chief Operating Officer	2.5% (1)	12.5% (15)
3. Senior Planning Officer	7.5% (3)	16.4% (23)
4. Operation Officer	20.0% (8)	22.9% (32)
5. Direct Report to Operation Officer	32.5% (13)	27.9% (39)
6. Indirect Report to Operation Officer	37.5% (15)	15.7% (22)

* The actual question wording indicated that:

2 . Chief operating officers were sometimes called president of company, superintendent, executive director

3. Senior planning officers were sometimes called senior vice-presidents, directors, assistant superintendents

4. Operation offices were sometimes called vice presidents, supervisors, principals

5. Direct reports to operation officers were sometimes called general managers, coordinators, assistant principals

Table 7A

Demographics for Secretary Survey Sample

Sex			Education		
Male	3.1%	(3)	Less than H.S. Degree	1.9%	(3)
Female	96.6%	(157)	High School Degree	42.0%	(68)
			Some College	17.8%	(29)
Race			College Degree	8.0%	(13)
Black	1.4%	(2)	More than College	29.2%	(49)
Hispanic	1.4%	(2)			
Native American	14.4%	(23)	**Income**		
Caucasian	81.7%	(132)	0-2,999	1.4%	(2)
Asian	0		03,000-5,999	3.3%	(5)
Other	0.8%	(1)	6,000-9,999	5.1%	(8)
			10,000-14,999	38.5%	(62)
Years Worked			15,999-19,999	36.6%	(59)
1-5	3.7%	(6)	20,000-24,999	10.1%	(16)
6-10	22.8%	(37)	25,000-29,999	3.9%	(6)
11-15	23.5%	(38)	30,000-34,999	0.8%	(1)
16-20	19.8%	(32)			
21-25	15.4%	(25)	**Job Tenure**		
26-30	7.4%	(12)	Less than 1 Year	13.6%	(22)
30+	6.8%	(11)	1-5 Years	40.1%	(65)
			6-10 Years	25.9%	(42)
Union Member			11-15 Years	9.9%	(16)
Yes	48.8%	(79)	16-20 Years	7.4%	(12)
No	51.2%	(83)	20+ Years	3.1%	(5)

Table 8A

Secretaries' Job Titles

	Interviews	Surveys
Secretary I, II, III	63.3% (19)	35.0% (55)
Clerk-typist/Stenographer/ Receptionist	6.7% (2)	14.0% (22)
Executive Secretary/ Administrative assistant	30.0% (9)	16.5% (26)
Officer Manager/Manager		8.2% (13)
Para-professional (Legal Assistant, Library Assistant, etc.)		15.4% (25)
Computer Operator/Keypuncher		3.2% (5)
Other		1.9% (3)

The Rise of Marginal Voices

Table 9A

**Secretary's Perceptions of Supervisor's Behaviors
by Sex of Supervisor**

Supervisor:	Women Supervisors				Men Supervisors			
	always	often	some-times	never	always	often	some-times	times
never								
Inquires about career goals*[a]	44.0%	38.0%	16.0%	2.0%	58.7%	27.9%	9.6%	3.8 %
Work to improve job title/position	40.0	34.0	20.0	6.0	51.5	31.7	11.9	5.0
Gives tasks to improve level/skills	20.0	44.0	26.0	10.0	32.0	39.8	20.4	7.8
Encourages school[a]	51.1	34.0	10.6	4.3	65.3	13.9	10.9	9.9
Allows school on company time	71.1	15.6	11.1	2.2	62.1	26.3	6.3	5.3
Cooperates with maternity leave	42.6	17.0	29.8	10.6	46.9	19.8	26.3	11.5
Gives credit for work*	28.8	30.8	36.5	3.8	29.8	32.7	31.7	5.8
Shows* appreciation for work	32.7	23.1	38.5	5.8	29.8	28.8	33.7	7.7
Shows consideration	38.5	26.9	30.8	3.8	33.0	35.9	26.2	4.9
Consults about decisions*[b]	19.2	48.1	23.1	9.6	29.1	47.6	19.4	3.9
Treats as equal*	25.0	26.9	34.6	13.5	19.4	26.2	38.8	15.5
Works as team member*[b]	33.3	25.5	31.4	9.8	28.4	31.4	31.4	8.8
N		50					101	

*Significant (.05 level) predictor of overall evaluation of supervisor.
[a]Significant difference .05 level.
[b]Significant difference .10 level.

Table 10A

**General Community Assessments
of Behaviors of Men and Women Supervisors**

Supervisor:	Women Supervisors				Men Supervisors			
	very true	some-what true	not very true	not at all true	very true	some-what true	not very true	not at all true
Gives credit	35.0%	36.9%	20.4%	7.8%	35.3%	31.0%	23.0%	10.6 %
Is considerate	37.9	34.0	24.3	3.9	40.2	33.3	18.1	8.3
Includes worker in decisions	15.5	32.0	34.0	18.4	19.8	31.0	27.6	21.6
Pushes work onto others	4.9	13.6	28.2	53.4	10.1	8.7	28.1	53.0
Insists you follow rules	27.2	26.2	22.3	24.3	33.5	27.2	17.1	22.3
Leaves you alone	40.8	41.7	5.8	11.7	48.0	32.5	11.5	7.5
Knows what to do	48.5	32.0	13.6	5.8	49.6	31.4	11.5	7.5
Insists follow rules	47.6	32.0	12.6	7.8	49.15	26.6	17.1	7.2
In touch with you	43.7	35.0	15.5	5.8	43.5	31.7	17.3	7.5
Works hard	54.4	32.0	3.9	9.7	50.6	28.7	13.2	7.5
N			103				348	

The Rise of Marginal Voices

Table 11A

General Community
Perceptions of Supervisors by Sex of Respondent

Supervisor:	Men				Women			
	very true	some-what true	not very true	not at all true	very true	some-what true	not very true	not at all true
Gives credit	32.2%	30.8%	26.5%	10.4%	39.0%	34.4%	17.2%	9.4%
Is considerate	39.2	31.2	21.5	8.1	40.1	36.5	17.2	6.3
Includes worker in decisions	22.3	29.6	26.9	21.2	14.1	33.3	31.8	20.8
Pushes work onto others	11.1	9.2	28.8	50.8	7.3	10.4	27.1	55.2
Insists you work hard	32.3	26.9	17.3	22.7	31.3	26.6	19.3	22.9
Leaves you alone	48.8	33.9	10.4	6.9	42.7	35.9	9.9	11.5
Knows what to do	46.5	33.5	12.3	7.3	52.6	29.2	11.5	6.8
Insists you follow rules	46.9	28.8	16.5	7.3	51.0	26.5	15.1	7.3
In touch with you	43.1	33.8	17.3	5.4	44.3	30.7	16.2	9.4
Works hard	48.1	30.4	14.2	7.3	55.7	28.7	6.8	9.4

Table 12A

**Male and Female Assessments
of Men and Women Supervisors**

| Supervisor: | WOMEN WORKERS | | | | | | | |
| | Men supervisors | | | | Women Supervisors | | | |
	very true	some-what true	not very true	not at all true	very true	some-what true	not very true	not at all true
Gives credit	34.4%	37.7%	21.1%	6.7%	43.1%	31.4%	3.7%	11.8 %
Is considerate	36.7	35.6	23.3	4.4	43.1	37.3	11.8	7.8
Includes worker in decisions	14.4	32.2	33.3	20.0	13.7	34.3	30.4	21.6
Pushes work onto others	5.6	12.2	27.8	54.4	8.8	8.8	26.5	55.9
Insists you follow rules	27.8	26.7	22.2	23.3	34.3	26.5	16.7	22.5
Leaves you alone	40.0	41.1	6.7	12.2	45.1	31.4	12.7	10.8
Knows what to do	48.9	32.2	14.4	4.4	55.9	26.5	8.8	8.8
Insists you follow rules	46.7	33.3	12.2	7.8	54.5	20.8	17.8	6.9
In touch with you	43.3	34.4	15.6	6.7	44.1	27.5	16.7	11.8
Works hard	54.5	32.2	3.3	10.0	56.9	24.5	9.8	8.8
N			90				102	

The Rise of Marginal Voices

Table 12A Continued

MEN WORKERS

Supervisor:	Men supervisors				Women Supervisors			
	very true	some-what true	not very true	not at all true	very true	some-what true	not very true	not at all true
Gives credit	38.5%	30.8%	15.4%	15.4%	32.1%	30.9%	26.8%	10.2 %
Is considerate	46.2	23.1	30.8	0	39.0	31.7	20.7	8.5
Includes worker in decisions	23.1	30.8	38.5	7.7	22.4	29.7	26.4	21.5
Pushes work onto others	0	23.1	30.8	46.5	10.7	8.6	28.8	51.9
Insists you follow rules	23.1	23.1	23.1	30.8	33.2	27.5	17.2	22.1
Leaves you alone	46.2	46.2	0	7.7	49.2	32.9	11.0	6.9
Knows what to do	46.2	30.8	7.7	15.4	46.9	33.5	12.7	6.9
Insists you follow rules	53.8	23.1	15.4	7.7	46.9	29.0	16.7	7.3
In touch with you	46.3	38.5	15.4	0	43.3	33.5	17.6	5.7
Works hard	53.8	30.8	7.7	7.7	48.0	30.5	14.6	6.9
N		13			246			

Table 13A

**Characteristics of Highly Educated Women Sample:
Type of Degree, Year of Degree, Year of Birth**

Type of Degree		Year of Degree		Year of Birth	
Ph.D	72.5%	Before 1966	8.3%	Before 1920	3.9%
Ed.D	.2%	1966-1969	17.4%	1920-1929	15.0%
M.D.	10.6%	1970-1972	28.7%	1930-1939	32.3%
J.D.	6.6%	1972-1975	41.5%	1940-1949	44.7%
D.V.M.	4.9%	1976 +	4.0%	1950 +	4.0%
D.D.	.2%				
M.B.A.	2.1%				
Other	2.9%				
N	472	N	470	N	461

Table 14A

Field of Study of Doctorates

Agricultural	.9%
Anthropology	1.2%
Art	.9%
Astronomy	.3%
Biology	5.4%
Business	1.2%
Chemistry	3.6%
Classics	.9%
Communication	2.1%
Education	26.8%
English	5.7%
Foreign Language	5.4%
Geology	.6%
History	2.4%
Home Economics	12.0%
Linguistics	.9%
Mathematics	1.2%
Music	.6%
Philosophy	.9%
Physical Education	6.6%
Political Science	.9%
Psychology	9.3%
Social Work	.3%
Sociology	2.1%
Speech & Hearing	1.8%
Theater	1.2%
Other Sciences	1.5%
Interdisciplinary	.3%
N	332

Table 15A

**Highly Educated Women's
Self-Reported Behaviors as Supervisory Women**

	Always	Usually	Sometimes	Seldom	Never
Difficulty delegating	.7%	6.3%	42.8%	36.9%	12.5%
Consult subordinate in decisions	13.1%	62.5%	20.4%	2.9%	.7%
Establish check points for delegating work	23.8%	52.4%	17.6%	4.8%	1.1%
Work very hard	44.4%	46.9%	6.5%	1.1%	.7%
Insistent subordinates work hard	14.0%	57.9%	22.1%	5.5%	----
Give subordinates autonomy	2.6%	44.9%	41.2%	8.5%	2.6%
Give subordinates credit	60.3%	36.5%	2.9%	----	----
Show appreciation to subordinates	52.7%	43.2%	3.3%	.5%	----
Let subordinates set own pace	8.4%	56.9%	27.4%	6.9%	----
Encourage teamwork	50.7%	41.4%	6.7%	.7%	.4%
Set high standards	60.1%	36.2%	2.9%	.4%	----
Listen to job related problems	54.5%	39.6%	4.4%	1.1%	----
Work to improve subordinate performance	32.7%	49.8%	16.0%	1.1%	----
Consider needs of subordinate	38.5%	54.5%	5.8%	.7%	----

Table 16A

**Highly Educated Women's
Reports of Supervisor's Behaviors****

Women's Supervisor:	Always	Usually	Sometimes	Seldom	Never
1. Finds it difficult to delegate*	2.6%	8.4%	27.2%	43.2%	18.6%
2. Let's her work on own	30.8%	53.9%	11.7%	3.1%	.6%
3. Shows appreciation	19.6%	35.8%	27.4%	11.7%	5.6%
4. Establishes checkpoints*	8.2%	22.6%	27.4%	26.8%	15.0%
5. Takes credit for her work	2.9%	7.2%	17.5%	26.7%	45.7%
6. Pushes to work hard	9.4%	14.9%	21.1%	31.6%	23.1%
7. Works hard*	36.9%	40.6%	10.9%	8.3%	3.4%
8. Shows consideration	17.4%	41.4%	26.0%	9.4%	5.7%
9. Encourages teamwork*	20.1%	35.1%	25.0%	14.9%	4.9%
10. Listens to job problems*	26.4%	38.2%	21.6%	8.9%	4.9%
11. Is concerned about position	24.5%	23.6%	22.2%	22.2%	7.5%
12. Pushes work onto subordinates*	5.3%	15.2%	33.3%	32.7%	13.2%
13. Is too emotional*	2.6%	3.7%	17.0%	38.9%	37.8%
14. Is insensitive	6.3%	8.5%	27.4%	37.6%	20.2%

*Significant difference by sex of supervisor
**All but 6. significantly related to evaluation of supervisor

Table 17A

**Differences Between Managers and Non-Managers
in Life Experiences**

Supervisory Status	Job Satisfaction				
	Very Satisfied	Satisfied	Neutral	Dissatisfied	Very Dissatisfied
yes	40.6%	43.8%	7.4%	5.3%	1.4%
	115	124	21	15	4
no	34.6%	49.2%	9.2%	3.8%	3.8%
	45	64	12	5	5

$X^2 = 6.986$ Significance = .4303

Supervisory Satus	Life Satisfaction				
	Very Satisfied	Satisfied	Neutral	Dissatisfied	Very Dissatisfied
yes	37.5%	45.4%	7.5%	8.2%	1.4%
	105	127	21	23	4
no	34.9%	45.0%	9.3%	6.2%	4.7%
	45	58	12	8	6

$X^2 = 4.746$ Significance = .3143

Table 17A Continued

Income

Supervisory Status	3,000-	6,000-4,999	10,000-9,999	15,000-14,999	20,000-19,999	25,000-24,999	30,000-29,999	35,000-34,999	40,000-39,999	45,000-45,999	50,000+49,999
yes	.4% 1		1.1% 3	3.5% 10	3.9% 11	6.7% 19	9.6% 27	9.9% 28	10.6% 30	8.5% 24	45.4% 128
no	1.5% 2	3.1% 4	4.6% 6	3.1% 4	6.2% 8	11.5% 15	15.4% 20	19.2% 25	11.5% 15	6.2% 8	17.7% 23

$X^2 = 47.4563$ Significance = .0000

TABLE 18A

Mean Levels of Agreement[a]
with Achieving Styles Items
Among Wisconsin Administrators

	Women	Men
Intrinsic Direct		
Most gratifying to solve problem	6.03	5.87
More than anything, like challenges	5.60	5.58
Most exciting thing, work on tough problem	5.43	5.30
Go out of way to work on challenges	4.93	5.22
Greatest satisfaction, breaking through solution	5.60	5.67
Competitive Direct		
Winning most important	3.68	3.52
Winning in competition most thrilling	3.61	3.41
More competitive the situation, the better	3.88	3.57
Not happy until come out on top	3.83	3.93
Seek competitive situations, do better	3.83	3.69
Power Direct		
Want to be leader	5.30	5.19
Seek out leadership positions	5.07	5.19
Seek positions of authority	4.73	4.80
Want to take charge working with others	4.97	4.87
Being in charge exciting	5.13	4.96
Personal Instrumental		
Work hard so people think well of me	5.18	4.78
Strive to achieve so well liked	4.42	3.59
Try to be successful so respected	5.35	5.26
Strive to achieve for recognition	4.78	4.24
Work toward goals for others' admiration	4.35	3.76
Social Instrumental		
Get to know important people to succeed	3.63	4.22
Develop relationships to get what need	3.90	4.21
Establish relationships for benefits	4.00	4.02
Use relationships to get things done	4.50	4.81
Establish relationships to get to know others	3.27	3.21

Table 18A Continued

Relation Instrumental

To achieve something, look for assistance	4.83	4.96
Seek guidance when have task	5.05	4.89
Look for support with new task	5.10	5.02
Look for reassurance with decisions	4.68	4.11
When encounter problem, go for help	4.63	4.93

Collaborative Relational

Faced with task, use team approval	5.15	5.00
Real team effort best way	5.25	5.07
Group effort most effective	5.30	5.11
Working with others brings out best	5.22	5.17
Best achievements working with others	5.08	4.94

Contributory Relationship

Achieve through contributing to others' success	5.52	5.48
Achieve by guiding others to their goals	5.35	5.39
Achieve by coaching others to their success	5.18	5.02
Succeed by active part in helping others succeed	5.30	5.26
Achieve by helping others learn what they want	4.57	4.87

Vicarious Relational

Feel others success as my own	4.85	4.76
Feel failure when those I care about do poorly	4.67	4.11
Feel success when loved one succeeds	5.50	5.39
Greatest accomplishment when those I love succeed	5.27	4.74
Others accomplishments give me sense of accomplishment	5.34	5.04

Mean differences on scales

Intrinsic Direct	5.54	5.50
Competitive Direct	3.76	3.62
Power Direct	5.05	5.00
Personal Instrumental	4.82	4.33
Social Instrumental	3.84	4.09
Reliant Instrumental	4.88	4.78
Collaborative Relational	5.20	5.06
Contributory Relational	5.18	5.20
Vicarious Relational	5.12	4.81

ªScales were 1 to 7, where 1 was "never" and 7 was "always"

TABLE 19A

Perceiving Specific Problems
and Supports in Wisconsin Administrative Position

	Women	Men
Supports		
Resources*	5.5%	26.7%
Good Organization	36.4%	33.3%
Automony or control	6.4%	20.0%
Manageable workload	5.5%	10.0%
Good Supervisors	2.7%	21.7%
Good Peers	9.1%	13.3%
Good Subordinants	40.0%	46.7%
Management skills	14.5%	16.7%
Organizational ability	25.5%	21.7%
Comparison	5.5%	8.3%
Team approach	41.8%	31.7%
People skills[a]	21.8%	35.0%
Hardworking	12.7%	6.7%
Stamina	3.6%	10.0%
Humor	9.1%	3.3%
Keep perspective	27.3%	18.3%
Problems		
Bureaucracy	54.5%	61.7%
Resource limitations	76.55	68.3%
Poor organizational structure	7.3%	15.0%
No automony or authority*	1.8%	15.0%
Too much work	34.5%	25.0%
No time to focus	20.0%	12.7%
Problems with supervisors	9.1%	6.7%
Problems with subordinants	2.7%	11.7%
Problems with peers	5.5%	5.0%
Politics	21.8%	30.0%
Other interpersonal problems	5.5%	8.35
Lack of management skills	3.6%	11.7%
Too tough	1.8%	0
Not tough enough[a]	10.9%	21.7%
Tired, exhausted	3.6%	6.7%
Lack of balance in life	0	1.7%
Sexism	21.8%	1.7%
Ageism	1.8%	0
Racism	3.6%	0

* significant difference at .05 level
[a] significant difference at .17 level

TABLE 20A

Demographics of Wisconsin Women and Men Administrators

	Men		Women	
Age				
Under 30	0		1	1.9%
30-39	9	15.0%	15	28.0%
40-49	19	31.7%	24	44.5%
50-59	25	41.6%	10	20.6%
60+	7	11.7%	3	5.6%
Marital Status				
Never married	1	1.7%	10	18.5%
Married	49	81.7%	33	61.1%
Remarried	6	10.0%	5	9.3%
Divorced	2	3.3%	5	9.3%
Widowed	2	3.3%	1	1.9%
Number of Children				
0	3	5.0%	21	37.5%
1	6	10.0%	6	10.7%
2	20	33.3%	16	28.6%
3	19	31.7%	8	14.3%
4	7	11.7%	3	5.4%
5	5	8.3%	1	1.8%
Race				
White	58	96.7%	51	91.1%
Black	1	1.7%	2	3.6%
Hispanic	0		2	3.6%
American Indian	1	1.7%	0	
Asian	0		1	1.8%

TABLE 21A

Work Related Demographics for Wisconsin Women and Men Administrators

Education	Men		Women	
High School	0		2	3.6%
College	8	13.3%	11	19.6%
Masters	16	26.7%	19	33.9%
Ph.D	36	60.0%	24	42.9%
Work Status*				
Full Time	60	100.0%	51	91.1%
Part Time	0		5	8.9%
Type of Institution				
Four-year	52	86.7%	43	78.2%
Two-year	8	13.3%	12	21.8%
Level of Management*				
Upper	31	51.7%	12	22.2%
Middle	24	40.0%	35	64.8%
First Line	4	6.7%	3	6.5%
Professional	1	1.7%	3	5.6%
Job Tenure*				
1-5 years	26	43.4%	34	64.1%
6-10 years	11	18.3%	16	30.2%
11-15 years	16	26.6%	3	5.7%
16-20 years	5	8.4%	0	
20+	2	3.4%	0	
Income*				
10,000-14,999	0		2	3.6%
15,000-19,999	0		1	1.8%
20,000-24,999	0		1	1.8%
25,000-29,999	3	5.0%	4	7.3%
30,000-34,999	1	1.7%	8	14.5%
35,000-39,999	6	10.0%	0	18.2%
40,000-44,999	6	10.0%	14	25.5%
45,000-49,999	9	15.0%	2	3.6%
50,000-54,999	7	11.7%	6	10.9%
55,000-59,999	5	8.3%	2	3.6%
60,000-64,999	9	15.0%	2	3.6%
65,000-69,999	3	5.0%	0	
70,000-74,999	3	5.0%	0	
75,000-79,999	3	5.0%	1	1.8%
80,000+	5	8.3%	2	3.6%

*Gender differences significant at .05 level

TABLE 22A

Wisconsin Administrator's
Self-Reported Managerial Behaviors

	Men					Women				
	Always	Usually	Some-times	Seldom	Never	Always	Usually	Some-times	Seldom	Never
Difficulty delegating	0	5.0%	50.0%	33.3%	28.7%	0	3.6%	37.5%	44.6%	14.3%
Work very hard	50.0%	48.3%	1.7%	0	0	48.2%	46.4%	3.6%	1.8%	0
Insist subordinates work hard	10.0%	66.0%	26.7%	1.7%	1.7%	26.0%	61.8%	10.9%	3.6%	3.6%
Give subordinates autonomy	5.0%	62.3%	26.7%	5.0%	0	3.6%	60.7%	28.6%	5.4%	1.8%
Consult subordinates about decisions	15.0%	71.7%	11.7%	1.7%	0	10.7%	64.3%	21.4%	3.6%	0
Establish check points for delegated work	8.3%	55.6%	26.7%	8.3%	1.7%	21.4%	57.1%	14.3%	5.4%	1.8%
Give subordinates credit*	58.3%	35.0%	6.7%	0	0	78.6%	21.4%	0	0	0
Let subordinates set own pace*	1.7%	75.0%	20.0%	3.3%	0	12.5%	51.8%	35.7%	0	0
Encourages teamwork	36.7%	43.3%	16.7%	3.3%	0	48.2%	42.9%	8.9%	0	0
Set high standards	53.3%	35.0%	11.7%	0	0	48.2%	48.2%	3.6%	0	0
Listen to job related problems	55.9%	39.0%	5.1%	0	0	56.4%	36.4%	7.3%	0	0
Work to improve subordinate performance	33.3%	45.0%	18.3%	3.3%	0	42.9%	46.4%	10.7%	0	0
Consider needs of subordinates	26.7%	63.3%	10.0%	0	0	30.4%	76.9%	1.8%	0	0
Shows appreciation to subordinates	40.0%	51.7%	8.3%	0	0	55.4%	42.9%	1.8%	0	0

*Significant difference at .05 level

TABLE 23A

Wisconsin Administrator's Reports of Their Supervisor's Behaviors

Supervisor:	Men Supervisors					Women Supervisors				
	Always	Usually	Some-times	Seldom	Never	Always	Usually	Some-times	Seldom	Never
1. Finds it difficult to delegate*	0	11.6%	14.7%	45.3%	28.4%	4.3%	13.0%	0	56.5%	26.1%
2. Let's person work on own*	33.7%	57.9%	6.3%	2.1%	0	17.4%	56.5%	21.7%	4.3%	0
3. Shows Appreciation	28.4%	37.9%	22.1%	10.5%	1.1%	13.0%	43.5%	39.1%	4.3%	0
4. Establishes checkpoints*	4.2%	33.7%	32.6%	21.1%	8.4%	4.3%	65.2%	8.7%	13.0%	8.7%
5. Takes credit for person's work*	0	4.2%	10.5%	38.9%	46.3%	4.5%	4.5%	18.2%	50.0%	22.7%
6. Pushes to work hard*	4.3%	22.6%	25.8%	32.3%	15.1%	18.2%	40.9%	18.2%	13.6%	9.1%
7. Works hard*	39.1%	34.8%	13.0%	13.0%	0	49.5%	41.1%	7.4%	2.1%	0
8. Shows consideration	21.1%	43.2%	25.3%	9.5%	1.1%	13.0%	52.2%	21.7%	13.0%	0
9. Encourages teamwork	21.1%	40.0%	24.2%	13.7%	1.1%	21.7%	34.8%	21.7%	21.7%	0
10. Listens to job problems	45.3%	31.6%	12.6%	8.4%	2.1%	21.7%	47.8%	26.1%	4.3%	0
11. Is concerned about own position*	9.6%	19.1%	26.6%	34.0%	10.6%	34.8%	30.4%	21.7%	13.0%	0
12. Pushes work onto subordinates*	2.1%	10.6%	33.0%	43.6%	10.6%	13.6%	36.4%	27.3%	18.2%	4.5%
13. Is to emotional	0	4.3%	17.4%	47.8%	30.4%	1.1%	0	12.8%	35.1%	1.1%
14. Is insensitive*	0	13.0%	43.5%	21.7%	21.7%	3.2%	2.1%	18.1%	41.5%	35.1%

*Significant differences by sex of supervisor
Fem Sup = 11   Male Sup = 48

TABLE 24A

Wisconsin Men Administrator's Reports of Their Supervisor's Behaviors

Supervisor:	Men Supervisors					Women Supervisors				
	Always	Usually	Some-times	Seldom	Never	Always	Usually	Some-times	Seldom	Never
1. Finds it difficult to delegate	0	12.5%	14.6%	45.8%	27.1%	0	9.1%	0	63.6%	27.3%
2. Let's person work on own	31.3%	62.5%	4.2%	2.1%	0	27.3%	54.5%	18.2%	0	0
3. Shows Appreciation	25.0%	41.7%	27.1%	6.3%	0	9.1%	45.5%	45.5%	0	0
4. Establishes checkpoints	4.2%	37.5%	33.3%	20.8%	4.2%	0	72.7%	9.1%	9.1%	9.1%
5. Takes credit for person's work*	0	0	10.4%	43.8%	45.8%	0	0	18.2%	72.7%	9.1%
6. Pushes to work hard	2.1%	22.9%	29.2%	33.3%	12.5%	9.1%	45.5%	27.3%	9.1%	9.1%
7. Works hard*	50.0%	45.8%	4.2%	0	0	27.3%	36.4%	18.2%	18.2%	0
8. Shows consideration*	25.0%	45.8%	29.2%	0	0	9.1%	54.5%	18.2%	18.2%	0
9. Encourages teamwork	25.0%	43.8%	20.8%	10.4%	0	27.3%	27.3%	18.2%	18.2%	0
10. Listens to job problems	50.0%	33.3%	14.6%	2.1%	0	18.2%	54.5%	27.3%	0	0
11. Is concerned about own position	6.3%	18.8%	25.0%	41.7	8.3%	18.2%	36.4%	18.2%	27.3%	0
12. Pushes work onto subordinates*	0	10.4%	39.6%	41.7%	8.3%	27.3%	36.4%	18.2%	18.2%	0
13. Is to emotional*	0	0	16.7%	39.6%	43.8%	0	9.1%	18.2%	54.5%	18.2%
14. Is insensitive*	0	2.1%	18.8%	45.8%	33.3%	0	18.2%	45.5%	27.3%	9.1%

*Significant differences by sex of supervisor
Fem Sup = 11 Male Sup 48

TABLE 25A

Wisconsin Women Administrator's Reports of Their Supervisor's Behaviors

Supervisor:	Men Supervisors					Women Supervisors				
	Always	Usually	Some-times	Seldom	Never	Always	Usually	Some-times	Seldom	Never
1. Finds it difficult to delegate	0	11.1%	15.6%	42.2%	31.1%	9.1%	9.1%	0	54.5%	27.3%
2. Let's person work on own	37.8%	51.1%	8.9%	2.2%	0	9.1%	63.6%	27.3%	0	0
3. Shows Appreciation	33.3%	33.3%	15.6%	15.6%	2.2%	9.1%	45.5%	36.4%	9.1%	
4. Establishes checkpoints	4.4%	28.9%	31.1%	22.2%	13.3%	9.1%	54.5%	9.1%	18.2%	9.1%
5. Takes credit for person's work	0	8.9%	11.1%	33.3%	46.7%	9.1%	9.1%	18.2%	27.3%	36.4%
6. Pushes to work hard	6.8%	22.7%	20.5%	31.8%	18.2%	27.3%	36.4%	9.1%	18.2%	9.1%
7. Works hard	48.9%	35.6%	11.1%	4.4%	0	45.5%	36.4%	9.1%	9.1%	0
8. Shows consideration	17.8%	40.0%	20.0%	20.0%	2.2%	18.2%	54.5%	18.2%	9.1%	0
9. Encourages teamwork	17.8%	37.8%	24.4%	17.8%	2.2%	18.2%	36.4%	18.2%	27.3%	0
10. Listens to job problems	37.8%	31.1%	11.1%	15.6%	4.4%	18.2%	45.5%	27.3%	9.1%	0
11. Is concerned about own position*	13.6%	20.5%	29.5%	22.7%	13.6%	45.5%	27.3%	27.3%	0	0
12. Pushes work onto subordinates*	4.5%	11.4%	25.0%	45.5%	13.6%	0	36.4%	36.4%	18.2%	9.1%
13. Is to emotional	2.3%	9.1%	29.5%	59.1%	0	0	18.2%	45.5%	36.4%	0
14. Is insensitive*	6.8%	2.3%	18.2%	36.4%	36.4%	0	9.1%	36.4%	18.2%	36.4%

*Significant differences by sex of supervisor
Fem Sup 11   Male Sup = 44

TABLE 26A

Wisconsin Administrator's
Perceptions of Women Managers

Women Managers are:

	Men					Women				
	Strongly Agree	Agree	Neutral	Disagree	Strongly Disagree	Strongly Agree	Agree	Neutral	Disagree	Strongly Disagree
More Considerate*	0	11.9%	47.5%	35.6%	5.1%	2.0%	31.4%	45.1%	19.6%	2.0%
More Appreciative*	1.7%	10.2%	35.6%	45.8%	6.8%	5.8%	34.6%	38.5%	19.2%	1.9%
More Demanding	0	3.4%	50.8%	40.7%	5.1%	5.8%	13.5%	48.1%	30.8%	.9%
Harder Working*	0	6.8%	30.5%	50.8%	11.9%	15.4%	42.3%	30.8%	9.6%	1.9%
Less Likely to Delegate*	0	3.4%	42.4%	47.5%	6.8%	0	30.8%	40.4%	23.1%	5.8%
More Thorough*	0	5.1%	42.4%	45.8%	6.8%	5.8%	40.4%	38.5%	11.5%	3.8%
Harder to Work For	0	5.1%	27.1%	54.2%	13.6%	0	7.7%	42.3%	34.6%	15.4%
More Emotional	0	6.8%	35.6%	49.2%	8.5%	0	15.4%	28.8%	38.5%	17.3%

*Significant gender difference

Table 27A

Demographics of African-American Sample by Gender

Women

Age	N	Education	N
31	1	AA degree, vocational training	2
36	1	Some college	1
40	1	College degree	1
41	1	Some grad. school	1
42	1	MA	1
43	1	MA, work on PhD	2
52	1	PhD	2
54	1		
55	1		
59	1		

Marital Status	N	Type of Workplace	N
		African-American Company	3
Married	4	Self-employed	2
Remarried	1	Specialized unit within bureaucracy	1
Divorced	5	Large bureaucracy	4
Never married	0		

Number of Children		Age of Children	
N		N	
0	0	1-5	1
1	1	6-12	3
2	3	13-18	3
3	3	18-25	5
4	3	26+	3

The Rise of Marginal Voices

Table 27A Continued

Men

Age	N	Education	N
27	2	AA degree, vocational training	0
32	1	Some college	1
37	1	College degree	1
42	2	Some grad. school	1
43	1	MA	2
47	1	MA, work on PhD	4
51	1	PhD	1
52	1		

		Type of Workplace	N
		African-American Company	1
Marital		Self-employed	3
Status	N	Specialized unit within	
Married	5	bureaucracy	2
Remarried	0	Large	
Divorced	2	bureaucracy	4
Never married	3		

Number of Children		Age of Children	
N		N	
0	1	1-5	2
1	3	6-12	6
2	4	13-18	4
3	2	18-25	2
4	0	26+	0

Table 28A

Demographics of Respondents in Wisconsin Indian Study

Tribal Affiliation	Gender		Position		
	Male	Female	University Program	Tribal Program	Traditional Position
Wisconsin					
Oneida 3	0	3	2	2	1
Menominee 4	2	2	1	3	1
Ojibwe					
Bad River 4	2	2	3	3	3
Lac Du Flambaeu 6	1	5	0	5	4
Mole Lake 2	1	1	1	2	1
Michigan 1	1	0	1	0	1
Winnebago (Ho-Chunk) 1	1	0	1	0	0
Potawatomi 2	2	0	0	2	1
Others					
Otl 1	1	0	1	0	0
Navaho 2	1	1	2	0	1
Abanakee 1	0	1	1	1	1
Seminole 2	0	2	0	2	2

Bibliography

Aburdene, Patricia and John Naisbitt. *Megatrends for Women*. New York: Villard Books, 1992.

Adler, Nancy. "Pacific basin managers: A *Gaijin*, not a woman," in *Women in Management Worldwide* (eds.) Nancy Adler and Dafna Izraeli. New York: M. E. Sharpe Inc., 1988.

Adler, Nancy and Dafna Izraeli. *Women in Management Worldwide*. Armonk, NY: M. E. Sharpe, Inc., 1988.

The Administrator, "Off the cuff: Creativity can be taught," July 9, 1990.

The Administrator, "Off the cuff: Workshops help women attain leadership positions," April 30, 1990.

The Administrator, "Off the cuff: So what's wrong with being irreplaceable?" January 8, 1990.

The Administrator, "Off the cuff: Do women make good managers?" December 9, 1989.

The Administrator, "Off the cuff: Doing administration," November 11, 1989.

The Administrator, "Off the cuff: Doing administration," November 11, 1988.

The Administrator, "Participative management, McKeesport style," 7: 1. June 13, 1988.

The Administrator, "Off the cuff: The fourth D: Delegate," March 28, 1988.

The Administrator, "Off the cuff: Falling off the ladder," November 9, 1987.

The Administrator, "Off the cuff: Lessons from gridiron," November 9, 1987.

The Administrator, "Off the cuff: It's all in the follow-through," October 12, 1987.

The Administrator, "Off the cuff: The adaptive organization," December 29, 1986.

The Administrator, "Off the Cuff: The ability to influence," June 22, 1986.

The Administrator, "Off the cuff: Inside-outside management," April 14, 1986.

The Administrator, "Out of touch?" 1986.

Aguilera-Hellwig, Max. "Camille Paglia and Susan Gordon meet face to face," *Working Women*. March, p. 76-79, 106, 1992.

Aiken, Michael, Louis Freeman, Harold Sheppard. *Economic Failure, Alienation, and Extremism*. Ann Arbor: University of Michigan Press, 1968.

Aiken, Susan Hardy, Karen Anderson, Myra Dinnerstein, Judy Nolte Lensink, and Patricia MacCorquodale. *Changing Our Minds: Feminist Transformations of Knowledge.* Albany, NY: State University of New York Press, 1988.

Albinski, Nan Bowman. *Women's Utopias in British and American Fiction.* New York: Routledge, 1988.

Alexander, Shana. "A woman undone," *Ms Magazine,* September, 40-45, 1986.

Allen, Paula Gunn. *The Sacred Hoop: Recovering the Feminine in American Indian Traditions.* Boston: Beacon Press, 1986.

Alperson, Myra. "The new corporate culture," *Building Economic Alternatives.* Summer, p. 5, 1988.

Alvarado, Rose. "Dual career couples: Anxieties of MBA couples with traditional couples," Report Graduate School of Business, Stanford University, Palo Alto, California, 1989.

Anderson, Bonnie and Judith Zinsser. *A History of Their Own: From Prehistory to the Present.* Vol. I. New York: Harper and Row, 1988.

Anderson, Sherry and Patricia Hopkins. *The Feminine Face of God.* New York: Bantam, 1991.

Anscombe, Isabelle. *A Woman's Touch: Women in Design from 1860 to The Present Day.* New York: Penguin Books, 1985.

Arditti, Rita. "Interview on envisioning a feminist world," *Women of Power,* Summer, Issue 2, 1985.

Astin, Helen and Carole Leland. *Women of Influence, Women of Vision.* San Francisco: Jossey-Bass, 1991.

Astrachan, Anthony. "On the job." *Ms Magazine.* August p. 62-63, 106, 1984.

The Rise of Marginal Voices

Auerbach, Nina. *Communities of Women: An Idea in Fiction.* Cambridge: Harvard University Press, 1978.

Austin, Beth. "Office madness: In corporate America, sanity is often the price paid for success," *Chicago Tribune.* October 19, 1986.

Badaury, M. K. "How women managers view their role in the organization." *Personnel Administration.* 23: 60, 62, 64-68, 1978.

Bailey, Julie. "Special report: Jobs for women in the nineties." *Ms Magazine*, p. 74-78, July, 1988.

Baker-Miller, Jean. "Women and power." Paper in progress: Wellesley College, Stone Center for Developmental Services and Studies, Wellesley, Massachusetts, 1982.

Baldwin, Deborah. "Quiet conviction," *Common Cause Magazine.* 34-38, March/April, 1990.

Ball, Aimee Lee. "Learning to love life at the top," *Working Woman,* 78-80, 132. June, 1989.

Balsamo, Anne. "Beyond female as variable: Constructing a feminist perspective on organizational analysis," *Women and Language.* 9:35-38, 1985.

Bandarage, Asoka. "From universal sexual subordination to international feminism: a critical assessment." Unpublished mimeo, Brandeis University, 1983.

Baron, Alma and Ken Abrahamsen. "Will he or won't he work with a female manager?" *Management Review.* November, 1981.

Baron, James N., William T. Bielby and Alison Davis-Blake. "The structure of opportunity: How promotion ladders vary within organizations," *Administrative Science Quarterly.* 31:248-273, June, 1986.

Baron, James N. and William T. Bielby. "Organizational barriers to gender equality: Sex segregation on jobs and organizations," in Barbara Reskin (ed.) *Sex Segregation in the Workplace: Trends, Explanations, and Remedies.* Washington, DC: national Academy Press, 1983.

Baron, James, P. Devereaux Jennings, and Frank R. Dobbin. "Mission control? The development of personnel systems in U.S. industry." *American Sociological Review.* 53: 497-514, 1988.

Barrett, Nancy. "Women in the job market: Unemployment and work schedules," in Ralph E. Smith (ed.) *The Subtle Revolution.* Washington, DC: The Urban Institute, 1979.

Bartol, K. R. "Male vs. female leaders," *Academy of Management Journal.* 17: 225-233, 1974.

Bateson, Gregory. *Mind and Nature.* New York: Dutton, 1979.

Beach, Betty. *Integrating Work and Family Life: The Home-Working Family.* Albany: State University of New York Press, 1989.

Beauvoir, Simone de. *The Second Sex.* Translated by H. M. Parshley: New York: Knopf, 1953.

Becker, Carol. "The invisible drama: Women and the anxiety of change," *The Chicago Tribune*, Tempo Section. February 1, 1987.

Belenky, Mary Field, Blythe McVicker Clinchey, Nancy Rule Goldberger, and Jill Mattack Tarule. *Women's Ways of Knowing: The Development of Self, Voice, and Mind.* New York: Basic Books, 1986.

Bell, Daniel. *The End of Ideology.* Glencoe, IL: The Free Press, 1960.

Bellah, Robert, Richard Madsen, William Sullivan, Ann Swidler and Steven Tipton. *The Good Society.* New York: Alfred A. Knopf, 1991.

Bendix, Reinhard and S. M. Lipset. *Social Mobility in Industrial Society*. Berkeley, Glencoe, N.J.: The Free Press, 1958.

Bennholdt-Thomsen, Viktoria. "Women's dignity is the wealth of Juditan (Oaxaca, Mexico)," *Anthropology of Work Review* 10: 3-4, 10, 1989.

Berk, Sarah Fenstenmaker. "Women's work and the production of gender." Paper presented to The American Sociological Association, Washington, D.C, 1985.

Beutel, Ann and Margaret Mooney Marini. "Gender and values," *American Sociological Review* 60:436-448,1995.

Bielby, Denise D. and William T. Bielby. "She works hard for the money: Household responsibilities and the allocation of work effort." *American Journal of Sociology*. 93: 1031-1059, 1988.

Billard, Mary. "Do women make better managers?" *Working Woman*. March: 68-71, 106-107, 1992.

Bird, Gloria W. "Family and career characteristics of women and men college and university administrators," in Patricia A. Furrant (ed.) *Strategies and Attitudes: Women in School Administration*. Washington, D.C.: NAWDAC, 1986.

Blanchard, Kenneth and Robert Lorber. *Putting the One Minute Manager to Work*. New York: William Morrow and Company, 1984.

Blanchard, Kenneth H. and Alice G. Sargent. "The one minute manager is an androgenous manager," *Training and Development Journal*. May: 83-85, 1984.

Bluestone, Barry, and Irving Bluestone. *Negotiating the Future: A Labor Perspective on American Business*. New York: Basic Books, 1992.

Blum, Linda and Vicki Smith. "Women's mobility in the corporation: A critique of the politics of optimism," *Signs*. 3: 528-545, 1988.

Bognanno, Mario F. "Women in professions: Academic women." In Karen Shallcrass Koziara, Michael H. Moskow, and Lucretia Dewey Tanner (eds.), *Working Women: Past, Present, Future*. Washington, D.C.: The Bureau of National Affairs, Inc, 1987.

Bologh, Roslyn Wallach. "Gender repression and liberation: an alternative feminist theory, method and politics." Paper presented to The American Sociological Association, Washington, D.C. 1985.

Bowen David. "Cross-sex mentoring." *Training and Development Journal*, February, 30-35, 1985.

Boyle, Charles, Peter Wheale, and Brian Surgess. *People, Science, and Technology: A Guide to Advanced Industrial Society*. Totowa, NJ: Barnes and Noble Books, 1984.

Bradford, David and Allan Cohen. "Management: Up with subordinants," *Working Woman*. May, 25-26, 1984.

Braverman, Harry. *Labor and Monopoly Capital: The Degradation of Work in the Twentieth Century*, New York: Monthy Review Press, 1975.

Bravo, Ellen. *The Job/Family Challenge: Not For Women Only*. New York: John Wiley & Sons, 1995.

Briles, Judith. *Woman to Woman: From Sabotage to Support*. Far Hills, N.J.: New Horizon Press, 1987.

Brothers, Joyce. *What Every Woman Should Know about Men*. Los Angeles: Simon and Schuster, 1982.

Brown, L. K. "Women and business management," *Signs: Journal of Women in Culture and Society*. 5: 267-288, 1979.

Brown, Linda and Julia Kagan. "The working woman survey," *Working Woman*, May, 92-96, 1982.

Brown, Phil and Faith Ferguson. ""Making a big stink' women's work, women's relationships, and toxic waste activisim," *Gender and Society* 9:145-172, 1995.

Bruyn, Severn. *A Future for the American Economy*. Stanford, CA: Stanford University Press, 1991.

Burawoy, Michael and Janos Lukacs. *The Radiant Past: Ideology and Reality in Hungary's Road to Capitalism*. Chicago: University of Chicago Press, 1992.

Business Ethics. "Trend Watch: If women made the laws," *Business Ethics*. September/October: 11, 1992.

Business Ethics, 1:3-18, 1987.

Business Week. "The new industrial relations," May 11 pp. 84-90, 92, 95-96, 98, 1981.

Cahill, Spencer. "And a child shall lead us? Children, gender and perspectives by incongruity." Paper presented to The Society for the Study of Symbolic Interaction, Chicago, IL, 1987.

Calano, Jimmy and Jeff Salzman. "Tough deals, tender tactics." *Working Women*, July p. 74-76, 96, 1988.

Campbell, A. *Worker-Owners: The Mondragon Achievement*. London: Anglo-German Foundation for the Study of Industrial Society, 1977.

Campbell, Joseph. *The Portable Jung*. Translated by R. F. C. Hall. New York: Viking Press, 1971.

Cann, Arnie and William D. Siegfried, Jr. "Sex stereotypes and the leadership role." *Sex Roles*. 17: 401-408, 1987.

Cantor, Dorothy and Toni Bernay with Jean Stoess. *Women in Power: The Secrets of Leadership.* Boston: Houghton Mifflin, 1992.

Capra, Fritjof. *The Turning Point: Science, Society, and the Rising Culture.* London: Wildwood House, 1982.

Capra, Fritjof. *The Tao of Physics.* London: Fontana, 1976.

Capra, Fritjof and Randy Hayes. "Green and peace: A visionary link." *Greenpeace Examiner.* 11: 14-15, 1987.

Carlson, Eugene. "Workers aren't the problem, theorist asserts: Bosses are," *Wall Street Journal.* May 8, 1981.

Carr-Ruffino, Norma. *The Promotable Woman: Becoming a Successful Manager.* Belmont, CA: Wadworth Publishing Company, 1985.

Carroll, Glenn R. and Yanschung Paul Huo. "Organizational task and institutional environments in ecological perspective: Findings from the local newspaper industry," *American Journal of Sociology.* 91: 838-873, 1986.

Cassedy, Elen and Karen Nussbaum. *Nine to Five: The Working Woman's Guide to Office Survival.* New York: Penguin, 1983.

Chafetz, Janet Saltzman. *Gender Equity: An Integrated Theory of Stability and Change.* Newbury Park, CA: Sage, 1990.

Chapman, Jenny. *Politics, Feminism, and the Reformation of Gender.* New York: Routledge, 1993.

Chase, Susan E. and "Interpreting women's narratives: Subjectivity and context." Paper presented to the Midwest Sociological Association, Chicago, April, 1990.

Chase, Susan E. and Colleen S. Bell. "Ideology, discourse, and gender: How gatekeepers talk about women school superintendents," *Social Problems*, 37: 163-177, 1990.

Cheatham, Annie and Mary Clare Powell. *This Way Daybreak Comes: Women's Values and the Future.* Philadelphia: New Society Publishers, 1986.

Chelte, Anthony, Peter Hess, Russell Fanelli and Wiliam Ferris. "Corporate culture as an impediment to employee involvement," *Work and Occupations.* 16: 153-164, 1989.

Chicago Tribune. Open for Discussion: The Executive Ladder. May 8, 1987.

Chicago Tribune. "Tempo: Losing ground: The road to happiness traveled at some expense." March 8, 1987.

Chodorow, Nancy. *The Reproduction of Mothering.* Berkeley: University of Californai Press, 1978.

Christman, Rebecca. "How I fought my own war over nuclear arms," *Working Women,* 54, 152, October, 1988.

Clemens, Elisabeth. "Organizational repertoires and institutional change: Women's groups and the transformation of U.S. politics," *American Journal of Sociology.* 98: 755-798, 1993.

Clough, Patricia Ticineto. *Feminist Thought: Desire, Power, and and Academic Discourse.* Cambridge: Blackwell, 1994.

Cohen, Bernard and Xueguang Zhou. "Status processes in enduring work groups," *American Sociological Review.* 56: 179-188, 1991.

Cohen, Julie. "Managing tomorrow's work force today," *Management Review.* 80: 17-21, 1991.

Cohen, Lynn. "Verbal (mis) communication between managerial men and women," in Bette Ann Stead (ed.) *Women in Management* 2nd Edition. Englewood Cliffs, NJ: Prentice Hall, Inc., 1985.

Cohen, Sherry Seib. *Tender Power.* New York: Addison-Wesley Publishing Company, 1989.

Collins, LaVerne Francis. "Speaking about working women's issues," Address to Community Women, sponsored by S. C. Johnson Wax and the Wisconsin Federation of Business and Professional Women, The Golden Rondell Theater, Racine, Wisconsin, May, 1990.

Collins, Patricia Hill. "Review of *Breaking Bread: Insurgent Black Intellectual Life* by bell hooks and Cornel West and *Segregated Sisterhood: Racism and the Politics of American Feminism* by Nancie Caraway," *Signs* 20:176-179, 1994.

Collins, Patricia Hill. *Black Feminist Thought: Knowledge, Consciousness, and the Politics of Empowerment.* Boston: Unwin Hyman, 1990.

Colwill, Nina. *The New Partnership: Women and Men in Organizations.* Palo Alto, CA: Mayfield Publishing Company, 1982.

Community Jobs (Staff). "The alternative workplace: Groups must practice the values they preach," *Community Jobs*, 5, February, 1990.

Conant, Jennet. "Broadcast networking," *Working Woman*, 58-61, August, 1990.

Conn, Sarah. "The self-world connection: Implications for mental health and psychotherapy," *Woman of Power.* Spring: 71-77, 1991.

Conscience: A Newsjournal of Prochoice Catholic Opinion. 9, 1988.

Cook, Mary F. "Is the mentor relationship primarily a male experience?" *The Personnel Administrator.* 24: 82-86, 1979.

Co-op America. *Building Economic Alternatives*, A Quarterly Publication. 14, Summer: 17-29, 1988.

Cox, Taylor. "The multicultural organization," *Academy of Management Review.* 5: 34-47, 1991.

Cullen, Dallas. "Self-actualization and organizational structure: Implications for women in management research," Paper presented to the Administrative Sciences Association of Canada, Quebec, 1992.

Culp, Kristine. "Envisioning whole, holly life: Feminist theology reconstructs redemptive community," Paper presented to the Conference on Women in The Year 2000: Utopian and Dystopian Views, Indianapolis, Indiana, April, 1988.

Cussler, Margaret. *The Woman Executive.* New York: Harcourt, Brace, & Co, 1958.

Daly, Mary. *Pure Heart: Elemental Feminist Philosophy.* Boston: Beacon Press, 1984.

Daly, Mary. *Gynecology: The Metaphysics of Radical Feminism.* Boston: Beacon Press, 1978.

Dean, Dwight. "Alienation: Its meaning and measurement." *American Sociological Review.* 26: 753-758, 1961.

Deaux, Kaye. "Self evaluations of male and female managers," *Sex Roles.* 5: 571-580, 1979.

De Gre', Gerard. "Freedom and social structure," *American Sociological Review,* 11:529-536, 1964.

Denmark, Florence L. "Style of leadership," *Psychology of Women Quarterly.* 2: 99-113, 1977.

Denzin, Norman K. "Post-pragmatism: A review of *Pragmatism and Social Theory* by Hans Joas," *Symbolic Interation* 19:61-75, 1996.

Derry, Robbin. "Managerial perceptions of ethnical conflicts and conceptions of morality: A qualitative interview study." Paper presented to the National Academy of Management SIM Symposium, 1988.

de Valle, Teresa. *Gendered Anthropology*. New York: Routledge, 1993.

Dill, Bonnie Thornton. "Interview on envisioning a feminist world," *Women of Power*. Summer, Issue 2, 1985.

Dinnerstein, Dorothy. *The Mermaid and the Minatour: Sexual Arrangements and Human Malaise*. New York: Harper and Row, 1976.

Di Prete, Thomas A. and Whitman T. Soule, "Gender and promotion in segmented job ladder systems," *American Sociological Review*, 53:26-40, 1988.

Drinker, Sophie. *Music and Women: The Story of Women in their Relation to Music*. New York: Harold Ober Associates, 1948.

Drucker, Peter. *Post-Capitalist Society*. New York: Harper Business, 1993.

D'Souza, Dinesha. *Illiberal Education: The Politics of Race and Sex on Campus*. New York: Free Press, 1991.

Dubno, Peter. "Management attitudes toward women executives: A longitudinal approach." Working paper #83-95, New York University Graduate School of Business Administration, College of Business and Public Administration, 1983.

Eder, Donna. "Building cohesion through collaboration narration," *Social Psychology Quarterly* 51: 225-235, 1988.

Edson, Sakre Kennington. *Pushing The Limits: The Female Administrative Aspirant*. Albany, NY: SUNY Press, 1988.

Edwards, Audrey. "The inspiring leader of scholars [and dollars]," *Working Woman*, 68-69, 72-74, June, 1989.

Eisenstein, Hester. *Gender Shock: Practicing Feminism on two Continents*. Boston: Beacon Press, 1991.

Eisler, Riane, *The Chalice and The Blade: Our History, Our Future*. San Francisco: Harper & Row, 1987.

England, Paula, George Farkas, Barbara Kilbourne, and Thomas Dow. "Explaining occupational sex segregation and wages: Findings from a model with fixed effects." *American Sociological Review*. 53: 544-558, 1988.

Epstein, Cynthia Fuchs. *Deceptive Distinctions: Sex, Gender, and the Social Order*. New Haven: Yale University Press, 1988.

Epstein, Cynthia Fuchs. *Woman's Place*. Los Angeles: University of California Press, 1970.

Erkut, Sumru. "What is good for women and minorities is good for business: What corporations can do to meet the diversity challenge," Working Paper Series, Center for Research on Women, Wellesley College, Wellesley, MA, 1990.

Evansville Press. "Researchers find beauty a corporate disadvantage." December 4, 1984.

Executive Female. "Women on the move." January/February, 1985.

Fantasia, Rick. *Cultures of Solidarity: Consciousness, Actions, and Contemporary American Workers*. Berkeley: University of California Press, 1988.

Farmaion, Roxane Farman. "How to manage your career for lifelong success," *Working Woman*, 101-104, October, 1989.

Fausto-Sterling, Anne. *Myths of Gender: Biological Theories About Women and Men*. New York: Basic Books, 1986.

Faxen, Karl-Olof. "Disembodied technical progress: Does employee participation in decision making contribute to change and growth?" *American Economics Review* 68:131-134, 1978.

Feldberg, Roslyn and Evelyn Nakano Glenn. "Technology and work degradation: Effects of office automation on women clerical workers," in Joan Rothschild (ed.) *Machina aux Deux: Feminist Perspectives on Technology.* New York: Pergomon Press, 1983.

Feminism and Nonviolence Study Group." *Piecing It Together: Feminism and Nonviolence.* New York: War Resisters Intenational, 1983.

Ferber, M., Joan Huber, and Glenna Spitze. "Preference for men as bosses and professionals," *Social Forces.* 58: 466-476, 1979.

Ferguson, Kathy. *The Feminist Case Against Bureaucracy.* Philadelphia, PA: Temple University Press, 1984.

Fernandez-Kelly, M. Patricia and Anna M. Garcia. "Invisible amidst the glitter: Hispanic women in the southern California electronics industry," in *The Worth of Women's Work: A Qualitative Synthesis*, Anne Statham, Eleanor M. Miller and Hans O. Mauksch (eds.). Albany: SUNY Press, 1987.

Fiedler, Fred Edward and Joseph E. Garcia. *New Approaches to Effective Leadership: Cognitive Resources and Organizational Performance.* New York: Wiley, 1987.

Fiorentine, Robert. "Sex differences in success expectancies and casual attractions: Is this why fewer women become physicians?" *Social Psychology Quarterly.* 51: 236-249, 1988.

Firestone, Shulamith. *The Dialectics of Sex: The Case for Feminist Revolution.* New York: Morrow, 1970.

Fligstein, Neil. "The intraorganizational power struggle: Rise of finance personnel to top leadership in large corporations, 1919-1979," *American Sociological Review.* 52: 44-58, 1987.

Fogarty, Michael, A. J. Allen, Isobel Allen, and Patricia Walters. *Women in Top Jobs: Four Studies in Achievement.* London: George Allen and Unwin, 1971.

Food and Justice, United Farm Workers, LaPaz, Keene, CA, Volume 7, January, 1990.

Forest, Kay B. "Female role stress in a post-industrial era: The issue of control in women's work." Presented to the Conference on Women in The Year 2000, Indiana University - Purdue University at Indianapolis, 1988.

Frankl, Razelle. "Women in management: Expectations and reality." Paper presented to The American Sociological Association, Washington, D.C., 1985.

Freeman, Jo. "The tyranny of structurelessness," *Berkeley Journal of Sociology*, 17: 151-64, 1972.

Freeman, Sue. *Managing Lives: Corporate Women and Social Change.* Amherst: University of Massachusetts Press, 1990.

Freundlick, Paul, Chris Collins, and Mikki Weriig. *A Guide to Cooperative Alternatives: Community Participation, Social Change, Well-Being, Appropriate Technology, Networking, and Almost Anything Else Hopeful in America.* New Haven, CT and Louisa, VA: Community Publications Cooperative, 1979.

Friedan, Betty. *The Feminine Mystique.* New York: Dell Publishers, 1963.

Friedman, Martin with Jack Lichtenstein. *The Leadership Myth.* Pittsburgh: Dorrance Publishing, 1992.

Fritz, Leah. *Thinking Like a Woman.* New York: WIN Books, 1975.

Frost, Charles H. "Males teaching females how to work with females?" Paper presented to the Fifth Annual Conference on Women and Work, University of Texas at Arlington, Arlington, Texas, 1988.

Gaertner, Karen and Stanley Wallen. "The affects of employee relations practice on work unit effectiveness," in *Research in the Sociology of Organizations*, (ed.) Richard Magjuka. Greenwich, CT: JAI Press, 1989a.

Gaertner, Karen and Stanley Wallen. "Career experiences, perceptions of employment practices, and psychological commitments to the organization," *Human Relations*. 42: 975-992, 1989b.

Gardner, Kay. "Female composition," in *Women's Culture Renaissance of the Seventies*, Kaye Kimball (ed.). Metuchen, NJ: The Scarecrow Press, Inc, 1981.

Garland Howard and Kenneth H. Price. "Attitudes toward women in management and attributions for their success and failure in a managerial position," *Journal of Applied Psychology*, 62: 29-33, 1977.

Gassman, Roberta. *Women in Business Curriculum Materials: Overcoming Barriers and Building Upon Strengths*. Madison, WI: University of Wisconsin-Extension and Small Business Development Center, 1988.

Gendron, Mary. "Giants aims for 25% women store managers," *Supermarket*, 32: 4, 28, 1977.

Gerson, Judith M. and Kathy Peiss. "Reconceptualizing gender relations," *Social Problems*. 32: 317-331, 1985.

Ghilani, Beth W. "The velvet ghetto: Women, power and the corporation," in G. William Domhoff and Thomas R. Dye (eds.) *Power Elites and Organizations*. Beverly Hills: Sage Publications, 1987.

Gilligan, Carol. *In a Different Voice: Psychological Theory and Women's Development*. Cambridge: Harvard University Press, 1982.

Gioseffi, Daniella. *Women on War: Essential Voices for the Nuclear Age from a Brilliant International Assembly.* New York: Simon and Schuster, 1988.

Glaser, Barney and Anslem Strauss. *Grounded Theory,* New York: Aldine Publishing Co., 1967.

Godfrey, Joline. *Our Wildest Dreams: Women Entrepreneurs Making Money, Having Fun, Doing Good.* New York: Harper-Business, 1992.

Goffman, Erving. "The arrangement between the sexes." *Theory and Society.* 4: 301-336, 1977.

Gordon, Francine and Myra H. Strober. *Bringing Women into Management.* New York: McGraw-Hill Book Company, 1975.

Gordon, Linda. *Pitied But Not Entitled: Single Mothers and the History of Welfare.* Cambridge: Harvard University Press, 1994.

Gordon, Suzanne. *Prisoners of Men's Dreams: Striking Out for a New Feminine Future.* Boston: Little, Brown and Co., 1991.

Gordon, Suzanne. "Anger, power and women's sense of self: New thoughts as a psychology for the future from Jean Baker Miller," *Ms Magazine.* July, pp. 42-44, 112, 1985.

Gould, Carol C. *Beyond Domination: New perspectives on Women and Philosophy.* Sussex: Rowman and Allanheld, 1983.

Grant, Linda. "Peer expectations about outstanding competencies of men and women medical students," *Sociology of Health and Illness.* 5: 42-61, 1983.

Gray, Elizabeth Dodson. *Patriarchy as a Conceptual Trap.* Wellesley, MA: Roundtable Press, 1982.

Green, Rayna. "Native American women." Address to National Women's Studies Association, Minneapolis, June 1988.

Habben, David. "A note from the editor," *Anthropology of Work Review*, 9: 5-6, 1988.

Hacker, Sally. "Women workers in the Mondragon system of industrial cooperatives," *Gender and Society*, 1: 358-379, 1987.

Haessly, Jacqueline. "Commitment to our future: Education for peace," *The Nonviolent Activist*, 3-5, September, 1988.

Hall, Jay. *The Competence Process: Managing for Commitment and Creativity*. The Woodlands, TX: Teleometrics International, 1980.

Hall, Nor. *The Moon and the Virgin*. New York: Harper & Row Publishers, 1980.

Hancock, M. Donald, John Logue and Bernt Schiller. *Managing Modern Capitalism: Industrial Renewal and Workplace Democracy in the United States and Western Europe*. New York: Praeger, 1991.

Harding, Sandra. *Feminism and Methodology*. Bloomington, IN: Indiana University Press, 1987.

Harlan A. and C. Weiss. *Moving Up: Women in Managerial Career Ladders*. Working Paper No. 86. Wellesley College Center for Research and Women, Wellesley, Massachusetts, 1981.

Harley, Joan and Lois Ann Koff. "Prepare women now for tomorrow's managerial challenges." *The Personnel Administrator*, 25: 41-42, 1980.

Harrel, Thomas and Jane Baack. "Dual career couples: Anxieties of MBA couples compared with traditional couples," Report, Stanford University Graduate School of Business, Stanford, CA, 1989.

Harrigan, Betty. "Why corporations are teaching men to think like women," *Ms Magazine*, 62-63, 87-88, October, 1989.

Harriman, Ann. *Women/Men Management*. New York: Praeger Press, 1985.

Helgeson, Sally. *The Female Advantage: Women's Ways of Leadership*. New York: Doubleday, 1990.

Heller, Trudy. *Women and Men as Leaders: In Business and Social Service Organizations*. South Hadley, Mass: J.F. Bergin Publishers, 1982.

Hellneig, Basia. "The breakthrough generation: 73 women ready to run corporate America," *Working Woman*. April, 98-101, 146-150, 1985.

Hennig, Margaret and Anne Jardim. *The Managerial Woman*. New York: Anchor Press, 1977.

Herbert, Theodore and Edward Yost. "Women as effective managers: A strategic model for overcoming the barriers," *Human Resource Management*. 18-25, 1978.

Herrick, John S. "Work motives of female executives," *Public Personnel Management*. 2: 380-388, 1973.

Hersey, Paul and Kenneth H. Blanchard. *Management of Organizational Behavior: Utilizing Human Resourse*. Fifth Edition. Englewood Cliffs, NJ: Prentice-Hall, Inc., 1988.

Hersh-Cochran, Mona, Adalaide Griffin, Allen Mesch. *Executive Women in the Dallas/Fort Worth Metropolex: Significant Problems and Successful Strategies*. Business and Economics Monograph No. 1, Department of Business and Economics, Texas Women's University, Denton, Texas, 1987.

Himmelweit, Susan. "The real dualism of sex and class," *Review of Radical Economics*. 16: 167-183, 1984.

Hirsch, Paul M. "From ambushes to golden parachutes: Corporate takeovers as an instance of cultured framing and institutional integration," *American Journal of Sociology*. 91: 800-837, 1986.

Hite, Shere. *The Hite Report on the Family: Growing Up under Patriarchy*. New York: Grove Press, 1995.

Hochschild, Arlie Russell. "The totaled woman," *The New York Times Book Review*. May 11, 1986.

Hochschild, Arlie Russell. *The Managed Heart: Commercialization of Human Feeling*. Berkeley: University of California Press, 1983.

Holmes, Barbara. *Jump at the Sun*. Annandale, VA: Northern Virginia Community College, 1989.

Holroyd, Kenneth and Richard Lazarus. "Stress, coping, and somatic adaptation," in *Handbook of Stress* (eds.) L. Goldberger and S. Breznitz. p. 21-35. New York: The Free Press, 1982.

Hood, Jane. "The caretakers: Keeping the area up and the family together," in Anne Statham, Eleanor Miller, and Hans Mauksch (eds.) *The Worth of Women's Work: A Qualitative Syntheses*. Albany, NY: SUNY Press, 1987.

hooks, bell and Cornel West. *Breaking Bread: Insurgent Black Intellectual Life*. Boston: South End Press, 1991.

Hoover, Helen Santmyer. *And Ladies of the Club. . . .* New York: Putnam, 1982.

Houseknecht, Sharon, Suzanne Vaughan and Anne Statham. "Marital disruption among professional women: Timing of career and family events," *Social Problems*. 31: 273-284, 1984.

Howard, Dick. *The Marxian Legacy*. New York: Urizen Books, 1977.

Hoy, Pat, E. Schor, and R. Diyamni. *Women's Voices: Visions and Perspectives.* New York: McGraw Hill, 1990.

Huff, Jack. "Magic, science, and the principle of truth," *The Rosacrucion Digest.* Summer, 19-21, 1993.

Hughes, Helen. "I had extra burdens, but I had extra privileges, too." *Chicago Tribune*, Tempo Section, 3, October 9, 1988.

Hunsaker, Johanna and Phillip Hunsaker. *Strategies and Skills for Managerial Women.* Cincinnati: South-Western, 1991.

Hunt, Jennifer. "The development of rapport through the negotiation of gender in field work among police," *Human Organization. 43:283-296, 1984.*

Hyman, Beverly. *How Successful Women Manage.* American Management Associations Extension Service, 1981.

Hymowitz, Carol. "One firm's bid to get blacks, women: Corning battles to overcome ingrained biases," *Wall Street Journal.* February 16, 1989.

Iaconetti, Joan. "New manager dilemmas," *Business Week*, Special issue on careers. 5: 40-43, 1987.

Ice, Martha Long. *Clergy Women and their World Views.* New York: Praeger, 1987.

INC. "Being the Boss: How Jack Stack's approach to business lets him avoid the problems of the traditional manager," *INC.* October 49-50, 54-55, 61-65, 1989.

Ingle, Sud and Nima Ingle. *Quality Circles in Service Industries: Comprehensive Guidelines for Increased Productivity and Efficiency.* New York: Prentice-Hall, 1983.

Insel, Barbara. "The making of a top manager," *Working Woman.* May, 105-108, 191, 1987.

Instone, Debra, Brenda Major and Barbara B. Bunker. "Gender, self confidence and social influence strategies: On organization simulation," *Journal of Personality and Social Psychology.* 44: 322-333, 1983.

Izraeli, Dafna, Moshe Banai, and Yoram Zeira. "Women executives in MNC subsidiaries," in *California Management Review*, 23: 53-63, 1980.

Jacobson, Barbara and John M. Kendrick. "Elizabeth Cady Stanton's 'Last Struggle': The two spheres paradigm, religion and women's superior morality." Paper presented to The American Sociological Association, New York, NY, 1986.

Jaggar, Allison M. *Feminist Politics and Human Nature.* Sussex: Rowman and Allanheld, Publishers, 1983.

Jaggar, Alison M. and Paula Rothenberg. *Feminist Frameworks: Alternative Accounts of the Relations between Women and Men.* New York: McGraw-Hill, 1993.

Jensen, Gary F. "Mainstreaming and the sociology of deviance: A personal assessment." *Changing Our Minds: Feminist Transformations of Knowledge.* Albany, NY: State University of New York Press, 1988.

Johnson, Cathryn. "Gender and formal authority," *Social Psychology Quarterly.* 56: 193-210, 1993.

Jong, Erica. "Changing my mind about Andrea Dworkin." *Ms Magazine*, June, pp. 60-64, 1988.

Josefowitz, Natasha. "Management men and women: Behind closed doors," *Harvard Business Review.* September/October, 58: 4-7, 1980.

Josefowitz, Natasha. *Paths to Power.* Reading, MA: Addison-Wesley Publishing, 1980.

Jung, C.J. *The Portable Jung.* New York: The Viking Press, 1971.

Jurik, Nancy and Greg Halemba. "Gender, working conditions, and job satisfaction of women in a non-traditional occupation," *Sociological Quarterly.* 25:551-566, 1984.

Kagan, Julia. "Survey: Work in the 1980's and 1990." *Working Women.* April 26, 28, 1983.

Kagan, Julia and Julianne Malveaux. "The uneasy alliance of the boss and the secretary," *Working Woman.* May, 105-109, 134-135, 1986.

Kamerman, Sheila B. and Alfred J. Kahn. *The Responsive Workplace.* New York: Columbia University Press, 1987.

Kanter, Rosabeth Moss. *When Giants Learn to Dance.* New York: Simon and Schuster, 1989.

Kanter, Rosabeth Moss. "Women managers: Moving up in a high tech society." in Jennie Farley (ed.) *Women in Management: Career and Family Issues.* New York: ILR Press, 1983a.

Kanter, Rosabeth Moss. *The Change Masters: Innovations for Productivity in the American Corporation.* New York: Simon & Schuster, 1983b.

Kanter, Rosabeth Moss. *Men and Women of the Corporation.* New York: Basic Books, 1977.

Kanter, Rosabeth Moss. "Some effects of proportions on group life: Skewed sex ratios and responses to token women." *American Journal of Sociology*, 82: 965-990, 1977b.

Kanter, Rosabeth Moss. *Community and Commitment: Communes and Utopias in Sociological Perspective.* Cambridge: Harvard University Press, 1972.

Karsten, Margaret F. "Mary Parker Follett: Underrated contributor to modern management," Paper presented to the University of Wisconsin System Women's Studies Conference, Kenosha, Wisconsin, October, 1989.

Karsten, Margaret Foegen and Stephen W. Kleisath. "Team sports as a predictor of business success." *Central State Business Review.* 5: 2-4, 1986.

Kelly, Marjorie. "Vandals in the free-market temple," *Business Ethics.* November/December, p. 6-7, 1993a.

Kelly, Marjorie. "Business and the decline of kings," *Business Ethics.* September/October: 6-7, 1993b.

Kelly, Marjorie. "Living in the dream machine," *Business Ethics.* September/October: 6-7, 1992a.

Kelly, Marjorie. "The bad guy question," *Business Ethics.* November/December: 6-7, 1992b.

Kelly, Marjorie. "Civilization and nature," *Business Ethics.* July/August, p. 6-7, 1991a.

Kelly, Marjorie. "The ethics of prosperity," *Business Ethics.* September/ October, p. 6-7, 1991b.

Keys, David. "Gender, sex role and career decision making of certified management accountants," *Sex Roles.* 13: 33-46, 1985.

Kimball, Gayle. *Women's Culture: The Women's Renaissance of the Seventies.* London: Scarecrow Press, 1981.

Kimmel, Michael S. "Men's responses to feminism at the turn of the century," *Gender and Society* 1:261-283, 1987.

Kirkland, Lane. "Capitalism and communism: Mirror images," *Business Ethics.* July/August: 21, 1992.

Kleeman, Walter E.   "The future of the office,"   *Environment and Behavior*. 14: 593-610, 1982.

Koopeli, Bruce and George Lakey. *Leadership for Change: Toward a Feminist Model*. Philadelphia: New Society Publishers, 1990.

Korn and Ferry. *Korn and Ferry International's Profile of Women Senior Executives*. Los Angeles, CA: Korn and Ferry, 1982.

Kornhauser, William. "'Power elite' or 'Veto groups"?" in Seymour Martin Lipset and Leo Lowenthal (eds.) *Culture and Social Character*. Glencoe: The Free Press, 1961.

Kuhn, Thomas S. *The Essential Tension: Selected Studies in Scientific Tradition and Change*. Chicago: University of Chicago Press, 1977.

Kuhn, Thomas S. *The Structure of Scientific Revolutions*. Chicago: University of Chicago Press, 1965.

Kunitsina, Svetlana. "Glamour and sickle." *Ms Magazine*, August, pp. 30-31, 1988.

Kushell, Elliot and Rae Newton.   "Gender, leadership style and subordinate satisfaction: An experiment," *Sex Roles* 14:203-209, 1986.

Lannon, Judith M.   "Male vs females values in management," *Management International Review*. 17: 9-12, 1977.

Larwood, Laurie and Marlaine Lockheed.   "Women as managers: Toward second generation research," *Sex Roles*. 5: 659-666, 1979.

Lasch, Christopher. *The True and Only Heaven: Progress and Its Critics*. New York: W. W. Norton & Co., 1991.

Lawrence, Paul and Jay Lorsch.   *Organization and Environment: Managing Differentation and Integration*. Boston, MA: Harvard University Press, 1967.

Leavitt, Harold. *Corporate Pathfinders: Building Visions and Values into Organizations*. Irwin, CA: Dow Jones, 1986.

Leavitt, Harold J. and Jean Lipman-Blumen. "A case for the relational manager," *Organizational Dynamics*. Summer, 27-41, 1980.

Lehner, Devony. "Kenai River Cooperative river basic study," *Women in Natural Resources*. 14: 13-16, 1993.

Lembcke, Jerry. "A comment on David Habben's 'Studying new technology after Braverman: An anthropological review'" *Anthropology of Work Review* 9:10-11, 1986.

Levin, Harry. "Improving the creative potential of human resources with producer cooperatives: Employment, productivity, and self-actualization." Paper presented to the Sixth World Congress of the International Economic Association, Mexico City, 1980.

Lewin, Kurt. *Field Theory in Social Science*. New York: Harper & Row, 1951.

Lightfoot, Sarah Lawrence *I've Known Rivers*. New York: Addison-Wesley. 1994.

Likert, Remses and Jane Likert. *New Ways of Managing Conflict*. McGraw-Hill Book Company, 1976.

Lincoln, James and Arne Kalleberg. *Culture, Control, and Commitment: A Study of Work Organization and Work Attitudes in the United States and Japan*. Cambridge: Harvard Univerity Press, 1990.

Lindo, David. "Delegating decisions," *Executive Female*, Jan./Feb., 19-21, 1986.

Lipman-Blumen, Jean. "Women and the nature of power relationships." Keynote address presented to WWHEA Fall Conference, University of Wisconsin, Madison, Wisconsin, 1985.

Lipman-Blumen, Jean. *Gender Roles and Power*. Englewood Cliffs, NJ: Prentice-Hall, 1984.

Loden, Marilyn. *Feminine Leadership or How to Succeed in Business Without Being One of the Boys*. New York: Times Books, 1985.

Loden, Marilyn and Judy Rosener. *Work force America! Managing Employee Diversity as a Vital Resource*. Homewood, Il: Business One Irwin, 1991.

Lombardo, Michael M. and Cynthia D. McCauley. "The dynamics of management derailment," Technical Report 34, Center for Creative Management, Greensboro, NC, 1988.

Lorber, Judith. *Paradoxes of Gender*. New Haven: Yale University Press, 1994.

Loscocco, Karyn and Joyce Robinson. "Barriers to women's small-business success in the United States," *Gender and Society*. 5: 511-532, 1991.

Lowe, Graham. *Women in Administrative Revolution*. Toronto: University of Toronto Press, 1987.

Lunneborg, Patricia. *Women Changing Work*. New York: Bergin and Garvey Publishing, 1990.

Lusardi, Lee A. "When a woman speaks, does anybody listen?" *Working Woman* 92-94, July, 1990.

McAllister, Pam. *Reweaving the Web of Life: Feminism and Nonviolence*. Philadelphia: New Society Publishers, 1982.

McBroom, Patricia. *The Third Sex: The New Professional Woman*. New York: William Morrow and Company, 1986.

Maccoby, Eleanor and C. Jacklin. *The Psychology of Sex Differences*. Stanford, CA: Stanford University Press, 1979.

Maccoby, Michael. *The Gamesman: The New Corporate Leader.* New York: Simon & Schuster, 1976.

McGregor, D. *The Human Side of Enterprises.* New York: McGraw-Hill, 1960.

Machlowitz, Marilyn. *Success at an Early Age.* New York: Arbor House, 1984.

McIntosh, Peggy Means. "Curricular revision: The new knowledge for a new age," *Educating the Majority: Women Challenge Tradition in Higher Education,* Carol S. Pearson, Donna Shavlick, and Judith Touchton (eds.). New York: Macmillion Publishing Co., 1989.

MacKenzie, R. Alec. *The Time Trap.* New York: AMACOM, A Division of American Management Association, Inc., 1972.

MacKinnon, Catherine A. "Feminism, marxism, method and the state: An agenda for theory," *Signs.* 7: 515-544, 1982.

Maclaine, Shirley. *Dancing in the Light.* New York: Bantam House Books, Inc, 1985.

McLean, Adrian and Judi Marshall. *Cultures at work: How to identify and understand them.* Workbook prepared by The Centre for the Study of Organizational Change and Development, University of Bath, England, no date.

Madden, Tara Roth. *Women Vs. Women: The Uncivil Business War.* New York: American Management Association, 1987.

Major, Brenda, Wayne H. Bylsme, and Catherine Cozzarelli. "Gender differences in distributive justice preferences: The impact of domain," *Sex Roles.* 21: 487-497, 1989.

Makower, J. "Women managers: Moving up in a high tech society," in Jennie Farley (ed.), *The Woman in Management, Career and Family Issues.* pp. 21-33. New York: ILR Press, Cornell University, 1983.

350   *The Rise of Marginal Voices*

Mandell, Barbara and Susan Kohler-Gray. "Management development that values diversity". *Personnel* 67 (March): 41-47, 1990.

Markham, William T, Scott J. South, Charles M. Bonjean and Judy Corder. "Gender and opportunity in the federal bureaucracy," *American Journal of Sociology.* 91: 129-150, 1985.

Marshall, Gene W. *Repair or Replacement? An Essay on Ecological Politics.* Dallas, TX: Realistic Living Press, 1988.

Marshall, Judi. "Review of *The Power of Balance* by William Torbert," *Academy of Management Review.* 17: 365-368, 1992.

Marshall, Judi. "Viewing organizational communication from a feminist perspective: A critique and some offerings," *Communication Yearbook,* 1992.

Marshall, Judi. *Women Managers: Travellers in a Male World,* Chinchester: John Wiley and Sons, 1984.

Marshall, Judi and Adrian McLean. "Reflection in action: Exploring organizational culture," in *Human Inquiry in Action,* (ed.) P. Reason. London: Sage, 1988.

Martin, Patricia Yancey. "Feminist practice in organizations: Implications for management," in *Women in Management: Tends, Issues, and Challenges in Managerial Diversity.* Newbury Park: Sage, 1993.

Martin, Patricia Yancey. "Group sex composition in worth organizations: A structured-normative approach," *Research in The Sociology of Organizations.* 4: 311-349, 1985.

Martin, Patricia Yancey, Sandra Seymour, Myrna Courage, Karolyn Godkey, and Richard Tate. "Work-place policies: Corporate, union, feminist, and pro-family leaders' views," *Gender and Society* 2: 285-400, 1988.

Massengill, Douglas and Nicholas DiMarco. "Sex-role stereotypes and requisite management characteristics: A current replication," *Sex Roles*. 5: 561-70, 1979.

Mayes, Sharon M. "Women in positions of authority: A case study of changing sex roles." *Signs*. 4: 556-568, 1979.

Mayo, Elton. *The Social Problems of an Industrial Civilization*. Cambridge: Harvard University Press, 1945.

Meeker, B. F. and P. A. Weitzel-O'Neill. "Sex roles and interpersonal behavior in task-oriented groups," *American Sociological Review*. 42: 91-105, 1977.

Miller, Eleanor M. *Street Women*. Philadelphia, PA: Temple University Press, 1986.

Miller, Gary. *Managerial Dilemmas: The Political Economy of Hierarchies*. New York: Cambridge University Press, 1992.

Miller, Jean Baker. *Toward a Psychology of Women*. Boston: Beacon Press, 1976.

Miller, Joanne. "Individual and occupational determinants of job satisfaction," *Sociology of Work and Occupations*. 7:337-366, 1980.

Mills, C. Wright. *The Power Elite*. New York: Oxford University Press, 1956,

Mills, Janet L. and Margaret Fitch Hauser. "Features of the boss-secretary relationship." Paper presented to The Third Annual Women and Work Conference, Arlington, Texas, 1986.

Mills, Judy. "Great explorations," *Ms Magazine*, 58-62, June, 1989.

Milwaukee Journal. "Business and finance: Women on the ladder." January 9, 1983.

Mirides, Ellyn and Andre Cote. "Women in management: Strategies for removing the powers," *Personnel Administrator*. 25: 25-28, 48, 1980.

Moir, Anne and David Jessel. *Brain Sex: The Real Difference between Men and Women*. New York: Carol, 1991.

Molloy, J. *Women's Dress for Success Book*. New York: Warner, 1978.

Molm, Linda. "Gender, power and legitimation: A test of three theories, "*American Journal of Sociology*. 91: 1356-1386, 1986.

Moore, Gwen. "Women in the old-boy network: The case of the New York State government," in G. William Domhoff and Thomas R. Dye (eds.) *Power Elites and Organizations*. Beverly Hills: Sage Publications, 1987.

Morrison, Anne, Randall P. White and Ellen Van Velsor. *Breaking the Glass Ceiling: Can Women Make It to the Top in America's Largest Corporations*? New York: Addison-Wesley, 1987.

Moses, J. and Boehm, V. "Relationship of assessment-center performance to management process of women," *Journal of Applied Psychology*. 60: 527-529, 1975.

Ms. Magazine. "Letters: Up against the patriarchy," September, 16, 18, 1986.

Muldrew, Tressie W. and James A. Bayton. "Men and women executives and processes related to decision accuracy," *Journal of Applied Psychology*. 64: 99-106, 1979.

Naisbitt, John and Patricia Aburdene. *Re-inventing the Corporation*. New York: Warner Books, 1985.

Nash, June. "Nonwage work in the crisis of capitalism," *Anthropology of Work Review*, 10: 5-6, 10, 1989.

Navarie, Sylvia. "A case study of female managers: A new model of management and where women learned it." Paper presented to the Fifth Annual Women and Work Conference, University of Texas-Arlington, Arlington, Texas, May 1988.

Neuman, George, Jack Edwards, and Mamburg Raju. "Organizational development interventions: A meta-analysis of their effects on satisfaction and other attitudes," *Personnel Psychology*. 42: 461-489, 1989.

Newman, Louise Michele. *Men's Ideas/Women's Realities*. New York: Pergamon Press, 1985.

Nicholson, Nigel and Michael A. West. *Managerial Job Change: Men and Women in Transition*. Cambridge: Cambridge University Press, 1988.

Nickles, Elizabeth and Laura Ashcraft. *The Coming Matriarchy*. New York: Seaview Books, 1980.

Nieva, Veronica and Barbara Gutek. *Women and Work: A Psychological Perspective*. New York: Praeger Publishers, 1982.

Nin, Anais. *A Woman Speaks*. Chicago: The Swallow Press, Inc., 1976.

Nisbet, Robert A. *Community and Power: The Quest for Community*. London: Oxford University Press, 1953.

Noddings, Nel. *Caring: A Feminine Approach to Ethnics and Moral Education*. Berkeley; University of California Press, 1984.

Oakley, Ann. *Women's Work: The Housewife, Past and Present*. New York: Vintage Books, 1976.

Oerton, Sarah. "Exploring women workers' motives for employment in cooperative and collective organizations," *Journal of Gender Studies*. 3:289-297, 1994.

Ofosu-Amaah, Waafas and Wendy Philleo. *Women and the Environment: An Analytical Review of Success Stories.* Washington, DC: United Nations Environment Program and World WIDE Network, Inc., 1992.

O'Hara-Devereaux, Mary and Robert Johansen. *Globalwork: Bridging Distance, Culture, and Time.* San Francisco: Jossey-Bass Publishers, 1994.

Oitzinger, Jane. "American Indian ecological perspectives: An annotated list of key themes," Unpublished manuscript, University of Wisconsin Center-Marinette, Marinette, WI, 1994.

Ost, David H. and Darla J. Turale. "Appointments of administrators: Reflections of administrative and organizational structures,: *Initiatives* 52:23-30, 1989.

O'Toole, Patricia. "How do you build a $44 million company?" *Working Woman* 88-92, April, 1990.

Ouchi, William G. *Theory Z: How American Business Can Meet the Japanese Challenge.* Reading, MA: Addison-Wesley Publishing Company, 1981.

Overman, Stephanie. "Managing the diverse work force," *HR Magazine.* 36: 32-36, 1991.

Pearson, Carol S., Donna L. Shavlik, and Judith G. Touchton. *Educating the Majority: Women Challenge Tradition in Higher Education.* New York: Macmillan Publishing Co., 1989.

Penrose, Jon. "Women and man-made environments: The Dutch experience." *Women and Environments.* 9: 12-13, 26, 1987.

Perlingieri, Ilya Sandra. "Lost woman: Strokes of genius." *Ms Magazine.* 17: 54-57, 1988.

Perrow, Charles. *Complex Organizations: A Critical Essay.* Glenview, IL: Scott, Foresmen and Company, 1972.

Peters, Thomas J. *Thriving on Chaos: Handbook for a Management Revolution.* New York: Knopf: Distributed by Random House, 1987.

Peters, Thomas J., and Robert H. Waterman, Jr. *In Search of Excellence: Lessons from America's Best-run Companies.* New York: Harper and Row, 1982.

Peterson, Norma. "How do women manage?" *The Executive Female.* 7: 45-48, 1984.

Pheterson, Gail. "Alliances between women: Overcoming internalized oppression and internalized domination," in Elizabeth Minnich, Jean O'Barr, and Rachael Rosenfeld (eds.) *Reconstructing the Academy: Women's Education and Women's Studies.* Chicago: University of Chicago Press, 1988.

Philipson, Ilene. *On The Shoulders of Women: The Feminization of Psychotherapy.* New York: Guilford Press, 1993.

Photiadis, John and Harry Schwarzweller. *Change in Rural Appaliachia: Implications for Action programs.* Philadelphia: University of Pennsylvania Press, 1971.

Piercy, Marge. *Gone to Soldiers.* New York: Fawcett Crest, 1987.

Plant, Judith. *Healing the Wounds: The Promise of Ecofeminism.* Philadelphia, PA: New Society Publishers, 1989.

Pleck, Elizabeth H. "Two worlds in one: Work and family," *Journal of Social History.* 10: 178-195, 1976.

Pleck, Joseph. "The work family role system." *Social Problems*, 24: 417-427, 1977.

Polachek, G. S. "Occupational segregation among women: Theory, evidence, and prognosis." in C. B. Lloyd (ed.) *Women in the Labor Force.* New York: Columbia University Press, 1979.

Popcorn, Faith. *The Popcorn Report: On the Future of Your Company, Your World, Your Life.* New York: Doubleday, 1991.

Pope, Christie Farnham. "The future impact of feminist scholarship on higher education." Paper presented to Conference on Women in The Year 2000, Indiana University - Purdue University at Indianapolis, 1988.

Port, Pat. "The delicate art of criticism," *The Executive Female.* 9: 36-39, 1986.

Powell, Gary. "One more time: Do female and male managers differ?" *Academy of Management Executive.* 4: 68-95, 1990.

Powell, Gary N. *Women and Men in Management.* Beverly Hills: Sage Publications, Inc., 1988.

Pyun, Chang Soo. "The monetary value of a housewife: An economic analysis for use in litigation." *American Journal of Economics and Sociology.* 28: 271:-284, 1969.

Quick, Thomas. "Selling bad news," *Working Woman.* October: 33-34, 1982.

Ragins, Belle Rose and John Cotton. "Easier said than done: Gender differences in perceived barriers to gaining a mentor," *Academy of Management Journal.* 34: 939-951, 1991.

Ramos, Patricia. "Ethnic women managers' attitudes and views about their jobs: A preliminary report," *Mabuchay International Monitor.* August: 6-10, 1992.

Reed, Beth Glover and Charles D. Garvin (eds.). *Groupwork with Women/Groupwork with Men: An Overview of Gender Issues in Social Groupwork Practice.* New York: Haworth Press, Inc., 1983.

Renner, Michael. "Military security and global governance," *World Watch.* 8(July/August):37-38, 1995.

Renou, Marieke. "Changing lifestyles of women," Paper presented at The First International Conference on the Future of Adult Life, Noordwijkerhout, The Netherlands, 1987.

Renwick, Patricia Ann. "The effects of sex differences as the perception and management of superior-subordinate conflict: An exploratory study." *Organizational Behavior and Human Performance.* 19: 403-415, 1977.

Ridgeway, Cecilia and Joseph Berger. "Expectations, legitimation and dominance behavior in task groups," *American Sociological Review.* 51: 603-617, 1986.

Ridgeway, Cecilia and David Diekema. "Dominance and collective hierarchy formation in male and female task groups," *American Sociological Review*, 54:79-95, 1989.

Ridgeway, Cecilia and Cathryn Johnson. "What is the relationship between socio-emotional behavior and status in task groups?" *American Journal of Sociology*, 95: 1189-1212, 1990.

Rifkin, Jeremy. *The End of Work: The Decline of the Global Labor Force and the Dawn of the Post-Market Era.* New York: Jeremy P. Tarcher/Putman Books, 1995.

Riger, S. and P. Gilligan. "Women in management: An exploration of competing paradigms," *American Psychologist.* 35: 902-910, 1980.

Risman, Barbara. "A theoretical note on gender: Toward a structuralist perspective on intimate relationships." Paper presented to The American Sociological Association, Washington, D.C., 1985.

Rizzo, Ann-Marie and Carmen Mendez. *The Integration of Women in Management: A Guide for Human Resources and Management Specialists.* New York: Quoram Books, 1990.

Rizzo, Ann-Marie and Carmen Mendez. "Making things happen in organizations: Does gender make a difference?" *Public Personnel Management*, 17:9-20, 1988.

Roberts, Bruce and Howard I. Thorsheim. "Are women employed through different processes than men?: An interview research project with leaders and those they empower." Paper presented to Fifth Annual Conference on Women and Work, University of Texas at Arlington, Arlington, Texas, 1988.

Roche, Gerald R. "Probing opinions: A survey shows that top executives who have had a mentor derive greater satisfaction from their career and work." *Harvard Business Review.* 79: 14-18, 24, 26-28, 1979.

Roddick, Anita. "A kinder, gentler capitalism," *Business Ethics.* July/August: 28, 1992.

Rodriguez, Noelie Maria. "Transcending bureaucracy: Feminist politics at a shelter for battered women," *Gender and Society* 2: 214-227, 1988.

Roessing, Walter. "High marks for Hallmark," *Compass* 32-39, March, 1990.

Rogers, Judy L. "New paradigm leadership: Integrating the female ethos." *Initiatives*, 51: 1-8, 1988.

Rogers, Louisa. "Getting ahead: How to communicate with power," *New Woman.* September: 100-103, 1989.

Rosch, Leah. "Switching Careers -- and getting a good reception," *Working Woman*, 68-69, 72-74, June, 1989.

Rosen, B. and T. Jerdue. "Perceived sex differences in managerially relevant characteristics," *Sex Roles.* 4: 837-843, 1978.

Rosen, Marjorie. "The Hurd instinct," *Ms Magazine*, 66-71, September, 1989.

Rosenberg, Rosalind. *Beyond Separate Spheres: Intellectual Roots of Modern Feminism.* New Haven: Yale University Press, 1982.

Rosener, Judith. "Ways women lead," *Harvard Business Review*, 68: 119-125, 1990.

Rothschild, Joyce and J. Allen Whitt. *The Cooperative Workplace: Potentials and Dilemmas of Organizational Democracy and Participation.* New York: Cambridge University Press, 1986.

Rowbotham, Sheila. "Working for Women: Economic planning and the local state." *Women and Environments* 9: 14-16, 1987.

Rubin, Lillian. *Intimate Strangers.* New York: Harper and Row, 1983.

Ruddick, Sara. *Maternal Thinking: Toward a Politics of Peace.* Boston: Beacon Press, 1989.

Rushing, William. *Class, Culture, and Alienation.* Lexington, MA: D.C. Heath and Co., 1972.

Russell, Peter and Roger Evans. *The Creative Manager.* San Francisco: Jossey Bass, 1992.

St. Joan, Jackie. "Who was Rembradt's mother?" *Quest*, 73-74, Spring, 1976.

Sandell, Steven H. and David Shapiro. "Work expectations, human capital accumulation, and the wages of young women," Mimeo. Center for Human Resource Research. Ohio State University, Columbus, Ohio, 1978.

Sandroff, Ronni. "The manager who never says never," *Working Women*, 88-92, April, 1990.

Sandroff, Ronni. "Helping your company become family-friendly," *Working Woman*, 136-137, 196-197, November, 1989.

Sandroff, Ronni. "Marketing yourself." *Working Women*, pp. 98-101, June, 1988.

Sargaria, Mary Ann D. "The managerial skills and experiences of men and women administrators: Similarities and differences," *Journal of Educational Equity and Leadership.* 5: 19-30, 1985.

Sargent, Alice. *The Androgenous Manager.* New York: American Management Associations, 1981.

Satin, Mark. "The 1980s were better than we thought," *New Options.* Issue 64, Washington, D.C., January/February 1990.

Scanzoni, John. *Men, Women, and Change.* New York: McGraw-Hill, 1976.

Schacht, Richard. *Alienation.* Garden City, NY: Doubleday, 1970.

Schaef, Anne Wilson. *Women's Reality: An Emerging Female System in a White Male Society.* San Francisco: Harper and Row, 1981.

Schein, Virginia Ellen. "Relationships between sex role stereotypes and requisite management characteristics among female managers," *Journal of Applied Psychology.* 60: 340-344, 1975.

Schein, Virginia Ellen. "The relationship between sex role stereotypes and requisite management characteristics." *Journal of Applied Psychology.* 57: 95-100, 1973.

Scheman, Naomi. "Welcoming remarks," National Women's Studies Association, Minneapolis, June, 1989.

Scherbaum, Carol J. and Donald H. Shephard. "Dressing for success: Effects of color and layering or perceptions of women in business," *Sex Roles.* 16: 391-399, 1987.

Schmidt, Peggy J. "Sexist schooling," *Working Woman.* October, 101-102, 1982.

Schneer, Jay A. and Frieda Reitman. "Effects of alternate family structure on managerial careers," *Academy of Management Journal.* 36: 830-843, 1993.

Schumacher, E. F. *Small Is Beautiful.* New York: Harper and Row, 1975.

Schur, Edwin. *Labeling Women Deviant: Gender, Stigma and Social Control.* New York, NY: Random House, 1984.

Schwartz, Felice N. "Management women and the new facts of life," *Harvard Business Review* 67: 65-76, 1989.

Schwartz-Shea, Peregrine. "Gendered organization," in *International Encyclopedia of Public Policy and Administration.* (ed.) Jay Shafritz. forthcoming, 1995.

Scott, Marvin B. "The social sources of alienation," *Inquiry.* 6: 56-69, 1963.

Scott, Nancy A. and Sue Spooner. "Women administrators: Stressors and strategies," *Initiatives.* 52: 31-36, 1989.

Seeman, Melvin. "Alienation in pre-crisis France,: *American Sociological Review.* 37:385-402, 1972.

Seeman, Melvin. "On the meaning of alienation," *American Sociological Review.* 24: 783-791, 1959.

Seeman, Melvin. "A comparison of general and specific leader behavior description," *Leader Behavior: Its Description and Measurement.* R. M. Stogdill and A. E. Coors (eds.), Columbus, Ohio: College of Administrative Science, The Ohio State University, 1937.

Segal, Lynn. *Is the Future Female?: Troubled Thoughts on Contemporary Feminism.* London: Virago Press, 1987.

Sekaran, Uma and Douglas Hall. "Asynchronism in dual-career and family linkages," in *Handbook of Career Theory.* (ed.) Michael Arthur, Douglas Hall, and Barbara Laurence. Cambridge: Cambridge University Press, 1989.

362   *The Rise of Marginal Voices*

Sell, Jane, W. I. Griffith and Rick K. Wilson. "Are women more cooperative than men in social dilemmas?" *Social Psychology Quarterly* 56: 211-222, 1993.

Serlen, Bruce. "Muttering from the men's room," *Ms Magazine*. May, 113-115, 1983.

Shakeshaft, Carol. *Women in Educational Administration*. Beverly Hills, CA: Sage, 1987.

Shalin, Dmitri N. "Pragmatism and social interactionism," *American Sociological Review*. 51: 9-29, 1986.

Shepard, Jon. *Automation and Alienation: A Study of Office and Factory Workers*. Cambridge: MIT Press, 1971.

Sheppard, I. Thomas. "Delegations's hidden snares," *The Executive Female*, Feb., 1985.

Shipka, Barbara. *When The Canary Stops Singing*. New York: Burett-Kohler, 1993.

Silverstone, Rosalie and Romemary Towler. "Secretaries at work," *Ergonomics*. 27: 557-564, 1984.

Simmel, Georg. *Georg Simmel: On Women, Sexuality, and Love*. Translated by Guy Oakes. New Haven: Yale University Press, 1984.

Simpson, Peggy. "All the candidate's women." *Ms Magazine*, October, p. 75-79, 1988.

Simpson, Peggy. "Corporate women: Just how far have we come?" *Working Woman*. March, 99-104, 1984.

Sitterly, Connie and Beth Whitley Duke. *A Woman's Place: Management*. Englewood Cliffs, NJ: Prentice Hall, 1988.

Smith, H. and Grenier, M. "Sources of organizational power for women: Overcoming structural obstacles," *Sex Roles.* 8: 733-746, 1982.

Smith, Dorothy. "Women's perspective as a radical critique of sociology," *Sociological Inquiry.* 44: 7-13, 1974.

Smith, Eleanor. "Upward mobility: Black and white women administrators," *Journal of National Association of Women Deans and Administrators.* Spring, 28-32, 1985.

Smith-Penniman, Adele. "Interview on envisioning a feminist world," *Women of Power.* Summer, Issue 2, 1985.

Snyder, Mary Hembrow. *The Christology of Rosemary Bradford Ruether.* Mystic, CT: Twenty-third Publications, 1988.

So, Alvin Y. "The managerial revolution in socialist China: A study of reforms in Shenzhen special economic zone." Paper presented to The American Sociological Association, New York, 1986.

Sokoloff, Natalie. "The increase of black and white women in the professions: A contradictory process." Paper presented at SUNY Albany Conference on Women's Employment Policy, Albany, NY, 1985.

Solomon, Julie. "Role models, type E's and feminism: Top women executives compare notes," *Wall Street Journal*, April 27, 1989.

Songer, Nancy Branham. "Work force diversity," *Business and Economic Review.* April/June, 3-6, 1991.

Sprague, Melinda S. and Alice Sargent. "Toward androgenous trainers," in J. William Pfeiffer and John E. Jones (ed.) *The 1977 Annual Handbook for Group Facilitators.* LaJolla, CA: University Associates, 1977.

Spretnak, Charlene. "Female thinking: Revision," *The Journal of Consciousness and Change.* 9: 37-39, 1986.

The Rise of Marginal Voices364 The Rise of Marginal Voices

Spretnak, Charlene. *The Politics of Women's Spirituality: Essays on the Rise of Spiritual Power Within the Feminist Movement.* New York: Anchor Books, 1982.

Srole, Leo. "Social integration and certain correlaries: An exploratory study," *American Sociological Review.* 21: 709-716, 1956.

Stacey, Judith and Barrie Thorne. "The missing feminist revolution in sociology," *Social Problems.* 32: 301-316, 1985.

Staff. "Special report: The new industrial relations," *Business Week,* May 11: 84-98, 1981.

Starrett, Cam. "Listen to women: Council on economic priorities survey." *Ms Magazine,* November, pp. 45-52, 1987.

Statham, Anne. "Environmental identity: Symbols in cultural change," *Studies in Symbolic Interaction: A Research Annual.* 17: 207-240, 1995.

Statham, Anne. "The gender model revisited: *Sex Roles.* 16:409-429, 1987a.

Statham, Anne. "Women working for women: The manager and her secretary," in Anne Statham, Eleanor Miller, and Hans Mauksch. *The Worth of Women's Work: A Qualitative Synthesis.* Albany, NY: SUNY Press, 1987b.

Statham, Anne and Sheila Denise Neinhaus. "Race and gender as factors conditioning approaches to work among African American managers," Unpublished manuscript, University of Wisconsin-Parkside, Kenosha, 1993.

Statham, Anne, Laurel Richardson, and Judith A. Cook. *Gender and University Teaching: A Negotiated Difference.* Albany: SUNY Press, 1991.

Statham, Anne and Marian Swoboda. "Women managing in higher education." Paper presented to the National Association of Women Deans, Administrators, and Counselors, Nashville: March, 1990.

Statham, Anne, Suzanne Vaughan, and Sharon Houseknecht. "The professional involvement of highly educated women: The impact of family." *Sociological Quarterly*. 28: 119-133, 1987.

Stead, Bette Ann. "Women and men in management: Getting along," in *Women in Management*, 2nd edition, (ed.) Bette Ann Stead. Englewood Cliffs, NJ: Prentice Hall, Inc., 1985.

Stein, Maurice, Arthur Vidich, and David White. *Identity and Anxiety: Survival of the Person in Mass Society*. Glencoe, IL: The Free Press, 1960.

Stockard, Jean, J. C. Van De Kragt, and Patricia J. Dodge. "Gender roles and behavior in social dilemmas: Are there sex differences in cooperation and in its justification?" *Social Psychology Quarterly*. 51: 154-163, 1988.

Stogdill, R. M. *Handbook of Leadership: A Survey of Theory and Research*. New York: The Free Press, 1974.

Stryker, Sheldon. "The interplay of affect and identity: Exploring the relationships of social structure, social interaction, self, and emotion." Paper presented to The American Sociological Association, Chicago, 1987.

Swindall, Linda. "Delegate, delegate," *Working Woman*. July, 18-19, 1985.

Swoboda, Marian. "Behind the glass ceiling-women in medicine." Address given to the Association of American Medical Colleges, Itasca, Illinois, April 1988.

Swoboda, Marian J. and Jane Vanderbosch. "The politics of difference," *Journal of Educational Equity and Leadership*. 4: 137-147, 1984.

Swoboda, Marian and Jane Vanderbosch. "The society of outsiders: Women in administration," *Journal of National Association of Women Deans and Administrators.* Spring, 3-6, 1983.

Symons, Gladys. "Career lives of women in France and Canada: The care of managerial women," *Work and Occupations.* 11: 331-352, 1984.

Tarvis, Carol and Carole Wade. *The Longest War: Sex Differences in Perspective.* Second Edition. New York: Harcourt Brace Jovanovich, Publishers, 1984.

Tausky, Kurt and Anthony Chelte. "Workers' participation," *Work and Occupations.* 15: 363-373, 1988.

Taylor, Carol. "Moosewood: Many chefs spice this great stew of a restaurant," *Mother Earth News,* 50-52, May, 1990.

Teamster Conway Express. "The good, bad and ugly of 'quality teams'," June/July, #115, 1992.

Terborg, J. "Women in management: A research review," *Journal of Applied Psychology.* 62: 647-664, 1977.

Thoits, Peggy. "Self-labeling process in mental illness: The role of emotional deviance," *American Journal of Sociology.* 91: 221-249, 1985.

Thom, Mary. "Elections: Southern women hold the key," *Ms Magazine.* February, 22, 1988.

Thomas, R. Roosevelt. *Beyond Race and Gender: Unleashing the Power of Your Total Workforce by Managing Diversity.* New York: American Management Association, 1991.

Thompson, Wayne E. and John E. Horton. "Political alienation as a force in political action," *Social Forces.* 38: 190-195, 1960.

Thorne, Barrie. "Girls and boys together...but mostly apart: Gender arrangements in elementary schools," *Relationships and Development.* (Eds.) Willard W. Hartup and Zick Rubin. London: Lawrence Erlbaum 1986.

Thorne, Barrie and Zella Luria. "Sexuality and gender in children's daily worlds," *Social Problems.* 33: 176-190, 1986.

Thorne, Mary. "Elections: Southern women hold the key." *Ms Magazine,* p. 22, February, 1988.

Tocqueville, Alexis de. *Democracy in America.* Translated by Henry Reeves. New York: Schocken Books, 1961.

Toffler, Alvin. *Future Shock.* New York: Random House, 1970.

Torbert, William. *The Power of Balance: Transforming Self, Society, and Scientific Inquiry.* Newbury Park, CA: Sage, 1991.

Torpy, Kathleen A. "Move over, paternalism," paper presented to the National Women's Studies Association, Akron, Ohio, June, 1990.

Touchton, Judith. "Women chief executive officers in U.S. colleges and universities." Unpublished Table, Office of Women in Higher Education, American Council on Education, Washington, D.C., 1988.

Tronto, Joan. "Beyond gender difference to a theory of care," *Signs: A Journal of Women and Culture in Society.* 12:644-663, 1987.

Trost, Cathy. "Women managers quit not for family but to advance their corporate climb," *The Wall Street Journal,* May 2, 1990.

Trost, Cathy. "Women in media making slow progress, study finds," *Wall Street Journal* April 10, 1989.

Tucker, Sharon. "Careers of men and women MBA's: 1950-1980," *Work and Occupations.* 12: 166-185, 1985.

Tzu, Lao. *Tao Te Ching.* Translated by D. C. Lau. Baltimore: Penguin, 1963.

U.S. Bureau of the Census. *Statistical Abstracts of the United States.* Washington, D.C.: U.S. Department of Commerce, 1985.

U.S. Department of Labor. "The United Nations Decade for Women, 1976-1985: Employment in the United States, Report prepared for the World Conference on the United Nations Decade for Women, 1976-1985." Washington, DC: U.S. Government Printing Office, 1985.

Useem, Michael. *The Inner Circle.* New York: Oxford University Press, 1984.

Walby, Sylvia. *Theorizing Patriarchy.* Oxford: Basil Blackwell, 1990.

Walby, Sylvia. *Patriarchy at Work.* Minneapolis: University of Minnesota Press, 1986.

Wallach, Amei. "Arts and craftiness," *Ms Magazine,* July/August 24-26, 1989.

Wall Street Journal - Gallup Poll. "Executive women," October 30, 1984.

Walter, Lynn. "Feminist anthropology?" *Gender and Society.* 9:272-288, 1995.

Waring, Marilyn. *If Women Counted.* New York: Harper & Row, 1988.

Wartik, Nancy. "So long, Robespierre." *Ms Magazine.* October, 68, 1988.

Watson, Carol. "When a woman is the boss: Dilemmas in taking charge." *Group and Organization Studies,* 1989.

Watson, Carol and Bonnie Kasten. "Separate strengths?: How men and women negotiate." Working paper #1. Center for Negotiation and Conflict Resolution, Rutgers University-Newark, 1987.

Watts, Patti. "Lending a helping hand," *Executive Female*, 38-40, 65-67, July/August, 1989.

WEAL Report. Women's Equity Act Legue. Washington, D.C., 1984.

Weisinger, Hendrie. "How should you criticize your boss? carefully," *Working Woman* 91-92, 122, February, 1990.

Whyte, William Foote. "Making the breaks at RATH: Reflections on applied research in the new systems of work and participation program." Unpublished manuscript, N.D., Cornell University, Ithaca, New York, no date.

Wiley, Mary Glenn and Arlene Eskilson. "Coping in the corporation: Sex role constraints," *Journal of Applied Social Psychology*. 12: 1-11, 1982.

Wilhelm, Richard. *The I Ching or Book of Changes*. Translated by Cary Baynes. Princeton: Princeton University Press, 1967.

Williams, Christie. *Gender Differences at Work: Women and Men in Nontraditional Occupations*. Berkeley: University of California Press, 1989.

Williams, Terry Tempest. "The wild card," *Wilderness*. Summer: 26-29, 1993.

Winston, Diane. "Ethics: Scutwork," *Working Woman*. January 26, 1986.

Winther, Dorothy A. and Samuel B. Green. "Another look at gender-related differences in leadership behavior," *Sex Roles*. 16: 41-56, 1987.

Wolf, Wendy C. and Neil D. Fligstein. "Sex and authority in the workplace: The causes of sexual inequality," *American Sociological Review.* 44: 235-252, 1979.

Wood, M. and S. Greenfield, . "Women managers and fear of success: A study in the field," *Sex Roles.* 2: 375-387, 1976.

Woodman, Marion. "Addiction to perfection," *Yoga Journal,* 1988.

Woolf, Virginia. *Three Guineas.* Orlando, FL: Harcourt, Brace, Jovanovich, Inc. 1938

Yager, Jan. *Making Your Office Work for You.* New York: Doubleday, 1989.

Yankelovich, Daniel. *New Rules: Searching for Self-Fulfillment in a World Turned Upside Down.* New York: Random House, 1981.

Young, Bettie R. "The changing face of today's business leader," *Executive Female.* May/June, 26-27, 1984.

Young, R. A. and R. Richards. "Entrepreneurial women: A hermenentical approach," Proposal for Research, Vancouver, British Columbia: the University of British Columbia, 1987.

Young, T. R. "Class warfare in the 80's and 90's: Reganomics and social justice." *Wisconsin Sociologist.* 25: 68-75, 1988.

Zeitz, Gerald. "Bureaucratic role characteristics and member affective response in organizations." *Sociological Quarterly.* 25: 301-318, 1984.

Zimmer, Lynn. "How women reshape the prison guard role," *Gender and Society.* 1: 415-431, 1987.

Zweigenhaft, Richard. "Minorities and women of the corporation: Will they attain seats of power?" in G. William Domhoff and Thomas R. Dye (eds.) *Power Elites and Organizations.* Beverly Hills, CA: Sage, 1987.

Index

182, 187, 189, 192-193, 202, 214, 251

military concept of leadership, 179

shared leadership, 179, 182, 185, 189

transforming leadership, 235

Lehner, S., 31

Lewin, K., 7

Lightfoot, S. L., 160

Likert, R., 114-115

locus of influence, 211

Loden, M., 40-41, 161, 206-208, 223

logic of care, 222

Lunneborg, P., 204

Luria, Z., 24

Maccoby, M., 116, 229

McIntosh, P., 5

MacKinnon, C., 63

Madden, T. R., 71, 144, 220

male system, 225

management (see leadership)

Marshall, G., 24, 195, 232